DIVINE ABUNDANCE

DIVINE ABUNDANCE

Leisure, the Basis of Academic Culture

Elizabeth Newman

CASCADE *Books* • Eugene, Oregon

DIVINE ABUNDANCE
Leisure, the Basis of Academic Culture

Cascade Books
An Imprint of Wipf and Stock Publishers
199 W. 8th Ave., Suite 3
Eugene, OR 97401

www.wipfandstock.com

PAPERBACK ISBN: 978-1-5326-1776-8
HARDCOVER ISBN: 978-1-4982-4270-7
EBOOK ISBN: 978-1-4982-4269-1

Cataloguing-in-Publication data:

Names: Newman, Elizabeth, author.

Title: Divine abundance : leisure, the basis of academic culture / Elizabeth Newman.

Description: Eugene, OR: Cascade Books, 2018 | Includes bibliographical references and index.

Identifiers: ISBN 978-1-5326-1776-8 (paperback) | ISBN 978-1-4982-4270-7 (hardcover) | ISBN 978-1-4982-4269-1 (ebook)

Subjects: LCSH: Leisure. | God—Worship and love. | Christian universities and colleges—United States.

Classification: LC383 .N455 2018 (paperback) | LC383 (ebook)

Manufactured in the U.S.A.   08/14/18

In memory of William H. Poteat (1919–2000)

professor, mentor, and friend

"Wonder does not make one industrious, for to feel astonished is to be disturbed."

Josef Pieper

CONTENTS

ACKNOWLEDGEMENTS

I am thankful to colleagues at Saint Mary's College, Notre Dame and the Baptist Theological Seminary at Richmond for opportunities to reflect on the nature and purpose of the academy. I am particularly grateful to BTSR for granting me a yearlong sabbatical to work on this book and for the editorial assistance of my teaching assistant, John Randall. I appreciate those friends at the 2016 National Association of Baptist Professors Region-at-Large for offering helpful and supportive feedback on an early version of one of my chapters. I especially thank Douglas V. Henry and David L. Schindler for their early support, suggestions, and encouragement when this project was still in its infancy. Finally, I am deeply grateful to my husband, Jonathan Baker, a delightful critic and faithful companion.

INTRODUCTION

I consider it a tremendous blessing to have taught for twelve years at Saint Mary's College, Notre Dame. Perhaps it was in part because I was Baptist, teaching religious studies to mostly Catholic students and otherwise trying to find my feet in a Catholic context, that questions of "Christian identity and higher education" occupied my thinking. Some of my stories from this time appear in the pages that follow, but I include one in this introduction to set the stage: a simple story of hospitality, brokenness, and the academy.

Every year, Saint Mary's has a festive baccalaureate mass, a culminating moment in the life of the institution. Hundreds of students along with their friends and families attend. Since my arrival at Saint Mary's, I had been told that it was an acceptable practice for those who were not Catholic to receive a blessing in lieu of the bread and wine that was permitted only for Catholics. At my final baccalaureate service as a Saint Mary's faculty member, I decided to go forward to receive this blessing from the priest or eucharistic minister. A student leader happened to guide me to the bishop's line where the bishop gave a long and generous blessing. I found this hospitable gesture a powerful one since, however briefly, it attended in a grace-filled and healing way to the brokenness of the church.

But why tell this story in a book about the academy? True, it took place in an academic setting but what, if anything, did it have to do with the *intellectual* life of the school? If it is difficult to say, it is because most colleges and universities assume that worship takes place in a sphere having little to do with the academic disciplines or the pursuit of knowledge. How could it be otherwise? After all, faculty and students come from different faith backgrounds. Even more, the free pursuit of truth wherever it may be found ought not be fettered by the constraints of faith or dogma. What, after all, does the Eucharist have to do with biology? In what sense is the Nicene Creed related to the study of history? Or what difference could the incarnation possibly make for the study of psychology or sociology? The former are beliefs, the latter forms of knowledge.

This book is an effort to respond to these questions by placing the question mark deeper down. The key question facing the academy today is not "whether faith?" but "which faith?" As Edward Farley observes, the usual criticisms of education "do not amount to reform [because] their focus is more on the symptoms than on the disease itself."[1] The disease, I argue, is a malaise of long standing within the modern academy. The contemporary university resembles nothing so much as a landscape strewn with the parts of some machine with no design by which the whole might be understood. A mechanistic ontology fragments academic being even as it prevents the academy from seeing and, even more, enjoying its *telos* or end. As Walker Percy puts it, "You live in a deranged age, more deranged than usual, because in spite of great scientific and technological advances, man has not the faintest idea of who he is or what he is doing."[2] The fact that the academy no longer sees questions of purpose as central to its whole being but relegates these to the private or personal sphere is itself a symptom of a malaise so prevalent that it seems simply normal.

In what follows, I diagnose this disease more fully, describing how distorted stories (chapter 1) and a warped ontology (chapter 2) have fueled the modern academic imagination. My thesis is that leisure is necessary for the academy to flourish (chapter 3). Rightly understood, leisure both acknowledges and embodies the fact that communion is intrinsic to being. Following Josef Pieper, I argue that leisure—the heart of which is contemplation and Divine worship—is the true basis of academic culture. Being, as Augustine so vividly captures, has an ontological potency: "My heart is restless, O Lord, until is rests in Thee." This is no mere pious sentiment, but a description of the logic of all creation. All being is to some degree oriented toward a Divine plentitude, a logic also reflected and embodied in the baccalaureate mass. This logic stands in radical contrast to a mechanistic understanding of being that is intrinsically neutral, an assumption that leads inevitably to fragmentation among the academic disciplines as well as to a divorce between church and academy. The turn to leisure as both a practice and a way of being provides a different account of the academy, one that reconfigures both space (chapter 4) and time (chapter 5).

1. Farley, *Theologia*, 3.
2. Percy, *Lost in the Cosmos*, 76.

Given these assumptions, my approach is not so much how to fix a problem as it is how to understand a mystery. Fixing a problem implies an extrinsic relation to an entity or subject. The academy is not, as I have said, a machine requiring adjustment. The academy rather names both a quest and a way of being; it is a search for Wisdom even as it calls for becoming a people capable of receiving the gift of wisdom in all its richness and variety. The philosopher George Grant states that "there is such a thing as a problem to which there is a solution, but mysteries are things one lives in the presence of . . . there are some questions which I would call mysteries, and one of the great purposes of life is to spend one's life trying to enter more and more deeply into them."[3] Academic being before the mysterious presence of God requires not simply a technique or technological fix. It rather calls for the kind of habits and vision that enable us to see why the love of learning and the desire for God are one and the same (chapter 6).

3. Quoted in Cayley, *George Grant*, 171.

1

ACADEMIC STORIES
THAT HOLD US CAPTIVE

In a religious studies departmental meeting at a Catholic institution, a first-year colleague once surprised us with the following question: "Does anyone here teach as if God really exists?" Readers might find this an odd question, especially in a Catholic institution. Some members of my department were puzzled as well. Was our colleague asking about their personal faith? Teaching "as if God exists" could sound like a remedy for propping up piety rather than engaging critical thinking. What else could "teaching as if God really exists" mean? In this chapter, I argue that we have difficulty imagining a richer response to this question because we have accepted distorted stories about the academy and its purpose.[1] What if "teaching as if God really exists" refers not simply to one's personal faith but to the stories, practices, and habits that constitute the life of an academic institution? Do these academic stories and practices, in order to make sense, require the existence of God?

Animal trainer Vicki Hearne communicates the power of story both to distort and heal in her account of a horse named Halla, a nervous and quirky animal who most trainers regarded as impossible to control.

---

1. By "we" I mean first of all those who believe that the academy can be far more than it currently is. This conviction flows from an understanding that humans are created for communion, most fully communion with the triune God. While the "we" is Christian, my hope is that my analysis will also find some resonance and echo in other traditions that see humans and indeed all being as gift.

As Hearne tells it, however, Hans Winkler, a German trainer, "didn't see [Halla] as all that crazy" and was able eventually to ride Halla in a Grand Prix competition. Even though Winkler pulled a groin muscle during the competition, he continued sitting painfully in the saddle, trusting Halla's instincts to make the demanding jumps. They won the gold. Hearn states that Winkler had to have "a story about what appears to be horse insanity may be—even must be, most of the time—evidence of how powerful equine genius is, and how powerfully it can object to incoherence . . . ." She concludes, "The stories we tell matter, and not only do stories reclaim the beauty of crazy horses but also stories lead to insanity in the first place."[2]

Just as Winkler provided an alternative to equine insanity, in what follows I narrate an alternative to those stories that have diminished the true beauty of academic being. I identify four such stories—which I call "secularization," "disenchantment," "excellence," and "pluralism." These are not intended to be exhaustive but rather representative of ways the academic imagination has been stifled, and even suffocated. To the extent this is true, we are like those who have accepted the story of Halla as crazy.[3] Halla was only able to live into the beauty of who she was when she abandoned distorted stories through the imagination of her trainer. The same is true for the academy; imagining a more truthful story will make possible a beauty, truth, and goodness heretofore obscured.

The story of secularization

The famous clash between the church and Galileo vividly captures the story of secularization. As is well-known, Galileo's discovery that the earth rotates around the sun was in conflict with the long-held conviction that the earth stood still. In the familiar account, the church silences Galileo, who nonetheless was to have heroically uttered under his breath, "But still it moves." While this is admittedly a delightful line, the usual telling of the story starkly contrasts Galileo, the hero, standing up for truth against a slow and dogmatic authority. The moral of this familiar plot is that the quest for real knowledge must not be impeded by a benighted church. Organized

---

2. Hearne, *Adam's Task*, 39.

3. My aim is similar to George Grant's description of "[bringing] darkness into light as darkness." Grant uses this phrase to refer to the "darkness of modernity," and to the challenge of saying "what the present is as clearly as one can . . . ." Cayley, *George Grant in Conversation*, 170.

religion cannot stand in the way of scientific progress. At best, faith belongs in a sphere separate from knowledge.[4]

This secularization story does indeed seem to have taken hold in most colleges and universities. To offer but one example, as recently as fifty years ago many Catholic institutions would have had a large percentage of sisters, brothers, or priests from their respective religious orders serving as faculty and administrators.[5] Similarly, in Protestant institutions, ordained clergy and faithful members of the respective denominations served as faculty and administrators. At the vast majority of originally Christian institutions, this is no longer so. While the reasons for this are multifaceted, a dominant one is the growing conviction—now taken for granted—that the academy exists in a sphere separate from religion and the church. As early as 1966, a major Danforth study reported what was already obvious: "the intellectual presuppositions which actually guide the activities of most church colleges are heavily weighted in the secular direction." "Many academic people," the report continued, "do not think of religion as concerned primarily with the truth about ultimate reality. Rather, it is regarded as a moral code, as a set of ideals, or a quaint and antiquated body of ideas which educated people are supposed to have outgrown."[6] Today such assertions themselves sound almost quaint, like saying most people no longer use rotary phones.

For now, let's accept this secular story as an accurate description and register the wide range of responses to it. James T. Burtchaell, in his magisterial book *The Dying of the Light: The Disengagement of Colleges and Universities from Their Christian Churches*, carefully charts the devolution of seventeen colleges and universities away from their founding Christian denominations and traditions. Burtchaell clearly sees this "dying" as a deep

---

4. For an alternative account of this popular Galileo story, see Langford, *Galileo*. Langford states that "one can still find those who use the Galileo affair to argue against the doctrinal authority of the pope and to infer that the Church was, and is, a sworn enemy of modern science and human progress." Langford, *Galileo*, xiii. He argues, "The condemnation of Galileo was not inevitable," xv.

5. For example, in 1960 at Saint Mary's College, Notre Dame, 70 per cent of the faculty were religious or clerical. The number dropped dramatically over the years, following a common pattern in Catholic higher education. The last sister, Sr. Jean Klene, CSC, an English professor and 1959 graduate of the college, retired in 2005. Sr. Eva Hooker, CSC, has since been hired as an English professor and writer in residence. For a wider discussion of this change in Catholic education, see Dosen, *Catholic Higher Education in the 1960s*.

6. Cited in Sloan, *Faith and Knowledge*, 205. Sloan is quoting a major study of church-related colleges (1966) sponsored by the Danforth Foundation.

and profound loss. Likewise, George Marsden's excellent work, *The Soul of the American University*, analyzes how elite universities in our country moved from "Protestant establishment to established nonbelief." Marsden, too, interprets this as a significant loss, suggesting in a final chapter ways that Christian colleges and universities may yet contribute to a genuine pluralism in the academic landscape.

Others, however, have interpreted secularization as a good and necessary transition. Baptist historian Bill Leonard, for example, former Dean of Wake Forest Divinity School, has explicitly opposed Burtchaell's "dying light" image as an accurate description of Wake Forest.[7] Trying to cling to traditional identities, he argues, will only keep institutions mired in a past that is now fragmented. "Clearly Baptist culture itself is fragmented if not collapsing all together. Schools that cling to traditional Baptist identity may be 'left behind.'"[8] In Leonard's view, the dying of the light is better understood as the evolution of light: a Baptist and more broadly Christian culture has collapsed and schools that cling to it are living in the past and thus subject to its distortions. Catholics as well have embraced secularization as a positive way to move into the modern world. At the University of Dayton, for example, faculty as early as 1967 produced a report welcoming secularization as a coming of age, bringing the institution into "the time and forms of the city of man today. It means a new freedom for men to perfect the world in a *non-religious* way."[9] More recently, at least one critic of Burtchaell interprets the outcome of his analysis as an effort to retreat into the backwaters of sectarianism.[10] If secularization is related to governance, then Anthony J. Dosen, for his part, interprets the laicization (or secularization) of boards at Catholic colleges and universities not as a negative turn, but as a way institutions sought to survive and even thrive in the wake of Vatican II.

---

7. Leonard, "Hegemony or Dissent." In extemporaneous comments, Leonard objected to Burtchaell's characterization of Wake Forest as a place where the light is dying. For a fuller account of this, see English, "The New Academic Freedom."

8. Leonard, "Hegemony or Dissent."

9. Gleason, *Contending with Modernity*, 312. The report is titled "Academic Freedom at the University of Dayton: A Report of the President's Ad Hoc Committee for the Study of Academic Freedom at the University of Dayton, July, 1967." Emphasis in original. The context for the report had to do with debate about the relation between the university and the magisterium, a relation brought under stress when a philosophy professor accused other members of his department of teaching heresy.

10. Coughlan, Review of *The Dying of the Light*.

The secularization story revisited

Whether one welcomes secularization or grieves its advance, the secularization thesis is blind in one crucial way. It assumes that the categories "secular" and "religious" are largely self-evident. To become more secular is to become less religious and vice versa. As a number of scholars emphasize, however, this dichotomy is itself a modern invention. Not only is it invented, but opposition between the secular and the religious is not neutral. It rather relies upon particular storied convictions and an implicit, albeit distorted, theology.

Jonathan Sheehan points to this alternative narration in his discussion of how, since the 1990s, scholars of the Enlightenment have moved away from seeing the Enlightenment as the "cradle of the secular world." There is now, according to Sheehan, a communal discomfort with this standard story: "religion has never been left behind, either personally or institutionally. Instead, it has been continually remade and given new forms and meanings over time."[11] Sheehan thus argues that the Enlightenment is now better understood as a time when the notion of religion itself underwent drastic change. Far from being in predictable decline, religion was being reconstructed in such a way as to fit into the "fabric of modernity."[12] One significant change is that before the late eighteenth century religion "generally described the behavior practiced by Christians, Jews, Muslims and pagans, and *religio* was connected to the 'careful performance of ritual obligations.'"[13] This understanding faded, however, as religion came to refer to a set of propositions. Sheehan states, "Enlightenment comparative religion and its effort to understand the common roots of 'religion' (whether in nature, humanity, or God) was born and built atop this foundation."[14] As Sheehan indicates, the invention of the secular and the religious involved imagining separate spheres, intensified today, for example in the spiritual over against the political, academic, and so forth.

Timothy Fitzgerald gives some sense of how theological convictions inform this dualism in his discussion of the influence of deism in

11. Sheehan, "Enlightenment, Religion and the Enigma," 1063 and 1072. Sheehan develops his thesis as it impacted what he calls the "forging of the cultural Bible" in *The Enlightenment Bible*.

12. Sheehan, "Enlightenment, Religion and the Enigma," 1077.

13. Sheehan, "Enlightenment, Religion and the Enigma," 1074.

14. Ibid. Sheehan lifts this example up as one of many shifts that has enabled religion to fit into modernity.

the seventeenth and eighteenth centuries. The conviction that God was entirely separate from the world enabled deists to construct a "natural religion" based on reason. Fitzgerald thus observes that "deism was not really only about 'religion.'"[15] In other words, deistic convictions gave rise to a particular conception of religion as pertaining to a sphere. "It reflected and promoted a view of the world that corresponded very closely with emergent bourgeois values," and acted as a bridge to "bourgeois individualism."[16] With deism emerges 1) the "idea of ethical universalism and rational individuals," and 2) "the idea of private religious experience . . . ."[17] According to Fitzgerald, deist convictions contribute to the construction of various oppositions: "religion and the state, religion and politics, religion and economics, religion and civil society, and religion and science." Underlying all these dichotomies is a fundamental one: the "religion-secular dichotomy."[18] Fitzgerald emphasizes that "what ends up being classified as religious or nonreligious, or as natural or supernatural, is quite arbitrary, and now has significance not so much in terms of any positive conceptual content (note the impossibility of defining 'religion' satisfactorily) as an ideological operator that destabilizes any practices that seem to challenge the interests of American power."[19] Along with a number of other scholars,[20] Fitzgerald thus argues that modern definitions of religion tend to be highly biased and

15. Fitzgerald, *The Ideology of Religious Studies*, 29.

16. Fitzgerald, *The Ideology of Religious Studies*, 29.

17. Fitzgerald, *The Ideology of Religious Studies*, 28–29.

18. Fitzgerald, *Discourse on Civility*, 23. He adds that "the definitions of all these domains are highly contested, yet in the ease with which these terms are used there lies a tacit assumption that we all know what they mean even if we can't quite define them exactly. My argument will be that none of these categories has fixed meanings and that they are fundamentally rhetorical and strategic." Fitzgerald, *Discourse on Civility*, 23.

19. Fitzgerald, *Discourse on Civility*, 41.

20. See, for example, Cavanaugh, *The Myth of Religious Violence*, 59. Cavanaugh also notes that "attempts to say that there is a transhistorical and transcultural concept of religion that is separable from secular phenomena is itself part of a particular configuration of power, that of the modern, liberal nation-state as it developed in the West." It is rather the case, he notes, that "the religious-secular distinction accompanies the invention of private-public, religion-politics, and church-state dichotomies." Cavanaugh, *The Myth of Religious Violence*, 59. Alasdair MacIntyre likewise states that when the secular and sacred are divided, "then religion becomes one more department of human life, one activity among others . . . . If our religion is fundamentally irrelevant to our politics, then we are recognizing the political as a realm outside of God. To divide the sacred from the secular is to recognize God's action only within the narrowest limits." Cited in Rowland, *Culture*, 93.

ideological in a way that typically relegates "religion" to a non-public sphere separate from politics and the state.

David Bentley Hart likewise states that modernity was not merely "the result of a natural evolution from one phase of economic and social development to another." It was rather a cultural revolution: "a positive ideological project, the active creation of an entire 'secular' sphere that had never before existed and that (because it had not yet been invented) had never before sought to be 'liberated' from the bondage of faith."[21] The categories "secular" and "religious" are not simply natural. It is rather that the story of secularization makes a nonreligious domain thinkable while making a religious sphere plausible. The assumption is that secular reason is more foundational, taming irrational religious belief and practice, but this assumption is a development of specific kinds of theological convictions, such as deism.

For a particularly poignant example of the reimagining of religion to fit into a secular versus religion plot line, consider a 1964 address given by Dr. Ralph Scales, former President of both Oklahoma Baptist and Wake Forest Universities. The address, titled "The Christian Scholar," given at a Southern Baptist faculty conference in Hot Springs, Arkansas, is interesting for our purposes because of how Scales edits the original manuscript. Scales's additions are in square brackets.

> We must be ever mindful of the importance of the ~~Christian origins~~ [spiritual heritage] and the urgent ~~Christian~~ obligations of our work [in the task of character building] . . . . The first test of our ~~Christianity~~ [character] in ~~supporting a Christian college~~ [operating schools] is to see to it that ~~it is,~~ [they are], first of all ~~a good college~~ [schools] . . . . It is rank deception, and not at all ~~Christian~~ [spiritual], to engage in cut-rate education. And so the ~~Christian scholar~~ [honest teacher] must be first of all, competent professionally . . . . [I would say without hesitation that the teacher who is doing an honest job in teaching mathematics or science or reading is discharging his first spiritual obligation. He doesn't have to teach religion to be able to teach religiously.][22]

21. Hart, *Atheist Delusions,* 26.

22. Scales, "The Christian Scholar." At the time, Scales was president of Oklahoma Baptist University.

As we see, Scales drops all uses of "Christian" and substitutes "spiritual." Further, he equates teaching "religiously" with teaching honestly and sincerely.

These edits might seem harmless enough, and Scales most likely imagined he was creating a more expansive statement. We can see, however, in the shift from the original to the edited version that Scales is rehearsing modernity's story of religion. In so doing, Christianity does not pertain to knowledge as such but becomes 1) a subset of the spiritual and 2) loosely equated with moral duty.[23]

At one point, Scales does poetically describe education as oriented toward God: "The roots of the tree of education are not physical, not clubs or departments or objective testing, or alma mater songs, or even shelves of books. The roots of the tree of higher education are fundamental ideas which exalt and strike a divine spark in the individual. Those ideas about God and man and the universe are all important in giving direction to life."[24] To say that the ideas about "God and man . . ." are the roots of the whole academic tree flies in the face of the secular/religious divide. Yet, sadly from my point of view, Scales cannot quite believe his own words. He changes, "Those ideas *about God and man and the universe* are all important in giving direction to life," to "Those ideas, *whether expressed in great poetry or in laboratory experiments*, are all important in giving direction to life."[25] Christian convictions are kept at bay to make sense of oneself as a "Christian scholar."

Such an example is not intended to disparage Scales, who is rightly honored for a wide range of accomplishments. His words, however, provide a particularly illuminative example of Christianity becoming a religion in the modern sense of the word. It thus seems problematic to allow Christian convictions to shape academic practices or to provide a *telos* for the university.

One might argue that Scales is simply seeking to neutralize Christianity so as to allow for other beliefs. After all, the academy is or should be a place to welcome all religions or none at all. Such a position rightly sees the practice of welcome as crucial to the academy. Genuine learning requires

---

23. More specifically, Scales is extending a story refined both by Immanuel Kant, who associates religion with moral duty, and by Friedrich Schleiermacher, who describes the essence of religion as a kind of spiritual awareness.

24. Scales, "The Christian Scholar."

25. Scales, "The Christian Scholar," my emphasis.

the reception of others and of other knowledges. Modernity's "hospitality," however, turns on the conviction that faith belongs in the religious sphere and does not itself count as real knowledge. Such a welcome expects others, naturally, to accept where this line is drawn, a fact that illumines that all practices of welcome are sustained by some boundaries.

The more basic question about academic welcome and a university's boundary, however, is not "secular or religious?" but, "which theological convictions are in fact already shaping it?"[26] For now, we can simply note that the secularization story relies upon a dualism between the spiritual and the material. The spiritual is something other than the material world of politics, science, academics, and so forth. The secularization story thus *requires* a spiritualized religion in order to make sense of itself as secular. This is to say that certain theological convictions have been repackaged as a self-evident academic framework. I will discuss an alternative, one that enhances academic welcome and reception. For now, however, let us turn to a second distorted story about the academy.

A story of disenchantment

The use of "enchant" lends itself to a fairy tale. Our second story, placed in this genre, goes something like this: Once upon a time, a princess called Magica ruled the land with her delightful fairies. If demons threatened to destabilize the land with disease or disaster, priests and other witch doctors defeated them through supernatural words and rituals. "Just say the word and we shall be healed," the people chanted. One day, however, a young man arrived and renounced the magic of the land. Instead of mere words, he gave the sick medicine. Instead of fairies, he was accompanied by educated companions who explained the causes of disease and disaster. Princess Magica died and the young man was crowned Prince Realo. Though the people at times remembered the princess fondly, they were also relieved to no longer be at the mercy of powers in which they no longer believed.

Charles Taylor famously captures this tale of disbelief with the following question: "[W]hy was it virtually impossible not to believe in God in,

26. I am using "theological" to refer to those storied convictions about humans, the world, and gods or God. McClendon, following Willem F. Zuurdeeg, offers this helpful understanding of convictions: "A conviction is a persistent belief such that if X (a person or a community) has a conviction, it will not be easily abandoned, and it cannot be abandoned without making X a significantly different person or community than before." McClendon, *Ethics*, 22–23.

say, 1500 in our Western society, while in 2000 many of us find this not only easy, but even inescapable?"[27] Carl Sagan, for his part, sums up this disbelief as follows: "The major religions on the Earth contradict each other left and right. You can't all be correct. And what if all of you are wrong? . . . I'm not any more skeptical about your religious beliefs than I am about every new scientific idea I hear about. But in my line of work, they're called hypotheses, not inspiration and not revelation."[28] One would expect to hear this from Sagan, a self-proclaimed atheist. But Taylor's point is that an implicit atheism has seeped into the fabric of the modern world such that we can no longer be fully enchanted by demons, angels, or, most significantly, God.

No one has described and embraced this modern disenchantment better than Max Weber. Weber rejected "mysterious incalculable powers," arguing instead that "one can, in principle, *master* all things by *calculation*." For Weber,

> This means, however, that the world is disenchanted. One need no longer have recourse to magical means in order to master or implore the spirits, as did the savage, for whom such mysterious powers existed. Technical means and calculations perform the service. This above all is what intellectualization means.[29]

Disenchantment thus purifies reason of magic, superstition, and mysterious forces. It makes modern knowledge possible. In Weber's disenchanted world, the academic vocation is not about one's service to God, but about allegiance to a specialized field of inquiry. As Mark Schwehn describes this position, "To what human good or goods is specialized academic work directed? Simply to the end of *Wissenschaft* [academics]—making knowledge."[30]

Strangely, the disenchanting figure that Weber appeals to is the Jewish prophet. This is odd since the biblical prophets heard God's voice and said seemingly irrational things. Yet for Weber the honesty of the Jewish prophets was a sign of reason, in which "Judaism clearly represented an advance over the sacrificial practices of the mythological priesthoods of

27. Taylor, *A Secular Age*, 25.

28. Sagan, *Contact*, 162.

29. Karlberg, ed., *Max Weber*, 322.

30. Schwehn, "The Academic Vocation," 191. Schwehn translates *wissenschaft* as "academics" rather than "science" to indicate that the German refers to all knowledge, not only natural science.

the other ancient Near Eastern peoples."[31] As Anthony J. Carroll notes, for Weber the price paid for such uncompromising honesty "was separation from the ordinary life of the people in order to ensure the preservation of the integrity of his message." This ascetical picture of the prophets became Weber's ideal academic in the sense that he or she is a renunciatory hero, dispelling superstition and irrational belief for the sake of truth in one's particular field. On this view, the academy itself becomes a renunciatory hero, rejecting myths from an enchanted world, or at least translating them to fit into a disenchanted context.[32]

One finds an example of this disenchanted academic vocation in the assumption that Catholic sisters, brothers, or priests of a university's founding religious order who are not academics do not really share in the institution's vocation. A Protestant version of this sees the church as having an entirely different vocation than the academy. The result is that the two institutions must travel separate paths, often having little to do with each other. While it is important to make distinctions between the church and academy, Weber's understanding, now dominant, blinds both institutions from seeing how they share a similar *telos*, and therefore in some sense also a vocation.

Revisiting the disenchantment story

There are at least two dominant responses to this modern disenchantment in the university. On the one hand is the effort to get belief back into the academy, e.g. hire professors who believe certain things. On the other hand, some welcome disenchantment as an alternative to proselytism. While the first response might be helpful, it nonetheless fails fully to see how religion as personal belief is part of a disenchanted world. The second response, bewitched by Weber's rationalism, fails to register how all teaching is a kind of proselytism.

Stated more fully, neither response is able to see how the story of disenchantment is *in fact* a story of enchantment filled with a sense of quest,

31. Carroll, "Disenchantment, Rationality," 133.

32. Carroll, "Disenchantment, Rationality," 134. As Sheldon Wolin states, Weber's "form of renunciation is dictated by the demands of specialization that require him to abandon the delights of the Renaissance and Goethian ideal of the universal man who seeks to develop many facets of his personality and as many different fields of knowledge as possible." Cited in Schwehn, "The Academic Vocation," 192.

heroes, and endings. Weber does not depend simply on a rationalized world; he is in fact endorsing a rationalized myth with a beginning and an ending. Though Weber imagines that in a rationalized world he has surpassed enchantment, it is more accurate to say that he has traded one enchanted story for another. William H. Poteat describes this paradox when he writes, "the Enlightenment has intimidated us with its impeachment of myths, all the while preserving and fashioning myths of its own."[33]

Weber does give some sense of how his rationalized myth disenchants in his famous description of the "iron cage," where he admits that rationalization can give birth to certain irrationalities.[34] Here, he acknowledges, we find "specialists without spirit" functioning in a mechanized world, overdetermined by an inhuman technology. Weber's iron cage indicates that even a so-called rational world cannot disenchant all reality, ridding it of both mystery and terror.

Friedrich Schleiermacher

We see a particularly vivid example of modernity's disenchantment/reenchantment story in Friedrich Schleiermacher (1768–1834), known as the father of modern Protestant theology. On the one hand, Schleiermacher is clearly in the modern school of disenchantment, opposed to dry dogmatism, empty customs, primitive beliefs, and miracles inconsistent with the natural world. This kind of religion, Schleiermacher argues, is rightly in ruins, its fragments irrelevant to the modern world. But Schleiermacher is not completely content with such rational disenchantment. The original elements of religion, he argues, were not "dead dross" but "the molten outpourings of the inner fire."[35] If the cultured despisers of his day (the disenchanters) could grasp religion's true essence—a feeling of absolute dependence on the Whole—they would realize that they were actually the

33. Poteat, *A Philosophical Daybook*, 71.

34. Thus Weber writes, "No one knows who will live in this cage in the future, or whether at the end of this tremendous development entirely new prophets will arise, or there will be a great rebirth of old ideas and ideals, or, if neither, mechanized petrification, embellished with a sort of convulsive self-importance. For of the last stage of this cultural development, it might well be truly said: 'Specialists without spirit, sensualists without heart; this nullity imagines that is has attained a level of civilization never before achieved." *The Protestant Work Ethic*, 182.

35. Schleiermacher, *On Religion*, 216.

truly religious.[36] Schleiermacher maintains that religion is not a thinking or a doing (metaphysics or morals), but a feeling and awareness: not dry doctrine or mere morality, but a living experience. "Monk by the Sea," painted by Casper David Friedrich, Schleiermacher's favorite artist, captures the enchanting beauty of this vision. A solitary monk, a small figure, stands before a majestic sea, beauty and threat both palpable in the vast blue darkness of sea and sky. For Schleiermacher, this is not an isolating experience but a unitive one, enabling a connection with all humanity.[37]

Schleiermacher is particularly significant for our analysis because he was instrumental in founding the University of Berlin (1811), which became a model for universities across Europe and America. As Hans Frei observes, the University of Berlin "was organized around a coherent, rational ideal, encompassing all knowledge and *neutral* as to religion."[38] Given this neutrality (or disenchantment), what was the place of religion or theology? Where did it fit, if it belonged at all?

Schleiermacher argues that theology, because it is a positive science, does belong in the university.[39] A positive science, he states, "is an assemblage of scientific elements that belong together not because they form a constituent part of the organization of the sciences, as though by some necessity arising out of the notion of science itself, but only so far as they are requisite for carrying out a practical task."[40] This rather complicated definition rests on a distinction at the time between "positive" and "pure" sciences. Schleiermacher argues that theology studies something historical and specific and therefore "positive," rather than that which is universal or pure (as in philosophy).[41] He thus concludes that theology belongs in the

36. Schleiemacher thus seeks to persuade the cultured despisers of their misguided understanding of true religion: "How unjustly, therefore, do you reproach religion with loving persecution, with being malignant, with overturning society, and making blood flow like water. Blame those who corrupt religion, who flood it with an army of formulas and definitions, and seek to cast it into the fetters of a so-called system." Schleiermacher, *On Religion*, 154.

37. Schleiermacher, *On Religion*, 79.

38. Frei, *Types of Christian Theology*, 98. My emphasis.

39. "Theology is a positive science, the parts of which join into a cohesive whole only through their common relation to a distinct mode of faith, that is, a distinct formation of God consciousness." Schleiermacher, *Brief Outline*, 1.

40. Schleiermacher, *Brief Outline*, 1–2.

41. Edward Farley further notes that "Schleiermacher gives this meaning a new dimension when he says that the positive faculties originate in the need to give cognitive and theoretical foundations to an *indispensable practice*." Farley, *Theologia*, 86.

university because, like the study of medicine and law, which are also positive sciences, it trains people to serve in certain areas of culture.

Yet Schleiermacher also saw theology as providing a sense of the whole. As John M. Stroup notes, Schleiermacher along with Wilhelm von Humboldt (the founder of the University of Berlin) opposed the idea that "education should be dissolved into processes of technical training in which each discipline would be pursued in virtual isolation from all others according to norms of immediate social and economic utility."[42] In contrast to such fragmentation and utility, Schleiermacher understood theology as capable of drawing the disciplines together. Theology thus enables one to see that the true scientists, artists, and poets were, as we saw, the truly religious because they had an immediate sense of themselves in relation to the whole. As Hans Frei summarizes it, Schleiermacher "identifies theology in two ways: as a practical discipline whose unity lies in its aim, the training of people . . . for ministry in the community defined by specific Christian life and language use; and as a historical and philosophical inquiry into the 'essence' of Christianity, that is, as an academic discipline grounded in a unitary theory of explanation for all disciplines and in human nature."[43]

Schleiermacher's re-enchantment

Schleiermacher sought to translate an enchanted religion into the disenchanted world of modern rationalism. In so doing, some have argued, Schleiermacher secured a scientific place for religion in the academy, one not bound by proselytism or narrow ideology.[44] Such an understanding, however, comes from the perspective of a modern disenchantment in which religion proselytizes while scientific study does not.[45]

42. Stroup, "The Idea of Theological Education," 156.

43. Frei, *Types of Christian Theology*, 70. Underlying Schleiermacher's defense, Tice argues, is the conviction that the religious domain is a "separable, independent aspect of the human experience of self and world. Religious consciousness is capable of scientific description as to individual and social phenomena that express it or are somehow associated with it and that are capable of development." Tice, "Schleiermacher on the Scientific Study," 60–61.

44. Tice evaluates Schleiermacher's defense of religion by claiming that he secured a place for the scientific study of religion, "not for narrowly ideological purposes or as a means of proselytizing." Tice, "Schleiermacher on the Scientific Study," 64.

45. As John Milbank puts it, the assumption is that "religions are mystificatory [while] . . . secular liberalism is candid about itself." Milbank, "The Real Third Way," 29.

We can, at this point, ask more fully, "what is actually enchanting the academic imagination that Schleiermacher seeks to extend?" A key aspect of Schleiermacher's enchantment with modernity is his belief that the German people are most capable of being awakened to the truly religious (because most cultured).[46] Speaking to his German cultured despisers, he writes, "It is not blind predilection for my native soil or for my fellows in government and language, that makes me speak thus, but the deep conviction that you alone are capable, as well as worthy, or having awakened in you the sense for the holy and divine things."[47] Readers today might be tempted to see this nationalism as simply a romantic love of Germany that had little to do with Schleiermacher's actual thought. Was he not, even more, seeking to woo his audience?

Yet as Stanley Hauerwas and others have pointed out, Schleiermacher needed the German state to make his defense of religion coherent. "Theology could be part of the university, according to Schleiermacher, insofar as it meets, like medicine and the law, human needs indispensable for the state. Since the state needs religion, theology is justified for the training of clergy who are thus seen as servants of the state."[48] So understood, the study of religion serves the state by helping it run more smoothly. Michael Legaspi points out more generally that over "the course of the 19th century, academic theologians succeeded in assimilating theology to the realities of the modern state in order to ensure the continued survival of their discipline. The fate of theology at the university contains a paradox: by innovating, the Germans conserved."[49] Applied to Schleiermacher, we can say that he innovates; Schleiermacher defines religion in a way that does not violate the rules of a disenchanted neutrality. But in so doing he also conserves: he extends a deeper enchantment with the German state. Such enchantment comes with a heavy price. Edward Farley argues that the price paid by Schleiermacher's defense that religion will prepare cultural leaders, namely

46 Thus Schleiermacher claims that the Islanders are too focused on gain and enjoyment, on utility, whereas the French suffer from "barbarous indifference" and "witty frivolity." Schleiermacher, *On Religion*, 10.

47. Schleiermacher, *On Religion*, 9.

48. Hauerwas, *Sanctify Them in the Truth*, 31–32. As Edward Farley notes, areas of culture such as medicine, law, and theology were "under the protection and sponsorship of the state" and so "the education of leaders for these indispensable regions of practice likewise occurs under the state." Farley, *Theologia*, 86.

49 Legaspi, *The Death of Scripture*, 29. Legaspi goes on to describe this as a Faustian bargain with the rising power of the state.

ministers, was actually "the location of theology outside the university's circle of sciences. Its validity was as a special professional school."[50] In this sense, Schleiermacher ended up underwriting the very thing he wanted to avoid: the isolation of theology from the university. Schleiermacher's legacy in this regard, Farley continues, is that in the "religious studies movement, as in the European Enlightenment, theology's legitimacy in the university and even in the study of religion is highly suspect."[51]

Schleiermacher's efforts, brilliant in many ways though they were, nonetheless underwrote a deep enchantment with the German state that was theologically constructed.[52] As such Schleiermacher calls us to consider more fully: "Who or what is enchanting the academy?," a question to which I will return.

The story of academic excellence

For now, however, let us consider a third story, the story of academic excellence.[53] Colleges and universities rightly strive to be excellent institutions: hiring outstanding faculty, selecting a strong student body, building large endowments, seeking research grants, and so forth. In the dominant story of academic excellence, the best universities are the Ivy Leagues. As early as 1957, David Riesman described American higher education "as a snake with the leading research universities, such as his Harvard, at the head, and the other, lesser institutions following as the tail." Riesman noted that while

50. Farley, *Theologia*, 197. This consequence, Farley notes, remained relatively hidden since most colleges and universities were still related to their sponsoring religious communities. But once "American pluralistic culture created the secular, private and state university, the problem immediately surfaced." Farley, *Theologia*, 197.

51. Farley adds that "the clerical paradigm and the correlation of theology with clergy preparation" has only exacerbated the location of theology "outside the university's circle of sciences." Farley, *Theologia*, 197.

52. Karl Barth's "Concluding Unscientific Postscript on Schleiermacher" is a fascinating document along these lines. While having deep admiration for Schleiermacher, Barth nonetheless wonders how it is that ninety-three German intellectuals, some of them his former professors, were able to sign a manifesto supporting Kaiser Wilhelm II and Chancellor Bethmann-Hollweg's war policy for World War I. While Barth concludes that Schleiermacher would not have signed such a manifesto, he states that "the entire theology which had unmasked itself in that manifesto . . . was grounded, determined, and influenced decisively by him." Green, ed., *Karl Barth*, 71.

53. I engage this story of excellence as well in my essay, "Failure and the Modern Academy."

significant differences existed among institutions, "all took their leads from the head and tried to emulate it," each attempting to move up to a more prestigious place.[54] Normal schools became colleges; teachers colleges became state colleges; and colleges became universities. Moving up this ladder of excellence gave institutions legitimacy and prestige.

Criticisms that an institution does not fit into the story of excellence can be disconcerting. To take a well-known example, George Bernard Shaw once famously said that a Catholic university is an oxymoron. Shaw believed that "Catholic" negated the very idea of a university since Catholics had to acknowledge the authority of the church over academic freedom. Not only were Catholic universities subpar, they were not even real universities.

Catholic educators understandably responded to the kind of criticism leveled by Shaw. In the 1960s, most notably, a prominent group of North American Catholics, led by Fr. Theodore Hesburgh, CSC, then president of Notre Dame, gathered to reassess the Catholic university, especially its relation to the church. Catholic universities, they emphasized, were first and foremost places of excellence:

> The Catholic University today must be a university in the full modern sense of the word, with a strong commitment to and concern for academic excellence. To perform its teaching and research functions effectively the Catholic university must have a true autonomy and academic freedom in the face of authority of whatever kind, lay or clerical, external to the academic community itself . . . . The Catholic university adds to the basic idea of a modern university distinctive characteristics which round out and fulfill that idea.[55]

Such a statement sought to dispel any notion that a Catholic university was a lesser institution than any other. It did not, as some feared, contribute to a "ghetto mentality."[56] As Hesburgh later emphasized, "the church does not have to be present in the modern world of the university, but if it is

54. Cited in Sloan, *Faith and Knowledge*, 72.

55. "Statement on the Nature of the Contemporary Catholic University," which became known as the Land O'Lakes Statement (1967). Gleason identifies at least two causes leading to its development: the need for lay experience on university boards and the worry that "sectarian" institutions might not receive government aid. See Gleason, *Contending with Modernity*, 315–16. O'Brien positively evaluates this statement 1) as an extension of Vatican II and 2) as a necessary endorsement of "Americanism." O'Brien, "A Catholic Academic Revolution," 23–35.

56. For an excellent analysis of this history, see Gleason, *Contending with Modernity*.

to enter, the reality and terms of this world are well established and must be observed."[57] The university terms that Hesburgh identifies—recognized "throughout the world"—are 1) an emphasis on teaching and research, 2) a new function of service to humankind, 3) freedom and autonomy, and 4) a system of governance that involves "diverse layers of power and decision." Descriptions such as "Catholic or Protestant, British or American" qualify but do not supplant the idea of an excellent university.[58]

At the time of this statement, there was also a broader unease about Catholicism and American political culture. This concern is seen most vividly in John F. Kennedy's well-known speech in July 1960 before the Greater Houston Ministerial Association. A presidential candidate at the time, Kennedy famously assured his listeners that his Catholicism would have no direct influence on his politics; they were separate. "I believe in a President whose views on religion are his own private affair . . . and whose fulfillment of his Presidential office is not limited or conditioned by any religious oath, ritual, or obligation . . . ." He summarizes, "For contrary to common newspaper usage, I am not the Catholic candidate for President. I am the Democratic Party's candidate for President who happens also to be a Catholic."[59] The similarity between Kennedy's speech and the Land O'Lakes statement is that both seek to carve out a space for excellence—whether political or academic—in which excellence can be defined regardless of one's Catholic faith. Both statements wish to assure others that freedom is not compromised. The Land O'Lakes statement is far from describing religion as a private affair as does Kennedy. It describes Catholic identity as "operatively present" in the theological disciplines, interdisciplinary dialogue, concern with ultimate questions and warm relations between students and faculty. Even so, the statement assumes that being Catholic is not intrinsic to academic excellence.

This position is not unique to Catholics but represents concerns well embedded in Protestant colleges and universities. The excellent academy is one that moves beyond the backwaters of denominationalism, embracing instead academic freedom and the pursuit of knowledge wherever it may be found. Over the years, the qualifier "Christian" has come to refer to campus ministry, service opportunities, clubs, religion courses, or denominational representation on certain boards. In many instances, excellence

57. Hesburgh, ed., *The Challenge and Promise*, 4.
58. Hesburgh, ed., *The Challenge and Promise*, 3–4.
59. Kennedy, "Speech on His Religion."

means seeing an institution's "religious" identity as a heritage from which one might glean values, the study of ethics, or leadership training to add to its academic foundation.[60]

Evaluating the story of excellence

In his reflections on Hesburgh and the Land O'Lakes statement, David L. Schindler acknowledges, as do I, "the greatness of [Hesburgh's] achievements in so many obvious respects."[61] He questions, however, the inherent logic of positing the basic idea of a university to which a religious affiliation is then added. While chapel, service opportunities, concern for justice, and theology departments are all indispensable for a vibrant Catholic college or university, Schindler states that "none of them yet informs us what specifies a Catholic institution as a university . . . ." It is also necessary, he argues, for it "to develop a Catholic *mind*."[62]

Some readers might have problems with this sort of claim. In the Protestant world, for example, does it make sense to speak of a Baptist or a Methodist mind? Schindler argues, however, that the very way university excellence is framed in the above understanding *already* undermines a Catholic academic excellence. Schindler relates this supposedly neutral excellence to liberalism. As operative in the university, liberalism "stands for a certain priority of method over content . . . . [The] precise intention is to avoid any *a priori* assumption of content which would, *ipso facto*, prejudice the (putative) pure openness of the methods. The burden of critical methods, so conceived, is that they are, of their inner logic, equally open to, and thus neutral toward, all potential contents."[63] Schindler identifies this

60. For example, Thomas Hearn, then president of Wake Forest University (1983–2005), in speaking before the 1989 North Carolina Baptist State Convention, identified "our reputation for academic excellence, celebrated most recently in *US News and World Report* and *USA Today* . . ." with "an already firm liberal arts foundation." He assured his Baptist audience that "we will seek to strengthen those parts of the Wake Forest experience which are appropriate to our religious heritage and our institutional personality," which he identified as "attention to the inculcation of values and the study of ethics, leadership training, and development of character . . . ." Hearn, "Baptist State Convention Speech."

61. Schindler, *Heart of the World*, 144. For a rich account of Hesburgh's life and work, and for his profound gratitude to all the people that made that possible, see Hesburgh, *God, Country, Notre Dame*.

62. Schindler, *Heart of the World*, 147.

63. Schindler, *Heart of the World*, 153.

stance with "proceduralism" or the deflection of any debate about substance into a debate about freedom. Yet, formal methodological procedures already in their very form import content even though, as in the case with Hesburgh and company, the content might not be explicitly embraced or even acknowledged. Schindler describes this content as a Cartesian mechanizing of the intellect (in the order of facts) and a voluntarizing of the will (in the order of values).[64] That is, one engages reality through its various mechanical parts (in the form of sociology or economics or religion, for example) but with little sense of how the parts relate to each another or to a larger whole. At the same time, values become matters of the will. Schindler observes that such dualism is "of a piece with a primacy of doubt, a loss of a primitively theoretical or contemplative disposition toward the object . . . ."[65] That is, there is no acknowledgment of being as given, as gift, and resting in a reality more profound than one's chosen values. The latter understanding is not neutral but "weighted against authentic Catholicism."[66]

For an example of how a voluntarizing of the will is often enshrined in the modern college or university, we can turn to the popular focus on "core values." These might include such values as learning, diversity, excellence, or community. Such statements are no doubt well intended. They inadvertently, however, underwrite the misguided belief that values are one's personal choices. In so doing, they both promote and reveal that there is no shared good. For example, diversity, typically understood as a commitment to celebrate difference, is embraced "for diversity's sake."[67] The underlying assumption is not that we are "beings toward good,"[68] but that values are

---

64. Schindler, *Heart of the World*, 163. As Schindler elaborates, "Descartes wishes to devise a method which leaves one initially neutral with respect to any possible content drawn from objects." Schindler, *Heart of the World*, 162.

65. Schindler, *Heart of the World*, 163.

66. Schindler, *Heart of the World*, 161.

67. This clause is from a 2001 faculty proposal from Saint Mary's College, Notre Dame. In a similar vein, the following statement from the University of North Dakota is typical: "Education concerning values is important in general education—not seeking one right way to behave, but recognizing that choices cannot be avoided. Students should be aware of how many choices they make, how these choices are based on values, and how to make informed choices." Cited in O'Brien, "The Disappearing Moral Curriculum."

68. Grant, *Technology and Justice*, 43. In the last century, Grant notes, "'good' has largely been replaced in our ethical discourse by the word 'value.' The modern emptying of 'good' can indeed be seen in the emptiness of its replacement . . . . The vagueness has resulted in the word generally being used only in the plural—our 'values.'" Grant, *Technology and Justice*, 41. Such values, I would emphasize, are inherently Cartesian,

matters of personal choice. So understood, core values remain abstract ways to protect an assumed neutrality. That is, the institution is neutral in promoting choice and diversity rather than embodying a particular good. Or rather, the good that the institution is in fact promoting is the good of choice itself, a good deeply embedded in the market and the state.

In his reflection on Wendell Berry, Stanley Hauerwas states that there are two questions you cannot ask a university: "What is the university for?" and "who does it serve?"[69] Responses to these questions would require at minimum a conviction that there is a higher common good. The excellent university today, however, one that embraces academic freedom, imagines that any answer to these questions will inevitably be an imposition of one person's values on another. As we have seen, this position fails to see how it is already mired in a way of life oriented toward some notion, however un-articulated, of the good, albeit a distorted one. Adrian Pabst describes this shadow good vividly: "the dominant language of 'choice' legitimates the extension of free-market mechanisms (aided and abetted by the regulatory state) into virtually all areas of socio-economic and cultural life—including education, health, the family, and sex."[70] Such implicit academic forma-tion—into a market society—is one where human bonds are reduced to contract and self-interest, and where concepts such as the "common good" become simply incomprehensible.

For all the lip service, then, paid to diverse values and the encourag-ing of critical thinking, the modern academy easily serves one purpose: to prepare the student to compete. This is true not merely for those who must publish or perish. It applies equally to those who must take part in the global economy as lawyers, MBAs, or software engineers. Those in the "multiversity," Grant states, who come "from some tired tradition may not be much concerned with any discussion of 'faith and the multiversity.' They can accept the dominant paradigm with open arms because it is their ticket to professionalism and that is the name of the game."[71] While the dominant story of excellence imagines that questions of ultimate purpose and of the good can be postponed or placed in a private sphere, the reality is that some

---

relying upon the modern paradigm of knowledge (facts versus values) that empties the conception of good into uncertainty.

69. Hauerwas, *The State of the University*, 97.

70. Pabst, "Introduction," 19.

71. Grant, *Technology and Justice*, 68.

formation into a good, even if a deeply distorted one, is always at work in the imaginations of students and faculty, even if not fully articulated.

Academic freedom

Let us turn more fully, however, to the question of academic freedom and the centrality of this for excellence in the modern university. The Land O'Lakes statement represents the widespread view: academic freedom is necessary to protect an institution from "authority of whatever kind, lay or clerical, external to the academic community itself."

So understood, academic freedom names the ability for individuals or institutions to pursue their own interests without interference. In this sense, academic freedom is negative freedom, or freedom from whatever interferes with the institution or its members. Such freedom from interference is an important condition. Its inadequacy, however, lies in the fact that it has no concept of positive freedom. It cannot say what freedom is for. David Hart describes modernity's freedom:

> The modern notion of freedom is essentially 'nihilistic': that is, the tendency of modern thought is to see the locus of liberty as situated primarily in an individual subject's spontaneous power of choice, rather than in the ends that the subject might actually choose. Freedom, thus understood, consists solely in the power of choosing as such. Neither God, then, nor nature, nor reason provides the measure of an act's true liberty, for an act is *free* only because it might be done in defiance of all three.[72]

Hart contrasts this understanding with classical theology, which understood freedom "principally as the freedom of any being's nature from any alien constraint or external limitation or misuse that might prevent that nature from reaching its full fruition in the end appropriate to it."[73] On this understanding, negative freedom or freedom from refers to that which prevents a person or an institution from reaching its end. A truly excellent academy does not deny academic freedom but repositions it so that freedom in its fullness might be realized. Stated differently, it is not simply a matter of freedom from authority but rather, "which authority is an institution ultimately serving?"

72. Hart, *Atheist Delusions*, 224.
73. Hart, *Atheist Delusions*, 224–25.

John Milbank, for example, observes that while it might appear that "liberalism is primarily about individual freedom . . . it is the freedom of the state which is primary for liberalism, once it has been deconstructed. For the liberty of the subject is only allowed as a device of governmentality in order to increase the power of governance."[74] To the extent this is true, then academic freedom weds the university to the state rather than the church. Some might respond, "This is the point. Academic freedom enables an institution to be free from ecclesial authority." Such an objection, however, fails to register how the authority of the state remains in place, often in unacknowledged ways. One can look, for example, at how federal grants have obligated institutions to do a nation's bidding.[75] Beyond financial connections, however, the dominant concept of academic freedom *unites* the idea of the university with the idea of the nation. A truthful alternative will be one that enables the academy to serve its home country and fellow citizens by showing how freedom rooted in Divine abundance transcends that of any nation, and thus serves the nation more faithfully.

The story of pluralism

Isn't the academy a place where we learn from multiple stories? Isn't it better understood as a tournament of narratives coexisting side by side? Why should one story dominate? From this perspective, my argument for a more truthful plot line can seem like either a benighted nostalgia or an imposition of power.

Such questions represent what I am calling the story of pluralism, a word that can be used in at least one of two ways. On the one hand, it can refer to a plurality of views, habits, and ways of being. For example, there are a plurality of ways of eating, of practicing medicine, and of worshiping

74. Milbank, "The Real Third Way," 35.

75. Burtchaell discusses how federal monies offered to denominational colleges led them to loosen ties with their respective denominations or traditions, especially in light of what little funding they often received from their sponsoring churches. Even more, he notes that "the church has compliantly withdrawn to an impotent distance, while civil authorities at every level now make no apology for imposing their laws and regulations on zoning, gender and ethnic imperatives for enrollment, occupational safety, hiring and faculty appointments, the positioning of chapels, the array of varsity sports, et cetera." Burtchaell, *The Dying of the Light*, 834. Military training and development as well have become deeply embedded in the modern university in the form of research and ROTC programs.

a god or gods. Used in this non-controversial sense, pluralism is descriptive of how people in different times and places do and believe different things. On the other hand, pluralism can be used in a normative way to mean that a plurality of beliefs, values, and ways of being is itself the primary good. To imagine otherwise is to make one story superior to all others and thus to assume a posture of triumphalism. Normative pluralism therefore seeks to unmask attempts to suppress difference for the sake of allowing plurality to flourish. It is pluralism in this latter sense—as normative—that I am addressing here.

To describe normative pluralism more fully, I want to look at Martin Marty's 1986 lecture "Anticipating Pluralism: The Founders' Vision." Marty's account of pluralism is normative in that he advocates for pluralism as our essential good. To begin, Marty is careful to say what he does not mean by pluralism. He is not using it to refer to a philosophy that sees the universe as being metaphysically plural rather than as having a single source. Nor is he equating pluralism with a relativism in which there are "many truths out there, all equally true and thus equally false."[76] Marty rather describes pluralism as building on a diversity but in addition as referring to "a polity, a program, a way of life." As such, pluralism is "a value that helps assure civil concord when a republic is made up of individuals and groups who do not share each others' outlooks on life or on what Paul Tillich called matters of 'ultimate concern.'"[77] For Marty, at this point, pluralism names a way of life for getting along with others with whom one disagrees. Understood in this minimal sense, pluralism is not controversial. Most Christians and others would agree that learning to live alongside those with whom they differ—including those within one's own faith—is important. Marty, however, goes on to contrast pluralism with homogenization and it is at this point that problems arise.

Marty explains that "homogenizers" are those who believe a republic or a people must be built on sameness and who thus privilege one tradition. A homogenizer is someone like "Senex, M.A.," a New Englander who feared that Congress in 1791 would

> pass a declarative resolve granting universal toleration to all opinions and free liberty to Familists, Libertines, Erastians, Anto-trinitarians, Anabaptists, Antinomian, Arians, Sabellians, Montanists, Arminians, Socinians, Deists, Mortallians, Gnosticks . . . . In a

76. Marty, *Anticipating Pluralism*, 1–2.
77. Marty, *Anticipating Pluralism*, 2.

word, room for Hell above ground. What can be expected but that such Gehenical errors will turn Christ's Academy into the Devil's University.[78]

Senex, in his quest to avoid "Hell above ground," is a homogenizer, according to Marty, because he does not allow for the good of pluralism. By contrast, Marty describes pluralism as a normative way of life that stands against all tribalist or totalitarian temptations such as represented by Senek. On Marty's account, pluralism is the American vision; it provides coherence to the American way of life. "If one must choose between a society where those who are unified grant rights to dissent, or one where those who are diverse must find coherence, the American record suggests value in the latter."[79] We agree to be diverse.

A key difficulty with Marty's analysis, however, is his either/or contrast between pluralism and homogeneity. When pluralism as a "way of life" makes choice the highest good, then pluralism itself functions as a homogenizing force. In the academy, one sees the homogenizing effect of pluralism as "every challenge to a point of view is just another point of view," soon to be absorbed into the conformity called "diversity."[80] That this is so indicates how such pluralism blinds one to how particular homogenizing convictions are inevitably present. Seen in this light, "Anticipating Pluralism" is really a tale of the nation-state's struggle for freedom "situated within a still larger narrative of (for want of another name) the 'triumph of the will.'"[81]

Marty naturally embraces the nonestablishment clause of the constitution and the protection of religious liberty for all.[82] For Christians, understandings of freedom are not first of all rooted in the human will's choice but in the worship of a non-coercive God, a God who allows humans to go their own way and even more a God who calls the faithful not to be dominating lords but servants of others.[83] Most importantly, Christians

---

78. Cited in Marty, *Anticipating Pluralism*, 17.

79. Marty, *Anticipating Pluralism*, 22.

80. Mansfield, "Political Correctness," 269.

81. Hart, *Atheist Delusions*, 224.

82. As Marty points out, the same year that Senex argued against the "Devil's university," Congress passed a "declarative resolution" in the form of the First Amendment stating it "shall make no law respecting an establishment of religion, or prohibiting the free exercise thereof."

83. For a classic statement of this freedom as servanthood, see Luther, *On Christian Liberty*.

find political coherence not ultimately in their national identity but in the wider body of Christ, across time and place. One often hears that if it were not for the nation, then Christians would not be able to worship freely. This conviction is idolatrous, however, in that it makes the modern nation necessary for salvation.[84]

But the question remains in regard to Marty's defense of normative pluralism: how are diverse religions or other groups to engage one another? Professor of Law and Religion John D. Inazu points in a helpful direction when he argues that particular moral judgments are necessary for any robust conversation. Such judgments, he argues, "can focus on ideas and beliefs rather than on people. They can avoid stigmatizing others, but they will not avoid causing offense. We fall short of the aspirations of tolerance, humility, and patience when we stigmatize others. But we risk a false tolerance—and a false humility—if we insist that nobody can be offended."[85] Inazu relates moral judgments to certain virtues: humility, patience, and tolerance (by which he means, significantly, a kind of practical enduring.)[86] Marty, however, sees traditions of virtue themselves as a threat to pluralism. "Many of our most distinguished philosophers, among them Alasdair MacIntyre in *After Virtue* (1981) . . . give voice to criticisms of pluralism. The MacIntyres fear that no virtue can be forthcoming in a republic made up of a general muster of opinionists."[87] Marty fails to see how pluralism as bare opinion, unsustained by formation into a higher good can only produce fragmentation, a point I return to in chapter 4.

For now, however, I want to consider two key ways that pluralism has played itself out in the Christian academy. First, numerous Christian colleges and universities, for the sake of pluralism, have interpreted their own particular tradition as a negative, homogenizing force. The inevitable result, now well documented, has been the dislocation of Christian colleges and universities from their sponsoring churches. It has come to seem incoherent to privilege any one "sect" over another. As Christian colleges and universities have embraced normative pluralism, their allegiance has shifted unsurprisingly from the church to the guild and the nation. As James Burtchaell points out about this shift, "No one anywhere [has been]

---

84. The martyrs testify to the fact that Christians are always free to worship.

85. Inazu, *Confident Pluralism*, 101.

86. Inazu, "How Confident is Our Pluralism?"

87. Marty, *Anticipating Pluralism*, 6.

worried that to be American might be more sectarian [or more homogenizing] than being Methodist."[88]

A second way that Christian colleges and universities have extended the story of pluralism is by making it central to their own particular identity. Thus pluralism or diversity comes to be seen as lying at the heart one's particular denomination or tradition. "Diversity," in this context, does not mean racial or ethnic diversity, but rather a diversity of beliefs and views. Baptist historian Walter Shurden, for example, argues that diversity is one of the distinctive features of Baptist life and thought: "the Baptist passion for freedom is a major reason why there is so much diversity in Baptist life. Baptists differ, and their differences are often broad and deep . . . . While diversity is threatening to some and downright devastating to others, it flows naturally from the Baptist preoccupation with the right to choice."[89] Shurden thus sees freedom and diversity as central to Baptist identity. Catholics have made similar claims. Theologian Rev. John Shea, in his essay "Here Comes Everybody," points out the great plurality in the Catholic world. He states that "Catholic identity is ultimately located in a spirit, an ethos, a sensibility, a structure of imagination . . . . It is a spirit of inclusion which sees analogies rather than disjunctions between all beings. It has an affinity for both/and rather than either/or statements."[90] An emphasis on both/and is another way of claiming diversity as central to Catholicism. Likewise theologian Paul Lakeland states that "through diversity we (Catholics) express the essence of the sacramental imagination . . . ."[91]

Revisiting pluralism

A crucial question: how is it that two very different traditions have come to claim diversity as essential to their identity? If one considers, for example, the history of Baptists vis-à-vis Catholics, one sees substantial and at times highly contested differences. If diversity has been an essential mark, then why a history of divergence? Such questions suggest that certain ideological forces have overwhelmed theology reflection.

88. Burtchaell, *The Dying of the Light,* 837.

89. Shurden, *The Baptist Identity,* 2–3.

90. Shea, "Here Comes Everybody," 510.

91. Lakeland, "Otherness, Difference and the Unity of Purpose."

Certainly welcoming the other, the stranger, and even the enemy through the practice of hospitality is an extension of Christian convictions.[92] Scripture acknowledges that when one welcomes the other, he or she is welcoming Christ (Matt 25). Normative pluralism, however, reflects a logic at odds with such hospitality. As theologian Michael Baxter points out, to describe Catholicism as a "both/and" tradition is to fail to see how being "both/and" is a logical contradiction since a "both/and" position must include an "either/or" position. That is, a both/and position has no way to make discriminating judgments about convictions, ideas, or events that would not be included. Baxter asks, for example, "Do we really want to uphold the 'both/and' approach when it comes to an event such as the Holocaust? Is the Catholic impulse both for anti-Semitism and against it?"[93]

There is no question that encountering different persons, ideas, and beliefs enhances the learning process. Engagement with different beliefs, stories, and ways of thinking is a crucial aspect of what it means to be educated. This kind of diversity or plurality is a given. And yet normative pluralism has no resources for making wise judgments or for fully welcoming the other. It rather inscribes its adherents into a tale where the good is plurality itself, which, ironically, leads to scarcity. Adherents of pluralism might well object, comparing pluralism to a garden where wide-ranging beliefs and values are "like a colorful field in which wheat is growing and posies and cornflowers are blooming . . . ."[94]

Choice and availability alone, however, do not generate abundance. As Aquinas notes, "To possess the power to choose evil is a sign not of perfection but of weakness."[95] In other words, freedom must be grounded in something other than freedom of choice in order to produce abundance. Economist John C. Médaille argues, from a different angle, that "the moral question and the economic question are in reality one."[96] He emphasizes that "the assumption that all things can be based on self-interest destroys the very basis of virtue which is presumed by the market."[97] Choice or the market alone require a higher good in order to produce a flourishing life. Pluralism's "wealth" is its misguided assumption that difference and choice

92. Newman, *Untamed Hospitality*.

93. Baxter, "Review Symposium," 331.

94. Lohfink, *Does God Need*, 298.

95. Cited in Caldecott, *Beauty for Truth's Sake*, 91

96. Médaille, *Toward a Truly Free Market*, 5.

97. Médaille, *Toward a Truly Free Market*, 39.

alone—along with unmasking all that excludes difference—will produce abundance.

But what is the alternative? To return to our earlier question, isn't privileging one tradition at the expense of others inevitably a denial of academic freedom? Yet some tradition, including the tradition of pluralism, is always being privileged. My concern is to see how pluralism as the dominant story or tradition in the Christian college or university distorts academic being. The academic Good is not diversity itself. It rather results from becoming the kind of institution capable of serving God in all places. This is not a coercive or competitive project but an invitation to study and participate in a Wisdom not our own.

Conclusion

A beloved Greek professor of mine, Dr. Carl Harris, once recounted a heated faculty debate in which a professor stood up and asked, "Knowledge for what?" My professor did not tell us the context of the exchange but the way he told the story—the way he put the question before us—was compelling. George Grant poses similar questions: "How can we do a proper job of education unless we have some clarity as to what education is for? How can the purpose for which we study not determine what studies are carried on?"[98] The stories I have told in this chapter offer their own responses; the purpose of education is to abandon naïve beliefs, aim for excellence or embrace pluralism. But these stories, I have argued, distort our academic lives by leaving us with no resources to embrace a divine goodness that permeates all of creation.

Even after these distorted stories are exposed, however, we can still find ourselves "living under the press of our vague feelings" that their views

---

98. Grant, "The Paradox of Democratic Education," 173. Grant notes that common responses to these questions include 1) teaching students how to think, 2) instilling values, and 3) adjusting to the world. In response to the first, Grant argues that one must give "some view of what really matters in life." In other words, "why is it good to think?" To the second, Grant argues that values depend on what is real. "For example, if a man believes that the struggle for animal existence is the underlying truth of all nature and history, obviously the virtue of brotherhood will not seem valuable." Grant, "The Paradox of Democratic Education," 175. In response to the third argument that education is essentially functional, Grant says that this turns universities into "servants of the expanding economy." Grant, "The Paradox of Democratic Education," 169.

are correct. "We are immured in our unresolved, affective evaluations."[99] The habits and practices of modernity have deeply inscribed us into flattened ways of academic being. In the next chapter, I describe an alternative, one that grounds academic being in Divine abundance.

99. Poteat, *A Philosophical Daybook*, 71. Poteat is referring explicitly to the Enlightenment, especially in its regard for "myth."

2

THE LOGIC OF BEING

Recovering the Depth of Divine Abundance

I have argued that distorted stories leave the academy unable to address the following questions: knowledge for what? Who or what is the academy serving? What is its ultimate purpose? In this chapter, I aim to show how an inadequate ontology lies at the heart of the academy's distorted narratives. That is, the academy, like modernity more broadly, imagines being apart from any inherent orientation, logic, or depth, a position that inevitably leaves the academy stranded at sea with no compass. In what follows, I argue for a more truthful understanding, one in which divine abundance both grounds being and provides its telos. What does it mean to say being is abundant or that ontology has a certain depth? I turn to the thought of Aquinas as well as contemporary thinkers William H. Poteat, and David L. Schindler, all of whom describe created being—including academic being—as oriented toward a Good greater than itself.

A lack of being

First, however, let's consider more fully how being becomes diminished. In the myth of Narcissus, a beautiful young man fixates on himself so obsessively that he is impervious to the love of others. A nymph named Echo pines miserably for him. When Narcissus refuses even her love, the gods grow angry. They consign Narcissus to gaze forever at his own reflection. We typically understand this story as one of sheer egoism and self-absorption: Narcissus is the first narcissist. David Kettle, however, argues that while Narcissus "may seem at first sight to be too full of himself, to the exclusion of all others," the deeper story is one of "personal lack and of a futile longing."[1] The myth of Narcissus, Kettle argues, is ultimately one of scarcity and impoverishment because he is unable ultimately to affirm others and the world as distinct from himself. He cannot truly even affirm himself but is rather caught up in an unattainable or isolated false self. As such, the figure of Narcissus does not so much express self-confidence as its opposite: his stance a defense "against the threat of personal disintegration."[2] Seen in a theological context, Narcissus suffers from a lack of being: an inability to be receptive "to God, to fellow human beings, and ultimately to the conditions of created life under God."[3] Understood in this light, the myth of Narcissus shows how genuine being involves communion. Cut off from such communion, Narcissus ends up gazing at a self that he basically lacks.

Stratford Caldecott describes this lack of being as a loss of ontological depth. Caldecott applies this description more specifically to a contrast between "medieval man" and "modern man":

> A popular misconception has it that medieval man thought the world was flat, and modern science gave us a round world floating in an infinite space. But the truth is almost the opposite of this. Medieval man inhabited a three-dimensional cosmos which has now been largely replaced by a flat universe, with no ontological depth. It is not a question of size, or even of infinite spaces. An infinite field is still essentially flat. In pure modernity there can be no up or down, no getting closer to hell or heaven, and there are no sacred places and times which participate in the divine.[4]

In developing this contrast, Caldecott states that in modernity "nothing can exist but individual objects." The "vertical" and "interior" dimensions of reality such as final causality (ultimate purpose) or divine providence are effectively eliminated.[5] This lack of ontological depth prevents one from seeing things in this world—including one's own self—as "tokens of a real-

---

1. Kettle, *Western Culture*, 230.

2. Kettle, *Western Culture*, 228. In developing this point, Kettle engages the work of Christopher Lasch, particularly *The Culture of Narcissism*.

3. Kettle, *Western Culture*, 229.

4. Caldecott, *Beauty for Truth's Sake*, 139.

5. Caldecott, *Beauty for Truth's Sake*, 29.

ity that exceeds them infinitely."[6] To describe things in this world as signs of a reality that exceeds them is to acknowledge that being is not simply flat. To say that everything is a sign of something greater is to say that in some way the cosmos points or participates in something beyond itself. Caldecott is describing, we could say, the world—creation—as liturgical: its depths resting ultimately in the God who creates it.

One might argue that modern science rightly ignores such ontological depth. Its purpose is rather to study, classify, and dissect the world, not to engage in speculation about being. While I will return to this concern, suffice it to say for now that a flat ontology inevitably distorts all the disciplines, including that of science itself. To the extent that Narcissus fails to see his being as communion, he lives a shallow existence. Similarly, to the extent that the academic disciplines and the academy more broadly fail to see all being as tokens of an abundance that exceeds them, then they too are suffering from a certain lack.

William H. Poteat provides a vivid personal account of this lack of being. He writes about standing in a shopping mall where, for a brief moment, he is suddenly seized "by a mild and fugitive attack of amnesia."[7] This is no case of absentmindedness but a "deeper sense of estrangement from myself and from the world—for the brief moment that it lasts, more disturbing than a familiar instance of forgetfulness."[8] Why this disorientation? Poteat recounts that he looked for some clue as to why "this place is *this* place rather than some other." He realizes, "There is none. Indeed, this is not even a *place*." Every shop is part of a national chain, there are no local businesses, and the mall is one of a "theoretically infinite number of identical malls . . . nothing here speaks uniquely of or to the history of my forty-five years of

---

6. Caldecott, *The Radiance of Being*, 60. A rejection of this way of seeing, Caldecott goes on to argue, had its source in fourteenth-century Christian philosophy that separated science from faith, and God from nature in what came to be known as the "*via moderna* of the nominalist philosophers . . . ." Caldecott, *The Radiance of Being*, 29. He continues, "The last three hundred years have consequently been an increasingly empirical rather than metaphysical age: priority has been accorded to externals, to quantities, to experimental evidence (although this emphasis on the material externals masked a parallel absolutization of human consciousness as the sole source of certitude and value)." Caldecott, *The Radiance of Being*, 30–31.

7. Poteat, *Recovering the Ground*, 77.

8. Poteat, *Recovering the Ground*, 77.

life in these environs."[9] Upon reflection, Poteat states: "being is contracted into an abstract entity that is nowhere in particular at no particular time."[10]

Poteat uses the phrase "contracted being" to describe a radical dislocation in place and time. While Narcissus's loss results from an infinite abstracted gaze at his own reflection, Poteat's loss of self comes rather from being in the infinite space of a timeless mall. In both instances, however, one's being is diminished. If as Kierkegaard states "walking is the gait of finitude," then the infinite gaze—whether at the self or in a placeless mall—reflects a loss of being. Poteat reflects on his experience at the mall in order to describe a broader cultural malady, one that led Pascal years ago to ask, "What is a man in the infinite?"[11] Pascal was faced with Descartes's universe abstracted into mathematical formula in which there are no personal pronouns or references to particular places and times.[12] In this world, as Caldecott says, there can be "no up or down . . . no sacred places in times which participate in the divine."

A loss of ontological depth

To shed light on this loss of ontological depth, I want to engage an earlier debate concerning the univocity of being, specifically between John Duns Scotus (c. 1266–1308) and Thomas Aquinas (1225–1274). As a number of scholars have emphasized,[13] Scotus's understanding of being as univocal has come to influence how modernity imagines being. Scotus, known as the "subtle doctor," argued that terms could be univocally predicated of

9. Poteat, *Recovering the Ground*, 78.

10. Poteat, *Recovering the Ground*, 79.

11. Poteat, *Recovering the Ground*, 10.

12. Poteat relates this estrangement to Cartesianism: "a universe embodied in mathematical discourse in the formal elements of which there are no egocentric particulars for making explicit references to specific times and places in the actual world, no tenses for expressing the temporal distension and deployment in time of such a world, no demonstrative or personal pronouns." Poteat, *Recovering the Ground*, 9–10.

13. Scholars discussing the impact of Scotus on modernity include Taylor, *A Secular Age*, Milbank, *Theology and Social Theory*, Gregory, *The Unintended Reformation*, and Pickstock, *After Writing*. Hart in *Atheist Delusions* discusses specifically the impact of nominalism (associated primarily with William of Occam but who was influenced by Scotus). There are some disagreements among these thinkers. For example, Hart, in an otherwise positive review of Pickstock's *After Writing*, criticizes her interpretation of Scotus. Hart argues that Pickstock's analysis of Scotus is at times misleading and that he deserves better than to be treated as the "first modern." Hart, "Review Essay."

both God and creatures. To say that a word is univocal is to say that it has the same meaning when applied in reference to different things. For example, "Fido barks" and "Spot barks." Both of these sentences use "bark" in the same way. By contrast, with equivocal language two concepts mean entirely different things: "Fido has a bark" and "the tree has bark."[14] Finally, analogy refers to a relationship between two terms or things which are partly different and partly the same.[15]

In defense of a univocity of being predicated of God and creation, Scotus had two admirable goals: 1) to deal with the possibility of knowledge of God, and 2) to develop an understanding of theology as a science.[16] Scotus argued that God could be known—at least in part—through reason, and that theology itself is a science like any other discipline in the university. Scotus developed his argument in response to what he saw as a certain latent agnosticism in his peers: Henry of Ghent and most famously Aquinas. For Scotus, use of analogous language for God led to agnosticism: unless there was univocity of some sort, then one would be left completely in the dark when speaking of God. As Scotus saw it, if we only have analogical language to speak of God, then understanding something of God through the natural order would not be possible.

Scotus's key argument against analogical language (though he allowed for it in some cases) is that one must have a shared sense of a word (univocity) in order for it to be meaningful. Thus, Scotus states, "If the same word names (or signifies) different things, then it must do so by a feature they hold in common. Analogical usage, then, must ultimately reduce to a solid univocal core of meaning as its justification."[17] For example, if we

---

14. Bauerschmidt, *Holy Teaching*, 68. Bauerschmidt is commenting on ST 1.13.5.

15. How Aquinas uses "analogy" is the subject of wide debate. As we will see, a key rationale for his use of analogy is to avoid both univocal and equivocal language when speaking of God's being and created being.

16. As one commentator puts it, "If, in his argument, Scotus can show that the human mind has foundational access to reality, and if that reality provides an adequate basis for natural knowledge of God, then theology can be understood as a science, whose content does not exhaust the truth about God." Ingham and Dreyer, *The Philosophical Vision of John Duns Scotus*, 40. Gregory states, "Starting from the traditional position of the radical distinction between God and creation, Scotus asked what could be said about God strictly on the basis of reason or philosophy." Thus, Gregory continues, Scotus's concern was to defend a bridge between "what observation could discover or philosophy could discern about God on the one hand, and Christianity's central claims about God's actions in history on the other." Gregory, *The Unintended Reformation*, 36.

17. Cited in Rolnick, *Analogical Possibilities*, 104.

say God is wise, then we must have some conception of what being wise is so that we know something of what it means when we apply it to God. Scotus argued, in fact, that analogy depends upon univocity. That is, "if of two things one is the measure of the other, then they must have something in common that permits the first to be the measure of the second, and the second to be measured by the first." Or again, "Things are never related as the measured to the measure, or as the excess to the excedent unless they have something in common . . . ."[18] In other words, even though God far exceeds humans, one still needs a common or shared meaning of wisdom, goodness, and so forth to be able to speak truthfully. How can we speak of God as wise, after all, unless we have some prior (univocal) understanding of wisdom? Scotus thus argued that it is possible for terms related to moral and intellectual perfections, such as wisdom or goodness, to be predicated or affirmed univocally of both God and creatures.

Of particular interest for my analysis is Scotus's understanding of the concept of *being* itself as univocal. It is possible, he claimed, to have a concept of being that is neutral as pertaining to the being of God and the being of creatures, but that is contained in both. Thus, Scotus states, "The intellect of a person in this life can be certain that God is a being though doubtful as to whether he is a finite or an infinite being, a created or an uncreated being. Hence as regards God the concept of being is other than this concept [i.e. of infinite or uncreated being] and that concept [i.e., of finite or created being]. And thus in itself the concept is neither of these and is included in each. Hence it is a univocal concept [of being]."[19] Scotus is arguing that being has a prior meaning that can be applied to both God and humans. The difference is that infinite being applies to God and finite being applies to humans. The words "finite" and "infinite" are included in this concept of being but not reducible to it.

Scotus thus assured his readers that in contrast to any agnostic approach, it is possible to form a concept of being that applies to both God and humans. This concept of being is logically antecedent to "finite" or "infinite." Being is the neutral category onto which such distinctions infinite or finite are mapped. Significantly, this qualification of being is a description about the *way* something is, what Scotus calls "intrinsic modes[s] of being."

---

18. Cited in Evans, *The Medieval Theologians*, 253.

19. Cited in Evans, *The Medieval Theologians*, 254.

So, for example, Scotus himself compares "infinite being" to "intense whiteness."[20] By extension, finite being would be less intense but still white.

As we noted, Scotus is seeking to establish a basis for knowledge of God that rests on the natural order of being. In so doing, he aims to move away from a kind of analogical agnosticism and toward a way of talking about God that makes sense in the natural world.[21] As commentators Ingham and Dreyer put it, for Scotus the "univocity of being is, first, the condition for the possibility of any metaphysics as well as of any theology."[22] At first glance, this might seem a good move since it allows space for God-talk in the otherwise natural academy. In reality, however, it has the opposite effect.

In contrast to this univocity of being, Aquinas famously argued for an analogical understanding. Aquinas saw both univocity and equivocity as problematic; the first reduces God to human concepts while the second leaves one unable to speak about God at all. On the one hand, a univocity of being domesticates God to one being among others. As Brad Gregory describes, "insofar as God's existence is considered in itself and in its most general sense, Scotus agreed that God's being does not differ from that of everything else that exists."[23] By domesticating God to one being among others, univocity eventually makes Divine being superfluous.[24] If God is one being among others—even though infinite—there is no real difference between God's being and ours.

On the other hand, as univocity places God as infinite being outside the order of finite being, God becomes increasingly mystified: the difference between infinite and finite equivocal. Catherine Pickstock states that "the univocity of being paradoxically gives rise to a kind of equivocity, for

---

20. Evans, *The Medieval Theologians*, 264.

21. It is important to emphasize that Scotus did not think such natural knowledge sufficient in terms of complete knowledge of creatures vis-à-vis God. For example, he did not believe that humans could know their final end from nature; "it is necessary, therefore, that there be imparted to him some supernatural knowledge." Cited in Micklem, *Reason and Revelation*, 9. At the same time, Scotus maintained that "whether [necessary truths] are known to us by faith or by special or general revelation, [they] can be known by natural cognition." Cited in Micklem, *Reason and Revelation*, 9.

22. Ingham and Dreyer, *The Philosophical Vision*, 47.

23. Gregory, *The Unintended Reformation*, 37.

24. Schindler makes a similar point in discussing the naturalism of Baius (1513–89) and Jansenius (1585–38). A concept of pure being or pure nature, he states, leads to a pernicious separation between the natural and supernatural, "rendering the latter (seemingly) superfluous." Schindler. "Introduction," xviii.

the difference of degree or amount of Being disallows any specific resemblance between them, and excludes the possibility of figural or analogical determinations of God that give us any degree of substantive knowledge of his character."[25] That is, a univocity of being allows for no relation between infinite and finite being. Rather all being is the same, thus in the end mystifying God.

The plot for how modernity has come to understand created being vis-a-vis God's being is of course profoundly complex. We can nonetheless begin to see an emerging challenge that makes it difficult if not impossible to speak of being as communion. The modern academy, for its part, is held captive by a picture of being as univocal. For example, in response to whether a quasi-Christian institution is "secular or sacred," a university president responds as follows: "'Everything is what it is, and is not another thing.' That principle of identity leads us to conclude that [this university] is what it is. We should never be tempted to turn from the unique and promising path which is ours alone."[26] One could hardly find a more perfect example of a flat ontology. Whether intended or not, the president is espousing a ultimately nominalist conviction. If being is "simply there," then nominalism maintains that "there is nothing real outside of disconnected individual things . . . ."[27] The academy "is what it is"; it has no ontological density, no higher good that might relate it to other institutions or, even more, to the very Source of its own being.

Abundant being, Aquinas, and analogy

In contrast to such univocity, Aquinas held that since God is the source of all being, then Divine being must be radically other than creaturely being. God is not one being among others but the fount of being. Aquinas thus argues that God does not *have* being but *is* being. Created reality, by contrast, participates in being, but is not itself being. We partake of being; we do not possess it since it is always a gift. We thus share in being: we "participate in God exactly to the extent that we exist at all."[28] Aquinas develops this

---

25. Pickstock, *After Writing*, 123.

26. Hearn, "To Dream with One Eye Open," 15. Hearn is citing the eighteenth century philosopher Joseph Butler

27. Barron, *The Priority of Christ*, 14. Barron is here specifically describing William of Occam's understanding.

28. Griffiths, *Intellectual Appetites*, 79.

understanding through the use of two key Latin words: *esse* (existence) and *quid* (essence). *Esse* or existence refers to the act or activity of being, the fact of existing. *Quid*, the essence or nature, refers to what a thing is. Every created thing that exists (*esse*) has an orienting essence or nature (*quid*), which is also a potential. Aquinas transforms these Aristotelian terms to emphasize two key aspects of created being: 1) all created being by virtue of its existence and essence is pure gift and 2) all created being has a basic ontological potency. Not only is creaturely being utterly groundless because it is a gift, Aquinas holds that created being is oriented toward receptivity and communion. This is creation's ontological potency and potential.

The distinction between existence and essence parallels Aquinas's use of actual and potential. But these distinctions, says Aquinas, cannot apply to God. This is because God has no potential; God is already fully actual. Therefore God's existence and essence are one. As Frederick Bauerschmidt states, for Aquinas God's existence is "radically free from all possibility of becoming. Or, as Thomas is wont to put it, God is 'pure act.'"[29] In saying God is "pure act," Aquinas is describing a Divine fullness that cannot be exceeded. God is already fully who God is and always will be. In this sense God does not need anything in order to be complete: God's being and God's becoming are already completely one. Aquinas calls this the "simplicity" of God, meaning that differences like the difference between existence and essence do not apply to God.

We can emphasize, as does David Bentley Hart, that such an understanding of Divine being is Trinitarian. The relations of Father to Son or Spirit are "not extrinsic relations 'in addition to' . . . the divine essence; rather, they are the very reality by which the persons subsist. Thus the Father is eternally and essentially Father *because* he eternally has his Son, and so on." Hart is emphasizing that Divine being does not involve some essence onto which relations are then added. Rather, Divine being *is* triune communion: "nothing in the Father 'exceeds' the Son and Spirit. . .to be known and to be loved are all one act." Thus one can say that " . . . the God who is also always Logos is also eternal Being."[30] The significance of the identification of Logos and eternal Being is a radical departure from a neutral or unknown being

---

29 Bauerschmidt, *Holy Teaching*, 60. As Aquinas states, "Therefore, since in God there is no potentiality . . . it follows that in Him essence does not differ from existence. Therefore His essence is His existence." Aquinas, *ST* 1.3.4.

30. Hart, "The Destiny of Christian Metaphysics," 407.

that is infinite. Hart is rather pointing to how Divine being is inherently Logos, but always in a way that exceeds human grasp.

Such convictions lay the groundwork for Aquinas to claim, in contrast to Scotus, that God is not a being alongside other beings, but the One who is present to and sustains all created being. To say God is pure act is to say that God is the Agent apart from whom all created being would cease to exist. For Aquinas, then, analogous language is not equivocal or agnostic, as Scotus imagined. Rather analogy makes it possible "to say true things about a God who exceeds our capacity for comprehension. In creation, God imparts to us an existence that *shares* in God's own existence, while also being fundamentally *different* from God's existence (since our existence has a source outside of us, whereas God's does not)."[31] Aquinas's analogous use of existence/essence to describe being avoids reducing God to another being (univocal) while also refusing to completely separate God and created being (equivocal). The use of existence/essence (or actual/potential) allows for an acknowledgment of God as radically other than created being while also showing how God is intimately present to all being, closer to us than we are to ourselves.[32] Aquinas can thus say that "God is in all things; not, indeed, as part of their essence, nor as an accident, but as an agent is present to that upon which it works . . ." God is able to be "in all things, and innermostly."[33]

Aquinas's analogy of being also allows one to say that God's being cannot be depleted. God's being is complete abundance so that no giving can diminish God. So understood, Divine being is underived. Aquinas refers to Exodus 3:14, where God says to Moses, "I am who I am," in the context of describing the "existence" of God.[34] To call God the unmoved Mover, then, is not to posit a distant, stoic-like God. Rather to describe God as underived (not coming from anywhere else) and unmoved (not being caused by something outside of God) is to say that God is the one who moves all else, the sun and stars and indeed all creation.

Some have worried that analogical language (*analogia entis*) opens the door to domesticating God: to ignoring that God is Wholly Other.

31. Bauerschmidt, *Holy Teaching*, 68.

32. As Griffiths puts it, "God is *interior intimo tuo*, interior to what is most intimate to you; but God is also vastly and immeasurably different, other, and superior to what is most exaltedly yours." Griffiths, *Intellectual Appetites*, 79.

33. Aquinas, *ST* 1.8.1.

34. Aquinas, *ST* 1.2.3.

As Hart points out, however, an equivocity of being between God and creation disallows any understanding of the incarnation: God could not become human but would have to become a hybrid or something radically opposed to human being: "an amalgamation . . . not the God-man but a monstrosity, a hybrid of natures that in themselves, would remain opposed and unreconciled."[35] The difference between God and humans is not quantitative (as in univocity), but is rather an "infinite qualitative difference." "Because the difference between God and creation is the difference between Being and created beings," there is in Christ "no diminishment of his divinity nor any violation of the integrity of his humanity."[36] Since the difference between "the divine and human really is an infinite qualitative difference, the hypostatic union involves no contradiction, alienation, or change in the divine Son."[37] Hart's christological engagement with being as analogical opens up space to see being as always an ever greater gift made possible by the triune God.

What then creates distance from God? As we have emphasized, for Aquinas God is never distant from us. What was true for Augustine is also true for Aquinas: "At the heart of each creature lies an enigma, as Augustine realized, for at the heart of each creature is a relation to God that makes the creature more than itself."[38] On the other hand, however, creatures can be distant from God. Aquinas says, "Hence nothing is distant from Him, as if it could be without God in itself. But things are said to be distant from God by the unlikeness to Him in nature or grace; as also He is above all by the excellence of His own nature."[39] In other words, creaturely distance from God has to do not with God, but with our unlikeness to God, our failure to reflect divine likeness.

To summarize, Aquinas uses analogy to show how created being is related to Divine being but in a way that reveals the richness of an incomprehensible dissimilarity. Aquinas's use of "essence" and "existence" of both creation and God illuminates the gift of created being and the triune source of all that is. To say that created being is both actual and potential is to say that all of creation "is already as itself *more than itself* . . . ."[40] An

---

35. Hart, "The Destiny of Christian Metaphysics," 409.

36. Hart, "The Destiny of Christian Metaphysics," 409–410.

37. Hart, "The Destiny of Christian Metaphysics," 410.

38. Hanby, "Creation and Aesthetic Analogy," 368.

39. Aquinas, *ST* 1.8.1.

40. Milbank, *Being Reconciled*, 368. My emphasis.

ontological depth marks creation. This depth points to the "more than" as mysteriously grounded in the abundance of God. All cosmic being is a sign that points to an evermore generous Giver. An ontological gratuity thus marks the heart of all created being that when actualized returns the world to its Source through communion with God. Thus we can say that "nature's de facto integration into a divine calling renders nature not less but *more* (i.e., more deeply and truly) natural."[41] In other words, the natural is not that which somehow exists in a domain apart from God; the natural is rather that which lives into the gift of being. Understandings of being blind to this ontological potency will inevitably become flat (Caldecott), contracted (Poteat), or unnatural (Narcissus and Aquinas). The difference such an analogical understanding makes to the academy is not that of adding a Christian perspective to an otherwise neutral being.[42] Since all being is oriented toward a telos, then gift, communion, and, dare we say, love animate being from the very beginning. This is why Aquinas can say that "goodness and being are really the same . . . ."[43] Grounded in Divine abundance, Aquinas's theology/ontology provides a way of seeing how such wealth might yet sustain the academy.

William H. Poteat: modernity's theater of solitude

To engage what I am calling ontological abundance from a different angle, I want to return to the thought of William H. Poteat (1919–2000), professor of philosophy, religion, and culture at UNC-Chapel from 1947 to 1957 and at Duke University from 1960 to 1987.[44] Poteat, as we saw from his mall experience, describes modernity as suffering from "self-inflicted amnesia." He describes this amnesia as a contraction of being. Such contraction indicates a reduction or a loss. As Poteat vividly states, a "wasting disease has afflicted

41. Schindler is describing Henri De Lubac, but his statement can apply to Aquinas as well. Schindler, "Introduction," xxiv.

42. Univocity predicated of both God and creatures easily gives way to the dominance of a choosing, arbitrary will for both God and creatures. Since God's being is totally inscrutable (equivocal) one is left to make sense of God as the One who simply wills x or y. At the same time, when being as communion or participation retreats, then the person identifies her being with her choices.

43. Aquinas, *ST* 1, 5, 1.

44. Poteat's major works include *Polanyian Meditations*, *A Philosophical Daybook*, and *Recovering the Ground*, as well as a collection of essays, *The Primacy of Persons and the Language of Culture*.

The Logic of Being

the human spirit, perhaps mortally, for now more than 300 years." Thus, we have "simultaneously believed that we are gods and that we are nothing. This pitiless dialectic rends our souls from our bodies and suspends us in a lethal skepticism that at once flatters us and isolates us from our human reality: isolates us precisely by flattering us; flatters us precisely by isolating us."[45] Isolation thus marks the modern condition.

One of the ways Poteat engages this isolation is by coining the term "theater of solitude." This theater is not only a place of profound loneliness; it has also mired us in deep distortions about ourselves and the universe. Poteat attributes this solitude in part to modernity's hyper-visualized print culture. He argues that we have an overwhelming tendency, especially in reflection, to imagine that we are "alone in the static, visible world of enduring, unmoving type; a disembodied intellect in a time that is no more dynamic than that during which the letters on the printed page endure."[46] Modernity is a culture dominated by an "opposition between my body in (visual) space and the static, perduring written or printed word before me [that] is the source of our conception of objectivity in the West."[47] Poteat contrasts this visualist picture with an oral/aural one in which speaking is dynamic and temporal. Whereas the theater of solitude leaves one in a dead slice of temporal space, an oral/aural context enables one to inhabit more fully a dynamic and temporal place. "No denizen of an oral culture," Poteat states, "even were he inclined and able to entertain an ecumenic view of his own practices, is likely, as was Descartes—that creature of print culture par excellence—to make the 'clear and distinct' the paradigm of an intuitively irresistible idea."[48] Descartes thus embodies the theater of solitude:

> [He] systematically severed his ties to the world established in his knowledge of ancient languages, fable, history, poesy, mathematics, morals, theology, philosophy and science (as then understood) to come at last—disarmed of everything save only the Latin and

45. Poteat, *Recovering the Ground*, 187.

46. Poteat, *A Philosophical Daybook*, 59.

47. Poteat, *A Philosophical Daybook*, 50. For a fuller engagement of speech, literacy, electronic images and their impact upon human place, see Jardine, *Technological Society*, 235–253. While some might argue that social media and modern technology are a kind of return to oral/aural sensibilities and culture, Jardine rather argues that such media intensify our visual orientation. This visual orientation, as Walter Ong noted early on in his studies of oral cultures, tends to interpret the real in terms of the seen, i.e., the objective, the permanent, the unchanging. I return to Ong in the following chapter.

48. Poteat, *A Philosophical Daybook*, 101.

French languages, formidable links to history to be sure, that
Descartes seemed not to have noticed were still conveniently at
hand—to surrender the existence of the external world and God.[49]

Such "an ecumenical *in principle* doubt" is one in which "we are as gods to
ourselves and to the world."[50] While Cartesianism has been criticized many
times over, Poteat states that it still inhabits our imaginations like "chronic
depression."[51]

One profound sign of this chronic depression is an inability to extract
ourselves from a range of devastating dualisms: literal versus metaphorical,
fact versus value, or logos versus mythos. Poteat notes that we almost always
come to imagine that we dwell in the first of these more seriously—more
really—than the second.[52] Facts are stable while values are adventitious.
Logic is reliable while myths are fabrications. The literal is real, the metaphorical an extension of our imagination.[53] According to Poteat, Galileo
spoke for the "whole of modernity" when he declared "that the book of
nature is written in the language of mathematics."[54] This "mathematization
of nature was to become and is today an at times cruel orthodoxy," one
that led to "the decisive distinction between 'hard' facts and 'soft' values."[55]
That is, nature was divided into primary and secondary qualities. Nature
is first of all "extended in three dimensions and either at rest or in mo-
tion at a meausurable velocity and therefore consisting of primary—i.e.,
inherent qualities . . . ." This is the nature "which *we* have endowed with
the adventitious, secondary qualities of colors, sounds and smells."[56] While
Poteat acknowledges that subtleties have been introduced into physical
theory, it is nonetheless this idea of nature which holds us in thrall: "nature
which 'is a dull affair, soundless, scentless, colourless'—and we can add,

---

49. Poteat, *Recovering the Ground*, 202.

50. Poteat, *Recovering the Ground*, 203.

51. Poteat that notes that this Cartesian presumption has been criticized many times
over, and, "it would be difficult to find voices which dissent from explicit formulations of
it." Poteat, *Recovering the Ground*, 203.

52 Poteat, *A Philosophical Daybook*, 7–8.

53 We easily imagine that the really real corresponds to what is "out there," an unchanging world beyond our mere time and place. Poteat relates this assumption to a
"name-relation" theory of meaning in *A Philosophical Daybook*, 8.

54. Poteat, *Recovering the Ground*, 218.

55. Poteat, *Recovering the Ground*, 218.

56. Poteat, *Recovering the Ground*, 218.

valueless . . . ."[57] Thus we come to imagine that mathematics, physics, and various branches of science are more stable and certain than values, which are relative and changing.

In his essay, "For Whom is the Real Existence of Values a Problem: Or, an Attempt to Show that the Obvious is Plausible," Poteat argues that such dualism to the contrary, we are in fact (*de facto*) always bonded to the world even though we may have in judgment (*de jure*) suspended this bondedness in our imaginations. "If the model for what it is for anything to be knowable is that it be a possible object opposing a subject, then this Being and the bond of my mindbody to it are not items of my knowledge, nor can they be."[58] What does Poteat mean? How is he using "mindbody"?

Recovering the ground

We can begin to respond to these questions by noting Poteat's debt to Michael Polanyi.[59] In Polanyi's "post-critical philosophy," he famously describes how all knowing involves a tacit dimension; in all acts of knowing we rely on clues. For example, when looking for a pen, Polanyi writes, "I know what I expect to find; I can name it and describe it . . . I know also that it is somewhere within a certain region though I do not know where."[60] The discovery of the pen depends upon tacit knowing. Or to solve mathematical problems, "we must find (or construct) something that we have never seen before, with the given data serving us as clues to it."[61] Polanyi maintains that tacit knowing is a feature of *all acts of knowing*. Explicit knowledge

---

57. Poteat, *Recovering the Ground*, 219.

58. Poteat, *Recovering the Ground*, 206.

59. Poteat discovered Polanyi's writings in 1952, and in 1955 during a trip to Manchester, Poteat examined at Polanyi's request his Gifford Lectures, later to be published as *Personal Knowledge*. Poteat describes reading the manuscript while on a train to Sheffield: "there were no seats to be had on board, so I stood in the aisle. There I propped the typescript on a stainless steel bar extending across the window at which I stood and read with mounting excitement the section on 'connoisseurship,' as the flooded English midlands rushed past, beyond the page from which I read." Poteat, *Polanyian Meditations*, 6–7. Subsequently, Poteat was instrumental in bringing Polanyi to the United States where, in 1964, Polanyi delivered a series of lectures at Duke 1964. For a description of Polanyi's influence on Poteat, see Mead, "A Symposium Encounter." Other key influences on Poteat include, among others, Blaise Pascal, Soren Kierkegaard, Ludwig Wittgenstein, Hannah Arendt, and Walker Percy.

60. Polanyi, *Personal Knowledge*, 125.

61. Polanyi, *Personal Knowledge*, 126.

relies upon the tacit even as tacit knowing is necessary in order to arrive at explicit knowledge.

Poteat observes that for Polanyi all knowing has a "genetic" history. Knowing includes appraising, puzzling, searching, coming to know, and upholding knowledge. As Poteat puts it, "the structure of [Polanyi's] way of knowing is a reduplication of the structure of his way of being in the world. For Polanyi then a theory of knowing must be inextricably implicated with a theory of being [an ontology]."[62] In other words, far from divorcing his knowing from his being in the world as did Descartes, Polanyi is relying upon the complexity of his being in his coming to know. Polanyi does not sever his ties with the world but relies upon them (thus his discussion of tradition, connoisseurship, commitment, and so forth). Perhaps such claims seem less controversial today as we are more aware of context and thus of the temporal shape of knowledge. Poteat, however, radically intensifies Polanyi's philosophy to claim the following: "language—our first formal system—has the sinews of our bodies, which had them first . . . ." All acts of knowing are generated out of "*our prelingual mindbodily being in the world, which is their condition of possibility.*"[63]

To engage this claim more fully, let us turn to Poteat's statement, "muscles make assumptions." Such a claim could sound either bizarre or highly metaphorical, especially given our habit of thinking of assumptions as primarily mental acts. When Poteat states that "muscles make assumptions," however, he means that the muscles that make up a motor skill, such as stroking a tennis ball, have a logical relation to that skill. That is, our muscles provide the ground from which the stroking of the tennis ball can occur. They are thus the assumptions that make possible assertions (stroking the ball). Only by "disattending from" the manner in which one is behind the rapidly approaching ball, and attending to its flight can one stroke the ball over the net. Poteat argues that this is what we do when we are making a particular point: we "disattend" from the convictions on which we inevitably rely in order to attend to the point we are making. It is not unlike how one note in a song "retrotends" a previous one even as it "pretends" those that follow. No one note is more *certain* or *stable* than another. The assumptions we make in a sophisticated argument are like those we make when playing tennis, listening to a musical composition, or when walking across a room. Poteat thus cites David Sudnow, "A descriptive foundation

---

62. Poteat, *Polanyian Meditations*, 15.

63. Poteat, *Polanyian Meditations*, 9. My emphasis.

for mathematics demands not the pursuit of perfection in the syllogisms of purified thinking but studies of the embodied calculus of such accomplishments as reaching for a doorknob and getting there on time."[64]

Poteat uses "mindbody" to show that any use of "mind" or "body" is itself derivative, just as hitting a tennis ball is derivative of our mindbody being in the world. Similarly, Poteat argues that all modes of knowing, seeing, understanding, and so forth derive from our mindbody's coherence, orientation, and intentionality. Poteat is thus pointing to "the tacit logos that is omnipresent in our quest for meaning and coherence . . . ."[65] While the logic of our various modes of pretension—from natural science to poetry to mathematics to myth to revelation—are different from one another, it is not that some are well-grounded, while others are not. Rather "they all have the *same* ground, the *same* reality bearing authority, when they are evaluated, as I am throughout claiming they ought to be, from the standpoint of our primitive mode of dwelling in the world."[66] For Poteat the stability of our various modes of knowing/being is not that some are more factual and unchanging than others. The stability lies rather in the logos and intentionality of our mindbodies, whether we are indwelling a musical sonata or examining a cell under a microscope.

This primitive mode of indwelling necessarily involves a bondedness to the world. As Poteat states:

> The developing infant is, in the womb, bonded to its mother, and this is a primordial—must we not say, the primordial—bond of our existence. The fact of our having been born into a world after nine months of uterine life is profoundly engraved upon, is ineradicable from the pre-history and still actively present in the history of our mindbodily being. No matter how far from this we may be abstracted into our later history, we still carry in our being as a living, present reality this archaic connection with the world . . . . Once born, we are bonded to our mother's breast, to our infant place, to our fathers, to our brothers and sisters, to the members of

64. As cited in Poteat, *Polanyian Meditations*, vii,. For Poteat's discussion of muscles making assumptions, see *Polanyian Meditations* 11–26.

65. Poteat, *Polanyian Meditations*, 117. Another way to put this, in Polanyi's terms, is that tacit knowing (like explicit knowing) does not pertain to the mind *over against* the body.

66. Poteat, *Polanyian Meditations*, 117–118.

an extended family, to our human fellows on the face of the earth,
to other animals and to all living things.[67]

Bondedness, as Poteat describes it, is constitutive of all being. Even the imagined theater of solitude cannot erase these bonds, such as the bonds of human language. That is, we necessarily rely upon or indwell our language in order to speak. Poteat thus claims that all knowing is a bonding, an indwelling. "For me to be bonded is for me to indwell an 'other,' sometimes prereflexively, sometimes in reflection, from within my mindbody."[68] Such bonds are ontologically radical.

At this point, then, we can say that Poteat, like Aquinas, is describing an ontological potency: an abundance that characterizes all being. Rather than focusing on essence/existence, however, Poteat describes this potency in terms of our mindbody being in the world as indwelling and bonding. Like Aquinas as well, Poteat relies upon an analogous, rather than univocal or equivocal, understanding of being predicated of God and creation. We see this most fully in Poteat's understanding of speaking, a resource he relies on to develop more fully an alternative to late modernity's amnesia and the ontology embedded therein.

The word: dabhar and logos

To develop his understanding, Poteat cites W. H. Auden, "a sentence uttered makes a world appear." We might be tempted to think that Auden's statement is true, but only of poetry or fiction. As J. L. Austin also famously claimed, however, words can be "performative." "I pronounce you husband and wife" is one familiar example; it makes a married world appear for the couple. Poteat notes, however, that Austin contrasts such performative speech with constatives, words that "describe" or "report," a distinction that Poteat finds problematic. To show why, Poteat imagines an interlocutor saying that performatives, however useful, are no more "palpable than the insubstantial fabric of social usage": performative speech is just a convention or merely relative. The interlocutor thus imagines, says Poteat, "a more substantial grounding for constatives than the 'mere felicities embodied in social usage.'"[69] That is, the interlocutor believes that words that describe

67. Poteat, *Recovering the Ground*, 204–5.

68. Poteat, *Recovering the Ground*, 208.

69. Poteat, *Polanyian Meditations*, 118.

and report (facts) are more substantive—more to be trusted—than merely performative words, which are fleeting.

Poteat argues otherwise. To explain, we can consider Poteat's analysis of asking for bread. He describes two different occasions for such a petition: one is a congregation of people saying together, "Give us this day our daily bread." The other is a person saying to a clerk in a bakery shop, "Here's my money. Give me my daily bread."[70] We imagine that the words spoken to the bakery clerk are direct and more efficacious than the figurative petition spoken in worship. Yet this literal/figurative distinction, Poteat argues, simply reinforces a modern prejudice, one in which the literal is real and the figurative is less so. By contrast, Poteat states, "The weight and force of the words 'Give us this day our daily bread,' uttered in the setting of prayer, are exactly what they are and not some other thing: As direct and unequivocal as can be, which no translation can improve or further legitimize."[71] How can Poteat claim this? After all, when we leave a store, having purchased the bread, we will have a real loaf of bread to take home and eat. After saying the Lord's prayer, we have no such tangible proof.

If one, however, tried to buy bread when saying the Lord's Prayer, practitioners would naturally assume that this person did know how to pray the prayer Jesus taught his disciples. This daily bread is not up for purchase, but is freely given. How does the congregation know this? They have repeatedly heard the salvific stories of bread: manna in the wilderness, the miracle of the fish and loaves, the Lord's Supper, and so forth. They have also been habituated to closing their eyes and bowing their heads while they pray, not pulling out their wallets to get money for bread. They have, if rightly formed, freely shared their bread with others. The words "give us this day our daily bread," then, are said in the midst of these kinds of bonds. The saying of these words is an acknowledgement that God is faithful and will *really* provide, even though the provision looks different than buying bread at a store. Both statements "make worlds appear": in one case, the commercial world of buying food, in another the grand narrative of a faithful God.

Poteat thus claims that the words "give us this bread" in the store and in the congregational setting are equally direct and real in their respective contexts. As he puts it, "To dwell in the imaginary is therefore not to dwell in the 'mind' or 'consciousness' or 'just in the head.' It is to dwell in

70. Poteat, *A Philosophical Daybook*, 9.

71. Poteat, *A Philosophical Daybook*, 10.

one of the forms taken by our mindbodily life, itself grounded in the real, and ceaselessly testifying to this ground."[72] We may dwell differently in the imaginary—in a poem, a song, a dance, a scientific examination, a mathematical equation, a prayer—but there is nothing inherently more real or superior about one of these ways of being and knowing. One is not more real or less imaginary than another. It is rather that the Enlightenment has "inclined us to *imagine* ourselves as being independent of, disentangled from, the world which is depicted as over against us, as an object to lucid reflection . . . ."[73]

To say, by contrast, that speaking makes a world appear is to acknowledge that "we are beings who exist in the midst of a plexus of bonds."[74] Even to listen to actors in a play is to enter into a quasi-ethical bond with them. We do not interrupt them, for example. Moreover, when we watch a dramatic performance—bonded as we are to the actors and to their words uttered before us—a world appears. But, "is this world really real?" we might ask, especially when we are held captive by modern prejudices. Poteat claims that there is no "context-neutral" sense that gives some words a better standing in regard to "real" over against "imaginary." Watching a play, praying, or buying bread are all places rooted in the orientation and coherence of our mindbodies that are "logically/ontologically antecedent to the distinction between fact and value."[75]

Again, an initial reaction might be that apart from the stability of "hard facts" then the world itself becomes unstable. But Poteat's point is that the reification of seeing—the theater of solitude (we could also call the god's eye view)—is rather the unstable place. It has led us to abandon the good ground of our incarnate being, speaking, and knowing. Bonding has become bondage, a gnostic heresy that holds us in its grasp.

At this point, it is helpful to see how Poteat traces our modern plight beyond the Enlightenment to a more ancient Greek understanding of reality. Within the Greek imagination, *logos* was "subject to the gravitational pull of the picture of the eternal passage of the planets through their orbital paths, never beginning, never ending . . . ."[76] Such a picture leads to an ontology that is like an eternal cycle, where words/facts are true to the extent

72. Poteat, *A Philosophical Daybook*, 15.

73. Poteat, *A Philosophical Daybook*, 15.

74. Poteat, *Recovering the Ground*, 204.

75. Poteat, *A Philosophical Daybook*, 46.

76. Poteat, *Polanyian Meditations*, 123.

that they correspond to an *extrinsic* reality. In this ancient understanding, an impersonal and eternal logos resided over the universe. While acknowledging the extraordinarily complex ways that *logos* is used, Poteat nonetheless observes that "it is characteristic of the Hebrews that their words *effect* and of the Greeks that the word *is*."[77] Stated more fully, ancient Greek thought lacks "a *paradigmatic* speaker, whose speech makes a world appear . . . ."[78] Whereas for the ancient Greeks, the world was ordered by impersonal and eternal cycles, for the Hebrews, Yahweh's word creates worlds. For "the Greeks the particularity and transiency of our particular truths are overcome in the eternal logos; for the Hebrews they are comprehended and affirmed in the dynamic but ever faithful will of Yahweh."[79]

An ever-faithful God who creates the world through the word (logos) provides the analogy that enables Poteat both to describe the mindbody as bonded and to describe our speaking as always making worlds appear. As Poteat puts it, "If one's analysis of what language is and does proceeds without reference to there being speakers and hearers of language it is most unlikely that one would discover the foundation of the meaning of words in our oral/aural exchanges. This foundation, our usage, is dynamic and survives the passage of time, *an analogy of God's fidelity*, securing the assertorial weight of our spoken word."[80] Our incarnate mindbody being in bringing forth worlds through speaking, dancing, drawing, gestures, and so forth is analogous to God's speaking worlds into being. In some ways like Aquinas's analogy of God as fully actual/potential, so also Poteat is saying that God's words are always promised/fulfilled. To be *creatures* in God's image is analogously to bring forth worlds through speech.

One might object, however, that God is faithful; humans are not. Our words deceive, distort, manipulate, and so forth. They are thus compromised and unstable. But the instability does not lie in the failure of our speech to match or correspond to some extrinsic grand text or an infinite static real. The failure of our words, radically unlike God's, lies in our unfaithfulness, our complicity, and our deception. Even so, these failed words

77. Thorleif Boman, cited in Poteat, *A Philosophical Daybook*, 121. Poteat acknowledges the complexity: "That *logos* could mean 'speech,' 'speaking,' 'story' and could be associated with the very physical activity of breathing, no less than the Hebrew *dabhar*, is beyond doubting." Poteat, *Polanyian Meditations*, 121.

78. Poteat, *Polanyian Meditations*, 121–22.

79. Poteat, *A Philosophical Daybook*, 66.

80. Poteat, personal correspondence, 5.

make worlds appear, albeit worlds in opposition to who we are as creatures before God. There is no more solid foundation than this.

Poteat gives a particularly powerful account of the logic of a "paradigmatic speaker" in his analysis of Hannah Arendt's classic, *The Human Condition*.[81] Arendt's concern is how to establish a hierarchy of labor, work, and action so that the uniqueness of humans can be established. The labor process, she argues, is like the cycles of nature with no beginning and no end and so cannot establish the uniqueness of humans. While work possesses a measure of durability and can survive the life cycles of generations, workers meet in the exchange market not as persons, but as producers. Arendt turns finally to the *vita activa*, where through mutual and convivial words and deeds, a person appears before another as a "who" rather than a "what." As Arendt states, "In acting and speaking, men show who they are, reveal actively their unique personal identities and thus make their appearance in the human world . . . ."[82] Thus, "this revelatory quality of speech and action comes to the fore where people are with others and neither for nor against them—that is, in sheer human togetherness."[83] Yet, a key problem that Arendt addresses is that our words even in the polis are fleeting; speaking by itself is one of the most futile of activities.[84] What saves our words from such futility? Arendt turns to the power of memory and stories. As Poteat states, for Arendt "it is in the memory of those hearers and in the stories which they come to tell that . . . one's uttered and lively words are rescued from sheer transiency and futility."[85] So while our words and deeds are impermanent and fleeting, the stories that the polis tells can keep them alive, and thus rescue our "who-ness" from futility.

---

81. Poteat, "A Skeleton Key." Poteat makes a similar argument in *Recovering the Ground*, 128–136.

82. Arendt, *The Human Condition*, 179.

83. Ibid., 180.

84 Arendt states, "The space of appearance comes into being wherever men are together in the manner of speech and action, and therefore predates and precedes all formal constitution of the public realm and the various forms of government, that is, the various forms in which the public realm can be organized. Its peculiarity is that, unlike the spaces which are the work of our hands, it does not survive the actuality of the movement which brought it into being, but disappears not only with the dispersal of men—as in the case of great catastrophes when the body politic of a people is destroyed—but with the disappearance or arrest of the activities themselves." Arendt, *The Human Condition*, 199.

85. Poteat, "A Skeleton Key," 2.

Poteat argues, however, that this move itself will not work. Stories about people might help a polis remember their words and deeds; it might even immortalize them as Odysseus is immortalized by Homer. "The fact that I am a who," however, "not to be reduced to the sum of all that can be predicated of me as a what, can only become fully manifest in the very particular act of speaking and owning these words before others who uptake them, these others must actually be present."[86] Stated differently, Poteat observes, "I can only fully appear as myself, as a who, in an existentially actual Polis."[87] Poteat notes that Arendt acknowledges this point, particularly in her reference to Augustine's *Confessions* where he addresses God "in whose eyes I have become a question for myself." Arendt notes, in a footnote, that "the answer to the question 'What am I?' can be given only by God who made man."[88] As Poteat notes, however, Arendt has nothing more explicitly to say about Augustine after this footnote, "even though her thesis cannot be made without the premise of Augustine's colloquy with God."[89] In the end she allows historical memory to determine the place where "who am I" is finally established.

Yet, as Poteat argues, historical memory cannot preserve the whoness of a person; only the presence of an actually present speaker/hearer can. He thus develops the significance of Augustine addressing his words to God. "If I fully enter the 'Polis' constituted in Augustine's Confessions and for myself vocatively address my questions to Yahweh, the never failingly faithful person ('I will be that I will be'), my lively speech will be covenantally uptaken and the unique 'who-that-I-am' will be everlastingly endorsed. Apart from this I do not have an endorsement. I can have no eternal validity."[90] Arendt, as we saw, argues that persons are rescued from futility in their appearance through words and deeds before others. Poteat logically extends this argument not through historical memory (as Arendt) but through the presence of a paradigmatic speaker, an always present "polis," an ever-faithful God. As creatures, we enter an "ongoingly contemporaneous 'history' in which a living and personal being is always actually appearing in the fabric of [our] actual activity of acting and speaking; and who hears and uptakes [our] words and deeds, holding [us] to account; and who, finally, is taken himself

---

86. Poteat, "A Skeleton Key," 2.
87. Poteat, "A Skeleton Key," 2.
88. Arendt, *The Human Condition*, 11.
89. Poteat, *Recovering the Ground*, 128.
90. Poteat, "A Skeleton Key," 3.

always to be faithful and never changing."[91] Significantly, Poteat states that his analysis is "not to be construed as a homily, but as a piece of cultural/conceptual analysis, showing that the concept of personhood, on one side of Arendt's argument, is parasitical upon these Biblical images."[92]

Within the modern academy, it is no surprise that a God whose words are ever-faithful will seem, at best, a personal belief, and at worse, beside the point. So also, Auden's "a sentence uttered makes a world appear" will sound like "once upon a time," perhaps generating stories to be studied but irrelevant for reflection on the academy as a coherent whole. But this is because, as Poteat notes, the bonds of our being have slipped from our reflective grasp. As such, fact is more real than value, science more certain than faith. Yet if dwelling and bonding are constitutive of our mindbodily being, then we are freed to abandon this gnostic impulse to turn away from our being in the world, the source of order, coherence, rhythm, form, and intentionality. We are free to see that petition for bread at a store is no more real than "give us this day our daily bread," though the reality may be of a different kind. This is not relativism but an affirmation of creation's goodness, a goodness generated by God's fidelity.

From within this understanding, we can turn to Poteat's discussion of the incarnate word in his essay, "The Incarnate Word and the Language of Culture." Though an early essay, we see already how Poteat is challenging

91. Poteat, "A Skeleton Key," 3.

92. Chief among these would be Arendt's discussion of our words bringing about genuinely new worlds, thus her description of speech as "revelatory" in the context of togetherness or covenant. We can note at this point that Poteat's language is analogous in the sense that it is a contrast with both univocal and equivocal understandings of human and divine being. Within Poteat's framework, we can equate univocal language and being with a modern, Cartesian abstraction from being, where the real appears separated from our incarnate being, in an atemporal space. At this same time, Poteat rejects equivocal speech as well. He notes that the phrase "wholly other" is often tossed around in "so facile a fashion as to put me off." He continues, "Either 'Wholly other' is quite without meaning, or its meaning derives from its real analogies with something in our experience in the world. For me this requirement is only met in the covenantal exchange, interpreted as here—let us say, the solemnization of marriage . . . . And how does this Yahweh, whom I encounter paradigmatically as this wholly other, bear upon the created world and upon my being in the world? He is, as creator, the faithful sustainer of what he has called forth out of nothing; and he is the mysterium tremendum et fascinans—the everlasting arms that grant their being to my sentient, oriented and motile mindbody . . . . It is worth noting en passante that, if Yahweh were indeed 'wholly other,' this fact could not be known." Poteat, "Some Remarks on Walter Mead's essay," 28–29.

certain dualisms, in this case that between real versus symbol. He turns again to Auden:

> By the existence of this Child, the
> proper value of all other existences is
> given, for of every other creature it can be
> said that it has extrinsic importance but of
> this Child it is the case the He is in no
> sense a symbol.[93]

Poteat elaborates: Christ is no symbol but "the most concrete reality there is."[94] In what sense can this be true? As we saw, Poteat emphasizes how we inhabit different sorts of real worlds all the time, i.e., playing sports, studying, worshipping, and so forth. How can one feature or person in this world be *most* real or concrete? Poteat states: "Any separation between the Father and the Son would have meant both that Jesus Christ was not related to the whole of human existence and that the one God had not been incarnate in that existence."[95] Poteat is not here defending Chalcedonion orthodoxy but engaging the implied logic of being. He is making a case analogous to the one he makes with Arendt. As we saw, Poteat states that one needs a paradigmatic speaker, ever present, to make logical sense of Arendt's description of personhood. In a similar sense, Poteat shows how the logos of our mindbodily being requires a Logos related to the whole of human existence, one in whom our being as bondedness, as logos, comes to fruition. Poteat can thus say, in a later work:

> Then you believe in the doctrine of transubstantiation? Well, no. What I believe—and I do not think of it as something I believe, it goes much deeper than that, in fact, all the way to the bone—is that the bread and wine are the *presently actual* body and blood of Jesus Christ; and that, if they are not, then the Son of God has nothing to do with the concrete person I am in *this* time and place; and if this be so, the whole of Christianity is but an elaborate system of symbols at no point engaged with the actual fabric of this world.[96]

Christ is no symbol but the most concrete reality there is because in him created being is fully comprehended and realized. Thus, "he is our

---

93. Cited in Poteat, *Primacy of Persons*, 108

94. Poteat, *Primacy of Persons*, 112.

95. Poteat, *Primacy of Persons*, 93–94.

96. Poteat, *Recovering the Ground*, 135.

present life renewed, in all its existential concreteness."[97] That Christ renews and fulfills all created being makes him then the most concrete reality there is, the telos of all creation. Here it is important to note that "concrete" has to do not only with matter or the material world but includes more fully purpose and goal inherent in being itself. To return to Caldecott, a flat or flattened world is not concrete but *abstracted* from the heights and depths of being as signs of a reality that exceeds it. A world of ontological depth, according to Poteat, is one in which the Logos is present in the actual fabric of the world, in our concrete place and time.

One might wonder why the need for a Logos present in the actual fabric of the world. While Poteat does not fully develop this, I would say that such an emphasis makes it abundantly clear that we are not gnostic spirits merely inhabiting bodies. As Irenaeus in his fight against the gnostics emphasized, "God's own creation, which depends for its existence on God's power and art and wisdom, has borne God."[98] To say creation has borne God is to point to a logos not in the purely spiritual realm, nor only in the world of the mind, nor merely in the world of facts. What is logical cannot be separated from creation as communion with God, revealed and realized most fully in Christ. As with Arendt, Poteat is here not making a homiletical or even strictly theological argument; he is rather making a descriptive one about the logic of being and the Divine word that ultimately sustains it.

While Poteat's thought is far richer and more complex that I can describe here, my analysis, I hope, is sufficient to give a sense of how he provides an alternative to the multiple dualisms that plague the academy: whether fact/value, real/symbol, knowledge/faith, all of which elevate one of these while denigrating or, at best, compartmentalizing the other. It might seem odd to describe the modern academy as a "theater of solitude." After all, so many are gathered in one place often doing good work together. And yet the deep unease that surrounds the modern university is palpable: why are we here? What are our values, entities we are now consigned to choose? What is our purpose?

Poteat helps us see that distinctive ways of being—whether doing math, reading a poem, or worshipping—are all dependent ways of making

97. Poteat, *Primacy of Persons*, 108. Poteat specifically cites St. Paul: "For me to live is Christ . . ." (Phil 1:21).

98. Irenaeus, *The Scandal of the Incarnation*, 54. Thus, as Tertullian emphasized, "the flesh is the hinge." Cited in Balthasar, "Introduction," 4. Balthasar states that this saying, while originally attributed to Tertullian, had decisive influence on Irenaeus and can be considered the center of his theology.

sense of the world. Our knowing/being as dependent upon and grounded in our mindbodily being is not some imperfection to overcome. It is rather the source of all order, form, and coherence. It is *essentially good*. Our aim in speaking, studying, discovering, and so forth is not to lay claim to the static, infinite real, to facts over against personal values. Our aim is rather, across diverse places and disciplines, to be faithful to one another and to the God who is faithful to us. An institution that acknowledges the logic of created being will thus abandon the theater of solitude for a theater of faithful speaking in which our bondedness to others, the world, and God is not ignored but embraced.

David L. Schindler: the death of God in the academy

We saw in chapter 1 how David L. Schindler critiques the dominant plot line of academic excellence, arguing against an understanding of an excellent university to which one adds "Catholic" or "Christian" after the fact. Schindler sees in this approach an implicit false assumption about the neutrality of the excellent university. One might be tempted to regard Schindler's analysis as ungenerous: as narrowing the universal reach of a true university. But that temptation is shortsighted. Schindler's criticism rests rather on what I am calling an ontology of abundance, one is which the logic of all being cannot be separated from gift and love.[99] Its scope, therefore, is more truly universal than a compartmentalized ontology that fragments our institutions as well as our lives.

Schindler is Dean Emeritus and Gagnon Professor of Fundamental Theology at the Pontifical John Paul II Institute for Studies on Marriage and Family at The Catholic University of America.[100] He also serves as editor of *Communio, International Catholic Review,* a journal originally edited by Henri de Lubac and associated with French Nouvelle Théologie school. This

99. Stated differently, love is a "transcendental," in the sense in which Aquinas used this term: transcendental refers to realities that necessarily accompany existence (such as goodness and truth) and as such are "convertible" with being. By contrast, Kant used "transcendental" to mean the conditions of the possibility of knowledge.

100 He is the author *Ordering Love, Heart of the World,* and *Freedom, Truth and Human Dignity: The Second Vatican's Council's Declaration on Religious Freedom*. Schindler has been influenced by a range of contemporary thinkers, including John Cobb, George Grant, Joseph Ratzinger (Pope Benedict XVI), Henri de Lubac, and Hans Urs von Balthasar. For a fuller intellectual autobiography, see Schindler, "Modernity and the Nature of a Distinction."

association is significant for my purposes as this school sought to overcome a neo-scholastic reading of Aquinas that sharply divided nature and grace. Rather than separate the natural from the supernatural, which tended to separate theology from philosophy and other disciplines, de Lubac and others in the school embraced the conviction that grace already effects all creation (the natural) from the very beginning by orienting it beyond itself, even as it makes possible a genuinely new creation in Christ.[101] Schindler develops how an understanding of grace and nature as *intrinsically* related can shape contemporary culture. As we will see, his ontology of abundance provides yet another lens for reframing and thus reimaging academic being.

In his essay, "On Meaning and the Death of God in the Academy," Schindler states that the academy (and more largely the West) is killing God, albeit in a cowardly and timid way. His analysis is no diatribe against self-proclaimed atheists in the modern academy. Schindler rather shows how Christians and others have accepted distorted assumptions about being that have undermined their deepest convictions. Citing Neitzsche, Schindler observes that the world "has become 'infinite' for us all over again, inasmuch as we cannot reject the possibility that *it may include infinite interpretations*."[102] What does it mean to say the world is infinite? Such a statement exposes what Schindler sees as modernity's characteristic flaw: "the dualism of an *originally indifferent world* awaiting an *originally creative human freedom* . . . ."[103]

To engage Schindler's diagnosis of modernity, I will explore each of these components in turn. First, Schindler relates an originally indifferent world to a mechanistic-technological ontology. A mechanistic view is one in which "the physical world and the body become machines conceived as originally neutral, hence 'dumb,' with respect to any distinctly human or divine ends, that is, in advance of the meaning yet to be conferred on them

---

101. Thus, as Schindler states in an introduction to de Lubac, if grace does not somehow always and already touch "the soul of every human being, the Christian fact would remain an essentially 'private' matter . . . . On the other hand, if the order of grace were not essentially gratuitous—then the Christian fact would lose its newness and it proper character as divine gift." Schindler, "Introduction," xvi.

102. Cited in Schindler, "On Meaning and the Death of God," 193.

103. Schindler is engaging the thought of George Grant. Schindler, *Ordering Love*, 281. My emphasis. In "On Meaning and the Death of God," Schindler discusses how Derrida's *closure* of the age of the sign underwrites the world becoming infinite in Nietzsche's sense.

through the constructive-controlling activity of the self."[104] As Poteat noted, such a mechanistic view has been criticized many times over, its dualism no longer explicitly endorsed. Schindler, however, like Poteat, argues that the world as originally indifferent—and thus as like a machine—continues to pervade late modern assumptions. Perhaps nowhere is this more evident than in how technology extends a mechanistic ontology. According to Schindler, technology is more than the human capacity to build televisions, computers, and so forth. A mechanistic-technological ontology, rather, interprets the world as neutral, like various parts of a machine with no design by which to understand the whole. "It is the essence of a technological worldview that it perceives technology more or less simply as the *sum of things that are made*—televisions, computers, automobiles and so on, but also economic and political institutions—and that it then begins to assess these only in terms of how they are *used*."[105] That is, one regards technology itself as first neutral (the sum of things made) onto which "values" are added. Thus the technological world is originally indifferent; human creativity and freedom determine its worth or value.

One might be tempted, at this point, to think that Schindler is moving in an anti-technological, or even nostalgic and ideal, direction. Some critics argue that one either has to accept the benefits of modernity with its ontological assumptions or, if one poses radical questions, one cannot with consistency appreciate the benefits of Western technology.[106] Yet Schindler argues that this kind of ideal versus real dichotomy is itself a modern failure of the imagination, as it leaves one to imagine that these are the only alternatives. Thus one assumes the real world is initially indifferent while values—whether pragmatic of "ideal"—are an imposed part of the nature of things. Thus the common argument that technology in itself is not good or bad but what matters is its use, while well intended, relies upon modernity's flawed ontology: an originally indifferent technological world and an originally creative human freedom.

This point leads to the second component of modernity's tragic flaw, as Schindler understands it: if the original constitution of the world is indifferent or neutral, then objects or subjects acquire meaning through originally creative human freedom. That is, freedom allows subjects to

---

104. Schindler, "The Meaning of the Human," 93.

105. Schindler, *Ordering Love*, 279.

106. Schindler engages this criticism in his discussion, "George Grant and Modernity's Technological Ontology," *Ordering Love*, 277–87.

create or choose value which itself is alien to an otherwise indifferent world. Schindler associates this understanding of freedom with liberalism inasmuch as it carries "a definite sense of the primacy of human agency or 'construction' of the self in its affective and cognitive relation to God and others."[107] The link between the form of culture in terms of a machine (originally indifferent) and the form of liberalism is the externality of relations. "What the language of the machine brings out is the preoccupation with power . . . and technique, and control and manipulation, which results from such externally conceived relations."[108] For Schindler the modern paradigmatic knower continues to be Descartes, for whom meaning comes through doubt and analysis—"staying at a distance"—and Bacon, for whom knowledge is power. Freedom, one assumes, has no content; it rather names the will's capacity to choose. Schindler emphasizes, however, that such freedom *in fact* relies upon a very definite content: an originally indifferent world awaiting originally creative human power. As mechanistic-technological-liberal ontology sees being as always available for manipulation; the worth of being comes to depend on its use.

In Schindler's view, the death of God in the academy is not about academics losing faith or not having faith. Nor is it about the failure to offer more explicitly Christian courses, diminished campus ministry programs, or weak mission statements, important though these might be. Schindler is rather attending to how modernity's flawed ontology has distorted the modern academy to the detriment of all.

As indifferent world awaiting an originally creative human freedom is one which relies upon an externality of relations. That is, relations are extrinsic to nature/being rather than intrinsic, a point to which I will return. For now, however, it is important to note, a god external to the cosmos ceases to be God at all. The "death of God" in the academy and beyond then refers not only to the absence of God in an institution. It refers to how the God placed in another sphere (or outside a particular world) is actually not-god. As Schindler observes, a god who is only transcendent (external, extrinsic, in another sphere) is in reality a *finite* god: a god who is limited because such a god cannot really be where we are. As Schindler states, "A God who remains outside of the cosmos is a God whose being leaves off

107. Schindler, *Heart of the World,* xiv. Schindler is here describing Anglo-American liberalism as against Continental or European liberalism. Schindler notes, however, that while the differences of these strands are not unimportant, they "bear in their deepest implications an ontological unity." Schindler, *Heart of the World,* ix.

108. Schindler, ed., *Catholicism and Secularization,* 18.

where the cosmos begins, whose being thereby reaches its boundary—its *finis*—where the boundary of the cosmos takes up."[109] An external god is thus reduced to finitude and a finite god is a dead god. While such atheism may be hidden from view, Schindler's point is that it nonetheless fuels an institution's entire way of being.

Relation as constitutive of being

"You have made us for yourself, and our heart is restless until it rests in you." This Augustinian quotation can serve as a point of departure for examining more fully Schindler's alternative. A key emphasis "is that relation to God on the part of finite beings is not *adventitious*; not something which is merely added on to their already constituted identity. On the contrary, relation to God is '*constitutive*' of finite beings."[110] That is, relation to God is not extrinsic. It is not what humans choose it to be; it is not simply a matter of the will. Relation to God cannot be isolated to a sphere or a transcendent category.[111] In saying relation to God is constitutive of finite being, Schindler is saying created being is a relation between God and all that is not God. About human being specifically, Schindler states, "human nature exists (*de facto*, not *de jure*) only as already *related* to the God of Jesus Christ."[112] This is not a judgment of what might be dependent upon human choice but a fact that already is, even if unacknowledged. The *logic* of all created being (*ontos*) already is a relation to God.

Schindler thus seeks to overcome a dualism between grace and nature. He notes that much of post-Tridentine theology, in the name of the transcendence of the order of grace, drew a sharp line between nature and grace to protect the integrity of the natural against certain Protestant emphases. On the other hand, much of post-Vatican II theology, in the name of immanence, "so absorbed grace into nature that nature and its activities were in effect no longer seen as requiring radical transformation in relation to

---

109. Schindler, "On Meaning and the Death of God," 198. Hart makes a similar point: ". . . for if the infinite can be opposed to the finite, it is itself, in the end, only finite, and in consequence merely the negation of the finite . . . ." Hart, *The Beauty*, 200.

110. Schindler, "On Meaning and the Death of God," 201, my emphasis.

111. Schindler relates this kind of focus on the will to voluntarism, a position often traced back to Duns Scotus's student, William of Ockham.

112. Schindler, ed., *Catholicism and Secularization*, 15. Schindler is here engaging the thought of de Lubac as well as Balthasar.

God, as needing judgment first from beyond themselves." The reality is, however, that these positions fold in on one another producing the same result: "a nature without God, a nature not ordered from within its depths to God."[113] By contrast, Schindler emphasizes that "the transcendence and the immanence of God are directly, not inversely, related."[114] It is not as if grace increases while nature diminishes. "It is because God has made us for himself, and thereby has already reached into us, that our hearts are restless until they rest in God."[115] If it is true that God has made us for himself, then it is no longer possible to have an autonomous or independent sphere where God is not already present precisely as One who calls us to communion.

What are the implications of this ontology for the academy? At this point, we can emphasize that for Schindler being and knowing are never neutral or indifferent. Being is intrinsically oriented toward communion, ultimately with God. This means that methods of knowing are never neutral. As Schindler emphasizes in his analysis of the death of God in the academy, "giving meaning the simple identity proper to a machine is but atheism unfolded into a 'method' . . . ."[116] In his essay, "Sanctity and the Intellectual Life," Schindler argues rather that

> no act of intelligence, however carefully packaged into whatever method of inquiry, can ever *remain simply neutral with respect to God*. God is somehow "implicated" in every act of knowledge, from the side at once of the subject (the act of knowing) and of the object (what is known: nature). Every methodical inquiry will therefore of necessity involve an *abstraction* of some sort from

113. Schindler, ed., *Catholicism and Secularization*, 11. This transcendent/immanent description is not only a peculiarly Catholic challenge. We can note analogous examples in the Protestant theological world: on the one hand, an immanent God as represented in the thought of F. Schleiermacher and on the other a transcendent God, "wholly other," as represented in some selections from the early Karl Barth. Schindler observes that both of these theologies give way to a form of secularization, whether liberal or conservative. He notes that de Lubac rightly observes that "neither of these theologies was capable of meeting the crisis of modernity in its deepest roots—which lay in modernity's driving impulse to order the world without God." Schindler, ed., *Catholicism and Secularization*, 12.

114. Schindler, ed., *Catholicism and Secularization*, 10. Schindler cites Kenneth Schmitz, "We may say, then, that, when said of the divine, the two terms 'transcendence and 'immanence' designate one and the same relation in reality . . . . The distinction of terms is a concession to the human mind as it deals with the real relation of creature to Creator," Schindler, ed., *Catholicism and Secularization*, 25.

115. Schindler, ed., *Catholicism and Secularization*, 11.

116. Schindler, "On the Meaning and Death of God," 204.

God, in a manner that carries *some definite sense of openness or closure to God.*[117]

The act of knowing is never neutral with respect to God. That God is implicated in all acts of knowing might sound like an outlandish claim. What does God, for example, have to do with mathematics, chemistry, history, or psychology? To respond, it is important to see that Schindler's analysis is not a mere pious claim but a logical one.[118] One's knowing and being will move with the logic of being as relation or against it. On the face of it, there is no reason why the method of the machine (simple identity) is more "critical" than a method of communion (relational identity). Both presuppose a relation to what is ultimate.

Schindler emphasizes that this understanding does not mean that "once armed with the truth of Christ, one would thereby be warranted in *determining for* each discipline its proper method and content." Rather the logic of created being relies on an analogical relation that "does not deny but on the contrary demands the distinctness proper to each created form of being (and just so far indicates a variety of disciplinary methods and contents). The point is that distinctness can never mean separation."[119] Different disciplinary methods need not be assimilated to a singular mold, but can and will display a rich variety. But this variety becomes—in an ontology of relation—not disparate and unrelated disciplines, but distinct ways of knowing being-as-communion. That is, folding the intellectual life into a divine calling, and thus a relational identity, makes it more fully itself even as it intensifies the genuine distinctiveness of the disciplines. Schindler's use of the word *holiness* or *sanctity* to describe the intellectual life is thus not first of all about an individual's personal beliefs or even his or her particular morally good actions. To say that holiness "comprehends the intelligence" is to allow the love of Christ to "assume not only their wills but their intellect and their thoughts."[120] The question that Schindler raises is whether academic knowing is open to being as communion as its true end or whether it relies instead on a closed ontology and a finite god.

117. Schindler, "Sanctity and the Intellectual Life," 217.

118. This way of stating the matter is not entirely adequate as it can underwrite a dualism between piety and logic. My argument, more fully, is seeking to show that all logic is grounded in some form of piety.

119. Schindler, "Sanctity and the Intellectual Life," 217.

120. Schindler, "Sanctity and the Intellectual Life, 215. Schindler specifically cites 2 Corinthians 10:5, "Take every thought captive to obey Christ."

The incarnation: filial being

For Schindler, the intellectual life becomes good, true, and holy inasmuch as we acknowledge not only that relation is constitutive of being, but even more, that all being is filial. Schindler uses "filial" to specify how being as relational is christological. To this end, he cites *Dominum et Vivificantem* (1986): "The Incarnation of God the Son signifies the taking up into unity with God not only a human nature, but in this human nature, in a sense, of everything that is 'flesh': the whole of humanity, the entire visible and material world. The Incarnation, then, also has a cosmic significance, cosmic dimension." So understood, Christ is not an ontological exception, but an index for understanding all of humanity, indeed the entire cosmos. Thus the "relation to the Father in Jesus Christ has been utterly freely passed on by Christ (through his Church in the Holy Spirit) to all creation."[121]

This incarnational emphasis clarifies that ontology as relation is not simply an explicit belief, a mental concept, or an ideal. It is rather embedded in the material world as gift even before we are able to have reflective thoughts. Schindler uses "filial" to emphasize how our being is from another before any act of will on our part. Thus, "relation to the world and to God is always-already *in* the self 'prior' to the self's doing and making."[122] Thus, "this implies that we are all receivers before we are achievers, in the manner of children. We are first not creators but (active) receivers of the relation to God and to the world that is always-already *in* our being."[123]

Following Balthasar, Schindler gives a key example of our filial nature in the relation between a mother and child. When the child smiles, Schindler asks, who is the agent? At one level, we might immediately respond, "the child." But the child is responding to the mother's prior love; the smile follows an attractiveness and a beauty embedded in the reality of love. The child is drawn into a truth. This structure of knowing, Schindler maintains, is true at "higher" levels as well in that as beings/knowers we are participating naturally in a prior giving and gift. Recovering a childlikeness, in this sense, is to recover wonder and thanksgiving typically characteristic of a child, not as mere psychological acts but as expressions of the "very ontology of the person as created, and as such are meant to be recapitulated

121. Schindler, "On Meaning and the Death of God," 205. Schindler is discussing this point in light of Mary's fiat; the logic of her "letting it be done according to the Word" is an extension and embodiment of the logic of being as relation and love.

122. Schindler, "The Meaning of the Human," 95.

123. Schindler, "The Meaning of the Human," 96.

in every act even of the adult . . . ."[124] Schindler calls this gratuitous structure of being not only filial but also primordially sacramental: one implies the other. A filial relationality is "a 'primordially sacramental' sign and expression of the ordered relationality first given by God and by other creatures in God."[125] The use of the term "primordially sacramental" stands in radical contrast to an evaluation of all being as flat or "value-neutral." Rather as created, all being is inherently receptive.

> It is because of this constitutive filial and nuptial relationality, of this being first a child of God and indeed of the universe of being itself, in and through one's own parents, that each one in each of his acts cannot but recuperate his being—in a basic if not wholly conscious way—as a generous-responsive "letting be" of oneself, and thus of God and of others, relation to whom is always already generously effective in one's self.[126]

Schindler argues that in and through Christ the being of creation is a relation of love, a relation exemplified most fully in a receptivity and response of wonder, gratitude, and love. Such a description may seem far indeed from the modern academy, possibly a warm and fuzzy idea that has little to do with study, research, and the mastery of a subject. But any ontology that distorts human being as relation, communion, and gift will inevitably also distort the worlds made possible through research and study. Schindler's call is not to abandon or somehow soften the intellectual life but to understand it ground and purpose.

At this point, we can engage at least two questions in light of Schindler's analysis. The first is, in light of sin, whether or not his understanding is overly optimistic. If sin impacts all of creation, then how does his understanding provide a genuine alternative if sin disrupts communion? Is his understanding not really an ideal after all, one unrelated to being in a fallen world? Schindler acknowledges the depth of original sin, of Adam's disobedience "lodged in the depths of the cosmos." As such, all societies will contain structural sin in some sense. Particular attention must be given, however, "to the distinct way in which modern liberal societies conceal their (ontological-spiritual) ambiguity and indeed 'voluntarize-privatize' their sin." They do so by claiming to have "carved

---

124. Schindler, "The Meaning of the Human," 96.

125. Schindler includes in the given, created relationality a "gender-differentiated nuptial relationality" as well. See, for example, Schindler, *Ordering Love*, 269.

126. Schindler, *Ordering Love*, 269.

out 'public-institutional-technical-procedural' space empty in principle of any ('evil') ideology, leaving evil to be exhaustively identified with an always (supposedly) *private* abuse of freedom."[127] The particular challenge of modernity, then, is to see how sin has become voluntarized and privatized. That is, "sin" is language easily relegated to a personal sphere. Inasmuch as the academy, however, is embedded in a flat ontology, then it is relying upon a sinful structure: one that disposes it to separation and fragmentation rather than communion.

Does not one need explicitly to accept the grace of Christ in order for it to be efficacious: to live into an alternative? In terms of my argument, I would say, "yes and no." Peter Maurin and Dorothy Day, founders of the Catholic Worker movement, sought to build a society in which it was "easier for people to be good." Similarly, I would say that Schindler is describing an ontology that makes an academic culture more possible in which it is easier for participants to be good. And good refers not simply to behavior; it encompasses studying, learning, and teaching in communion with others and ultimately God. Such an approach in no way denies personal responsibility, but rather enables one to be more responsive and more attuned to all cosmic being in its manifold richness.

This point leads to a second question pertaining to Schindler's use of the language of "primordial sacrament" to describe the natural world as created in its relation to God. Such language might seem puzzling, especially to those Protestants for whom the language of sacrament is rather alien. For them, it might bring to mind Catholic-Protestant debates about the number of sacraments or about how to speak of Christ's presence at the table. While these issues are important, they need not detract from Schindler's ontology in which "primordial sacrament" is a way of describing an alternative to dualist tendencies. Any denial of the world's natural "sacramentality" or any radical opposition between the natural and the supernatural makes "the world *grace-proof*, and ultimately lead[s] to *secularism*."[128] To say the world is primordially a sacrament is to say it is not a "dumb" machine onto which we impose our own values. As Brad Gregory puts it, "Descartes's mechanical universe devoid of God's presence is the antithesis of a Christian sacramental worldview."[129] All of creation—the entire cosmos—is a sign of God's generosity and excessiveness apart from which we would cease to be. The

---

127. Schindler, "The Meaning of the Human," 101.

128. Alexander Schmemann cited in Schindler, *Ordering Love*, 290.

129. Gregory, *Unintended Reformation*, 57.

language of primordial sacrament helps us see that a purely autonomous world ironically makes the world (the academy) less natural.

In this chapter, I have argued that academic being, like cosmic being more broadly, is not a neutral phenomenon onto which we subsequently add value or meaning. Aquinas, Poteat, and Schindler share in common a criticism of any dualism that separates being from purpose, mind from body, or nature from grace: all dualisms which leave the academy adrift in a sea of unending interpretation and unable to speak of purpose. Each of our thinkers describes, albeit in different ways, an understanding of being as both created and oriented toward God. Being and goodness (Aquinas), being and logos (Poteat), and being and communion/love (Schindler) are convertible. To be is to be oriented toward the One who is the abundant source of all that is. Such an ontology sees the world's destiny, as Augustine rightly understood, as resting in God. We will see in the next chapter how true leisure, as the basis of academic culture, orients the academy toward its true end.

3

LEISURE IN THE ACADEMY

A colleague in a biology department once told me of being asked at a conference about what it was like to teach biology at a Catholic institution. His response, "It makes no difference at all." He was surely defending the legitimacy of his work as real science, untouched by myopic or authoritarian religious teachings. Even so, he was rehearsing pervasive academic assumptions that place religion and faith in a sphere separate from the academic disciplines.

What would it take for the academy to produce a different kind of response than the one my colleague gave? Institutions have responded to a decline in Christian identity and higher education by focusing on service opportunities, campus ministry, core values, and hiring policies. These initiatives, however, while no doubt helpful, fail to address the deepest challenge in the academy today, which I have argued is an ontological one. My colleague was tacitly relying upon a closed ontology, one that prevents institutions from seeing the things in this world as "tokens of a reality that exceeds them infinitely."[1] In contrast to this closed ontology, I argue that leisure relies on an ontology of abundance and thus makes possible an academic culture that sees being as inherently gift and communion.

1. Caldecott, *The Radiance of Being*, 60.

Josef Pieper and Intellectual Work

In his classic *Leisure, the Basis of Culture,* Josef Pieper challenges misunderstandings of work and leisure. One of the most common is that work—academic or otherwise—is pure activity: if you want to know or accomplish something, then you must work. This seems like common sense. But Pieper argues that this assumption leads to the conviction: "If to know is to work, then knowledge is the fruit of our own unaided effort and activity; then knowledge includes nothing which is not due to the effort of man, and there is nothing gratuitous about it, nothing 'in-spired', nothing 'given' about it."[2] That is, to believe that knowing is only work is to believe that the academic life is a product of human effort and ingenuity alone.

Pieper relates this understanding to the thought of Immanuel Kant who, according to Pieper, held knowledge to be exclusively discursive, which is the opposite of contemplative and receptive. Kant thus regarded intellectual knowledge as activity and work. As such, Kant saw contemplation not as knowledge but as a "pseudo-philosophy."[3] Even more than the contrast activity/passivity, however, Pieper argues that Kant attached a *moral* significance to hard work. Kant regarded contemplation as questionable because it did not cost anything. Rather, for Kant "the good should be difficult, and . . . the effort of will required in forcing oneself to perform some action should become the yardstick of the moral good: the more difficult a thing, the higher it is in the order of goodness."[4] On this view, what gives intellectual activity *worth* is its difficulty. The logical conclusion is that contemplation, as non-activity, is worthless and a waste of time.

Pieper contrasts Kant with two key points from Aquinas: 1) "the essence of virtue consists in the good rather than in the difficult," and 2) "not everything that is more difficult is necessarily more meritorious; it must be more difficult in such a way that it is at the same time good in a yet higher way."[5] Pieper (with Aquinas) does not want to deny the difficult, but what makes an activity worthwhile, he argues, is not self-generated but a participation in goodness and love.

---

2. Pieper, *Leisure,* 2. Pieper refers specifically to Max Weber's study of capitalism where Weber states, "one does not work to live; one lives to work." Pieper, *Leisure,* 2.

3. Pieper, *Leisure,* 9.

4. Pieper, *Leisure,* 13.

5. Pieper, *Leisure,* 14–15.

Pieper turns to the command to love one's enemy in order to illustrate a confused tendency to identify the difficult with the good. The tendency to overvalue hard work and the effort of doing something difficult is so deep-rooted that it even infects our notion of love. Why should it be that the average Christian regards loving one's enemy as the most exalted form of love? Principally because it offers an example of a natural bent heroically curbed; the exceptional difficulty, the impossibility one might almost say, of loving one's enemy constitutes the greatness of the love.[6]

Pieper responds to this identification of the difficult with the good by quoting Aquinas: "It is not the difficulty of loving one's enemy that matters when the essence of the merit of doing so is concerned, excepting in so far as the perfection of love wipes out the difficulty. And therefore, if love were to be so perfect that the difficulty vanished altogether, it would be more meritorious still."[7] Loving our enemies is, of course, a worthwhile action; its difficulty, however, is not *essential* to its being worthwhile. What makes it worthwhile is love. Pieper relates this point to knowledge, the essence of which is not work but "unveiling reality." Thus, "just as the highest form of virtue knows nothing of 'difficulty,' so too the highest form of knowledge comes to man like a gift—the sudden illumination, a stroke of genius, true contemplation; it comes effortlessly and without trouble."[8] For Pieper then, true work is not pure activity. It is first of all contemplative precisely because it is oriented toward a greater Good that human effort alone cannot manipulate or control.

At this point, one might worry, as Kant did, that prioritizing so-called passivity, inspiration, and intuition over reason leads to a lazy mysticism. Kant believed that his opponents, whom he called "mystagogues," were "un-tuning" philosophy.[9] These were contemporary Neoplatonists who

---

6. Pieper, *Leisure*, 14–15.

7. Pieper, *Leisure*, 14–15. Hebert emphasizes that Pieper "points to a doctrine found in Aquinas, in the Church's recent Catechism, and in other writings of John Paul: that 'God is happy by way of His existence,' and not by virtue of his work; that God's creative and redemptive work is in fact an outpouring of his love, his self-enjoyment, and his happiness—not their condition . . . ." Hebert, "Be Still and See," 156.

8. Pieper, *Leisure*, 15–16.

9. Kant, "On a Newly Arisen Superior Tone in Philosophy." Kant's position on work is related to his distinction between the noumenal and the phenomenal, where the noumenal is ultimately unknowable, though the idea of God is a "postulate" for the moral law. The phenomenal realm—the realm of law and reason—is knowable and requires regimen and effort. Battersby rightly registers the equivocal ontological status between these two Kantian realms: "Like the moral law, nature must be constructed in a way that

Kant believed were not really working at philosophy but simply relying upon questionable speculation. In response, Pieper acknowledges that the highest forms of knowledge may be preceded by great exertion in thought but he emphasizes that ultimately "effort is not the cause; it is the condition" of knowledge.[10] Ultimately, the worth of knowledge and knowing does not rest on human effort or productivity, but has to do rather "with salvation, with the fullness of being, and thus ultimately with the fullness of happiness . . . ."[11] Salvation? This sounds strange, especially against the backdrop of our typical understanding of academic work. But Pieper is emphasizing that it is not sheer human effort that makes knowledge (or teaching or learning) worthy. The worth, rather, has to do with the receptivity of a gift outside ourselves which is always in some sense salvific and healing. Pieper's analysis points to the conviction that true knowing is inherently gift and will always point beyond the recipient toward a larger Good given for all of creation.

Leisure

If one had to name a sin in the academy today, "sloth," understood as laziness, might well come in first. Being productive is the hallmark of success. Departments or programs are closed on the basis of a lack of "efficiency and effectiveness."[12] In light of this understanding of work, leisure today is seen as useful for rest and restoration in order to work better and be more productive. Leisure is a vacation, taking time off, or entertainment.

In an astonishing passage, however, Pieper states that "no one who looks to leisure simply to restore his working powers will ever discover the fruit of leisure . . . ."[13] To understand the fruit of leisure, Pieper first turns to the nature of true sloth or *acedia* (the Greek word for "sloth"). Pieper argues

---

leaves its ontological status unresolved." Battersby, *The Phenomenal Woman,* n.p.

10. Pieper, *Leisure,* 16.

11. Pieper, *Leisure,* 17.

12. See, for example, the rationale for closing the Religious Studies graduate program at University of Pittsburgh in Schackner, "Pitt dropping." Pieper asks rhetorically: "Is there a sphere of human activity, one might even say of human existence, that does not need to be justified by inclusion in a five-year plan and its technical organization?" Pieper, *Leisure,* 19.

13. Pieper, *Leisure,* 31.

that laziness is rather a *symptom* of sloth as is constant busyness.[14] Both are symptoms of not wanting to be who God wants us to be, which ultimately means that we do not wish to be who we really fundamentally are.[15] He relates this definition to Kierkegaard's "despairing refusal to be oneself." Sloth thus refers to the refusal to be who we are before God, to be who God created us uniquely to be. The opposite of sloth, then, is "man's happy and cheerful affirmation of his own being, his acquiescence in the world and in God—which is to say love."[16] Both the workaholic and the indolent reject the gift of receiving their being from and before God.[17]

Pieper argues that the cure for *acedia*—the despairing refusal to be oneself—is leisure. But leisure is not simply taking a break. Rather the "the deepest of the springs by which leisure is fed" is divine worship. According to Pieper, worship creates a place of abundance, "a sphere of real wealth and superfluity, even in the midst of the direst material want—because sacrifice is the living heart of worship."[18] Whereas work understood as purely human effort results from and produces *acedia* (refusal to be before God and thus alienation from God), leisure produces wealth understood as receiving our lives as gift and communion with God.

"Sacrifice" might sound jarring in relation to wealth and superfluity. But Pieper is discussing how leisure is impossible on the basis of human construction alone. By contrast, "no one need expect a genuine religious worship, a *cultus*, to arise on purely human foundations, on foundations made by man; it is of the very nature of religious worship that its origin lies in a divine ordinance . . . ."[19] Worship is either something given or it does

14. As Pieper notes, the seven deadly sins are also known as "capital" sins, *caput* meaning "head" or "source." See *Leisure*, 25–26. Sloth or *acedia* is deadly because it is a source, sometimes hidden, that gives rise to other faults, like a contaminated lake flowing into and polluting surrounding streams. Laziness as well as busyness are like the streams; they are signs of sloth.

15. Pieper, *Leisure*, 24.

16. Pieper, *Leisure*, 25.

17. To affirm one's being in this sense is not a kind of self-help philosophy. Affirmation of being, for Pieper, is affirmation of a way of life that calls for humility, confession, forgiveness, reconciliation, all of which constitutes participation in Divine love.

18. Pieper, *Leisure*, 49 and 47.

19. Pieper, *Leisure*, 51. The idea that culture lives on religion through divine worship will easily strike modern ears as nonsensical. We tend to think of cultures as related to geography and particular habits of a group of people, where the boundaries of language are often those of a particular culture. Multiculturalism, on this understanding, means the mixing of lots of different groups: African American, Native American, Caucasian,

not exist at all.[20] In a Christian understanding, the gift that is "the sacrifice of the God-man" heals and restores fallen creation. Worship draws one out of a sphere of purely human construction and into "the heart and centre of creation" to see that every day is a feast day.[21]

Pieper's analysis of work, *acedia,* and leisure applies to the modern academy in the following ways. First, by far the dominant way of thinking about work in the modern academy has been Kantian. That is, work requires effort; it is difficult and, more often than not, its difficulty is what makes it or at least contributes to its worth. It is better for professors to have produced five books rather than one in terms of academic evaluation and prestige. Secondly, the common understanding of leisure in the academy is taking a break or vacation in order to be more productive. From Pieper's perspective, these are profound signs of an institution's despairing refusal to be itself. Finally, Pieper's analysis leads to the conclusion that a true academic life *requires* leisure. Rightly understood, leisure is the goal of work, not as some means end calculation but as the purpose of work. If leisure rooted in worship makes true work *possible*, it lies at the heart of an authentic academic culture.[22]

The kernel and the husk

Pieper, of course, is writing against the academic grain. Leisure fed by the spring of Divine worship has increasingly been seen as peripheral if not simply inconsequential in the academy, a sensibility vividly captured in the frequently used image of the kernel versus the husk. Adolf von Harnack (1851–1930) used this image to identify what in his view was at the heart of Christianity. In *What Is Christianity?* (published in 1900), Harnack argued that the essence of Christianity is found in Jesus' teachings, which he summarized as 1) the coming of the kingdom of God, 2) the Fatherhood of God and the infinite worth of the human soul, and 3) the command to love. Harnack interpreted the development of Christian dogma as mere

---

and so forth. By contrast, Pieper is relating culture to its etymological sense: cult, understood as related to cultic practices of worship.

20. Pieper, *Leisure,* 52.

21. Pieper, *Leisure,* 52 and 53.

22. As Pieper observes, we see this connection etymologically in the fact that in Greek, "leisure" is *skole* and in Latin, it is *scola.* Pieper, *Leisure,* 2.

husk, seeking instead to recover the true historical kernel.[23] In so doing, Harnack was eager to show that the essence of Christianity lined up with a truly scientific way of thinking. Theology is a *Wissenschaft*, he maintained, that investigates "God in inner experience within time and in the historical records that give us access to such experiences."[24] So understood, the *Wissenschaft* (science and true knowledge) of theology is a kind of phenomenology of human experience through historical records. Harnack thus asks, "Is there—admitting sloth, shortsightedness, and numerous ills—really any other theology than that which has a firm connection and blood relationship to science?"[25]

In seeking an essence of Christianity that could qualify as a *Wissenschaft*, Harnack was following his eighteenth-century predecessors and the Enlightenment more broadly. He was attempting to get at the primary qualities, the thing itself, rather than the secondary qualities, which were external and not essential to the phenomenon. Before Harnack, Friedrich Schleiermacher had argued against the cultured despisers of religion that true religion had nothing to do with its trappings: rituals and dogma. "If you have only given attention to these dogmas and opinions [theories about the origin and end of the world, analyses of the incomprehensible Being], therefore you do not yet know religion itself, and what you despise is not it. Why have you not penetrated deeper to find the *kernel* of this shell?"[26] For Schleiermacher, like Harnack, dogma as well as ritual made up the shell of religion. Later in the twentieth century, Rudolf Bultmann will continue this trajectory by seeking to demythologize the Bible: to go beyond the myth/dogma/husk and discover the true kernel of meaning. All of these thinkers stand in the shadow of Kant, especially his effort to describe religion "within the limits of reason." Kant found it necessary to deny knowledge of God, freedom, and immortality in order to find a place

23. "What is common to all the forms which it has taken, corrected by reference to the Gospel, and conversely, the chief features of the Gospel, corrected by reference to history will, we may be allowed to hope, bring us to the kernel of the matter." Harnack, *What is Christianity?*, 16.

24. Stroup, "The Idea of Theological Education," 168.

25. Harnack, "Fifteen Questions to Those Among the Theologians," 166. Barth responded, "If theology regained the courage to be objective, the courage to become a witness of the word of revelation, of judgment, and of the love of God, then it could also be that 'science' in general would have to look out for its 'firm connection and blood relationship' to theology, rather than the other way around." Barth, "Fifteen Answers to Professor von Harnack," 170.

26. Schleiermacher, *On Religion*, 15. My emphasis.

for faith.[27] In denying such knowledge, Kant was seeking to protect faith from the onslaught of scientific knowledge and enlightened reason. Thus, "God" and "immortality" are postulates that cannot be "objectively known," though they do provide the ground for a truly ethical attitude. Kant embraced a rational faith based on data contained in pure reason. Though well intended, we see in Kant a sharp division between objective reason, on the one hand, and irrational myth, on the other.[28]

This way of thinking—kernel versus husk—has taken root in Protestant as well as Catholic understandings of the academy. We can find such assumptions in both Protestant and Catholic struggles to articulate the nature of the university. For example, at a conference held at Urbana on religion and higher education in 1905, John Henry Gray of Northwestern argued for the "Christianizing" of the whole atmosphere by conveying not "the husks of denominational dogma" but the "essence of personal religious life."[29] In 1908, American educator Abraham Flexner vividly described the university as having "come down the mountain" in order to "take up its abode among men."[30] Flexner used this biblical imagery to convey the idea that the real place of the university is on the ground "among men," not up on the mountain, the place of benighted vision and myth. A milder version of this kernel versus husk understanding can be found in William Louis Poteat, biologist and president of Wake Forest University (1905–1927). Instead of using the word "husk," however, Poteat used the word "baggage" to refer to the accretions of Christianity over time, which were not the real

27. Kant states, "I cannot even make the assumption—as the practical interests of morality require—of God, freedom, and immortality, if I do not deprive speculative reason of its pretensions to transcendent insight . . . I must, therefore, abolish *knowledge*, to make room for *belief*." Kant, *Critique of Pure Reason*, 10.

28. As Jaspers notes, "[Kant] is one of the philosophers in the tradition of Lessing, who rationally interpret the content of religion, who 'demythicize' when myth sets itself up as knowledge, but who grasp myth in its essence and so enable us to make it our own." Jaspers, *Kant*, 86–87.

29. Cited in Johnson, "'Down from the Mountain,'" 554. The overall question of this conference had to do with how to respond to the loss of Christian life and practice in the face of rapidly expanding institutions of higher education, which had once been avowedly Christian.

30. Johnson, "'Down from the Mountain,'" 585. On the same page, Johnson comments on the inevitably of this dualism: "separation and autonomy . . . were no longer the problem. They were now the remedy."

thing. Poteat, at the time, was caught up in a controversy over evolution and was eager to separate faith from science.[31]

More recently, Fr. Theodore Hesburgh, CSC, claimed that the university is "the place where the Church does its thinking."[32] While this statement, frequently cited, affirms that the university serves the church, it also equates thinking with intellectual competence in a university that is free from the church.[33] Though Hesburgh likely did not intend it, this way of speaking implies that real thinking does not occur in the church; thinking occurs rather in the domain of intellectual competence free from hierarchy, dogma, and so forth. The university is not the church in that one space is free for intellectual pursuit and the other is not; one place focuses on the intellect while the other is about prayer, creeds, ritual, and worship. A realm of knowing (kernel) free from a realm of faith (husks) feeds this way of thinking.

We can expand the lens of the kernel versus husk image even more widely and notice how it represents dominant assumptions about the so-called secular and the religious. Talal Asad argues that "from the point of view of secularism, religion has the option either of confining itself to private belief and worship or of engaging in public talk that makes no demands of life."[34] The modern world is broken down into a duality: "a world of self-authenticating things in which we really live as social beings and a religious world that exists only in our imagination."[35] On this view, the real is the social, the political, and the public, while religion and worship are, at best, peripheral.

31. In 1925, Poteat delivered the John Calvin McNair Lectures, titled "Can a Man Be a Christian To-day?," "Baggage," and "Peace." For descriptions of these lectures see Linder, *William Louis Poteat: Prophet of Progress* and Hall, *William Louis Poteat: A Leader of the Progressive-Era South.*

32. This oft-cited quote can be found at http://hesburgh.nd.edu/fr-teds-life/an-extraordinary-life/biographical-essay/.

33. As we saw in chapter 1, Hesburgh is particularly concerned to defend Catholic universities as excellent universities rather than "ghetto" enclaves. Against this, Hesburgh claims that "a university does not cease to be free because it is Catholic" and "the best and only traditional authority in the university is intellectual competence . . ." in Hesburgh, ed., *The Challenge*, 4 and 5.

34. Asad, *Formations of the Secular*, 199. "In the discourse of modernity," Asad adds, "'the secular' presents itself as the ground from which theological discourse was generated (as a form of false consciousness) and from which it gradually emancipated itself in its march to freedom." Asad, *Formations of the Secular*, 192.

35. Asad, *Formations of the Secular*, 194.

The kernel versus husk image has settled into the walls of the modern academy. It assumes the kernel of the college or university is true knowledge associated with the academic disciplines (here understood as those specialties requiring critical and autonomous methods of interpretation), while piety, ritual, creed, and worship are the marginal husks. The kernel versus husk image thus reproduces a way of thinking about the academy that makes leisure tangential to institutional self-understandings.

Taught bodies

Pieper offers a brilliant analysis of true leisure. Yet, given the dominant modes of thought that relegate leisure to the husk, how can leisure become embedded in the academic culture? We can begin by looking at how learning leisure is a matter of "taught bodies," to use a term from Asad. Discussing the nature of belief, Asad argues that "changes in the grammar of 'belief' are connected with changes in forms of life . . . ."[36] This Wittgensteinian point indicates that different patterns of thinking require alternative habits of speech and practice. Asad thus calls for a focus not on the inner world of subjects, but on "how objective conditions in which subjects find themselves enable them to decide what one must think, how one can live, and how one is able to live."[37] By "objective conditions," Asad is describing how rituals, practices, and myths—far from being merely external shells—are rather what make thinking certain thoughts possible. Thus he claims that "the inability to enter into communion with God becomes a function of *untaught bodies*."[38] From this perspective, the so-called "husks" or "external" practices, rituals, and so forth are what make particular ways of thinking possible in the first place. Asad thus draws attention to how bodies are in fact being formed; rituals and patterns of speaking make certain thoughts and beliefs possible. From a certain perspective, this might sound bizarre as it challenges a modern assumption that the individual is free to choose his or her beliefs. But Asad's point is that beliefs are embedded in prior body formations that have already, in a sense, imposed a way of thinking on us.

To see how this is so, we can turn to George Grant's discussion of technology and modern thinking. Grant rejects that assumption that "the

36 Martin and Asad, "Genealogies of Religion, Twenty Years On," 14.

37 Martin and Asad, "Genealogies of Religion, Twenty Years On," 13.

38. Asad, *Genealogies of Religion*, 77, my emphasis.

computer does not impose on us the ways it should be used."[39] Grant's purpose is not to be reactionary, but rather to show how the logic of a certain paradigm of knowledge is part and parcel of the logic of technology and its use. He argues that the tools we use and the world we see and know cannot be separated. The liberation that leads us to believe "we freely create values, is a face of the same liberation in which men overcame chance by technology—the liberty to make happen what we want to make happen . . . . The whole of nature becomes more and more at our disposal as if it were nothing in itself but only our 'raw material.'"[40] One might object that technology has helped save or protect nature in a wide variety of ways. This is true, as is of course its opposite. But Grant's point is that now in regard both to the self and to nature, one stands as master. He is thus arguing that the paradigm of objective information over against subjective freely chosen values cannot be separated from practices surrounding modern technology.[41] Grant calls technology the "ontology of the age." His analysis, though briefly described here, helps us see how certain external conditions (technology) impose ways of thinking.

To take another example of taught and untaught bodies, we can look at the ritual of a typical faculty meeting. Faculty from different disciplines gather in one place; a faculty president convenes the meeting; a particular order is followed. Robert's Rules maintains a certain procedure and order. On many issues, faculty vote and the majority wins. Like the so-called neutral computer, the faculty ritual too seems like a neutral and innocuous process, the procedure simply a tool to get to the best outcome. But such proceduralism cannot be divorced from a certain paradigm of knowing, itself embedded in a liberal democratic politics. The assumption is that there can be no common good other than what the majority decides. In what sense is this an ontology? It relies on the assumption that freedom is about choosing our values, even as it fails to see how such proceduralism itself is not explicitly chosen (and as such reflects a value/fact dichotomy).

We can contrast this kind of faculty meeting ritual with one in which faculty do not vote. Such is the case at Earlham College, where its Quaker

39. Grant, *Technology and Justice*, 19.

40. Grant, *Technology and Justice*, 31.

41 As Grant puts it, "The new adage of rulers and educators is that to the mastery of non-human nature must now be added mastery of ourselves," in Grant, *Technology and Justice*, 16. Further, Grant states that because computers can only exist in societies with large corporate institutions, they "are not neutral instruments, but instruments which exclude certain forms of community and permit others." Grant, *Technology and Justice*, 26.

tradition of "waiting for light" still shapes faculty practice. Instead of voting, faculty engage in a process that requires periods of waiting. Faculty develop a practice of willingly yielding to others even when they do not fully agree. This kind of faculty ritual makes possible different sorts of habits and virtues. Generally speaking, it calls for faculty to attend more carefully to their colleagues. It calls for developing the virtue of patience since waiting itself in part of what it means to be at a faculty meeting. Most fundamentally, there is the conviction that light is not simply generated by the faculty themselves but comes from *outside*, from a Divine source. Whereas the dominant faculty ritual promotes the practice of choosing the good, the Quaker inspired meeting practices discerning the good for all in light of the Divine Good. This is not to say that voting is never a good practice; it is only to call attention to how certain practices make particular ways of thinking about the good possible.

Leisure and the grammar of singing

To learn how to practice leisure in the way that Pieper describes, then, it is necessary to learn renewed habits of speaking and bodily being. Singing might seem an odd place to begin. After all, singing in the academy tends to take place only in music departments or in extracurricular activities on campus. We do not sing in classrooms. Lectures are not sung. And yet, leisure and singing are intimately related; both rest is a particular sort of harmony that is constitutive of being itself.

Before developing this point more fully, however, it is helpful to recall how orality and literacy can shape the way we see and interpret the world. Perhaps the best-known interpreter of these different modalities is Walter J. Ong. In *Orality and Literacy*, Ong describes the invention of writing as a "technological revolution," one followed by the printing press and then by today's mass media. Ong narrates how this technological literacy provided a capacity to imagine oneself as an objective viewer in contrast to oral cultures where knowing is more embedded in a "human lifeworld." According to Ong, in highly technological cultures, individuals are more likely to think of themselves as autonomous subjects. As Ong puts it, "For an oral culture learning or knowing means achieving close, empathetic, communal identification with the known . . . , 'getting with it'. Writing separates the knower from the known and thus sets up conditions for 'objectivity', in the sense of personal disengagement or distancing."[42] Ong discusses how an "objective" (in this sense) view of the self tends not to be present in oral cultures. He gives the example of a thirty-six year old peasant who, when asked what sort of person he was, responded, "What can I say about my own heart? How can I talk about my character? Ask others; they can tell you about me. I myself can't say anything."[43] Such a response would be atypical in a technological literate culture.

Among other comparisons, Ong describes how oral memory differs from a primarily literate one. For example, oral peoples do not have the concept "line by line" nor even of "word" as a discrete entity apart from the flow a speech. Ong refers to at least once study, that of Albert Lord with South Slavic narrative poets, where the idea of a text as controlling the narrative actually interfered with the oral composing process. Their remembering rather had nothing to do with texts but were rather "the re-membrance of songs sung."[44] The memory feats in oral cultures are often phenomenal, the performers typically able to repeat lengthy stories for hours on end. Ong notes that it is typical for the oral poet to wait a day after having heard the story; "he needs time to let the story sink into his own store of themes and formulas, time to 'get with' the story."[45] This differs for a primarily literate culture where the passing of time can easily make remembering more difficult.

Ong's work has occasionally been criticized for its generalizations.[46] Even so, for my purposes it highlights how certain objective sorts of con-ditions (to use Asad's language) can deeply form one's sensibilities about knowing and being. That such is the case puts us in a better position to con-sider how the grammar and practice of singing enhances an understanding of leisure as the basis of academic culture.

To develop this, we can begin with Pope Benedict XVI's discussion of monastic culture where, he observes, human speech is not enough; mu-sic is required. It might seem as if music, while pleasant, adds nothing to the actual meaning or grammar of speech. But Benedict XVI emphasizes, "Wherever man praises God, the word alone does not suffice. Conversation with God transcends the boundaries of human speech, and in all places, it

42. Ong, *Orality and Literacy*, 45.

43. Ong, *Orality and Literacy*, 55.

44. Ong, *Orality and Literacy*, 59.

45. Ong, *Orality and Literacy*, 60.

46. Soukup, "Orality and Literacy 25 Years Later," 3–17.

has by its very nature called to its aid music, singing and the voices of creation in the harmony of instruments."[47] From this perspective, music and singing are not simple additions to spoken words adding no real content. They rather make possible a harmony heretofore unrealized.

Benedict XVI observes that the Psalms contain numerous instructions about how to sing the psalms and how to accompany such singing with instruments. He points to St. Benedict, for whom the decisive rule that governed the chant of the monks was a psalm: "In the presence of the angels, I will sing your praise" (138:1). In the Christian (Catholic) liturgy, participants join with the angels in singing the "Gloria," sung at the birth of Jesus, and the "Sanctus," the cry of the seraphim before the Lord. Such passages and practices illustrate how singing rests on "the awareness that in communal prayer one is singing in the presence of the entire heavenly court, and is thereby measured according to the very highest standards: that one is praying and singing in such a way as to harmonize with the music of the noble spirits who were considered the originators of the harmony of the cosmos, the music of the spheres."[48] So understood, singing harmonizes participants with the entire cosmos.

But how is this true? Augustine, in his classical treatment of music in *De Musica*, states that God *is* music. As Carol Harrison paraphrases, God "is supreme measure, number, relation, harmony, unity, and equality. When he created matter from nothing he simultaneously gave it existence by giving it music, or form—in other words measure, number, relation, harmony, unity, equality . . . ."[49] God himself is harmony and, through creating and redeeming, extends this harmony to all of creation, must fully through the Word becoming flesh (John 1:14).[50]

To sing "songs, hymns and spiritual songs" (Col 3:16) is therefore to participate in a cosmic harmony. Singing is thus a rational activity in that it orders one towards God. If the soul is not so ordered, it falls into nonbeing. To sing poorly, or not at all, is to enter "a zone of dissimilarity," a phrase Augustine used before his conversion, indicating that he was remote from God. He had become "dissimilar not only to God, but to himself, to

---

47. Benedict XVI, *The Unity of the Church*, 26.

48. Benedict XVI, "Address."

49. Harrison, "Augustine and the Art of Music," 31.

50. Irenaeus states that the Word becoming flesh signals the "harmonious music of salvation." Irenaeus, *The Scandal of the Incarnation*, 65.

what being human truly is."[51] So understood, "music is no longer simply a liberal art that teaches us about the nature of reality through a rational analysis of numerical relation; it is an art that must be practiced in every moment of a creature's existence if it is to remain in right relation to God and not fall back into non-being . . . ."[52] Music and singing are not mere additions to a curriculum, nor merely extra-curricular activities but crucial to the harmony of being itself. Rightly understood, "the culture of singing is also the culture of being."[53]

It is from this perspective that Stratford Caldecott argues for a relation between mathematics and theology. While he admits this sounds strange, he states that this is only because we have become fragmented in our thinking. In an earlier system of education—the *quadrivium*, which included arithmetic, music, geometry, and astronomy—the assumption was "that by learning the harmonies of the cosmos, our minds would be raised toward God," the source of unity for all harmony.[54] Yet, Caldecott notes, present education tends to eliminate the contemplation of such harmony, reducing knowledge to its component parts. Such reduction stands over against both ancient Greek and Scriptural wisdom as contained, for example, in the Wisdom of Solomon, "But thou hast arranged all things by measure of number and weight" (11:20).[55]

Singing forms a people to be present to the harmony of all creation. If a body does *not* sing, it will be deaf to this cosmic harmony. Such a position could sound overly romantic, as if singing a few psalms could suddenly resolve the fragmentation of the academy. There is a sense in which this objection is true. If singing is simply an extra-curricular activity disconnected from an institution's intellectual life, then, yes, it will make little difference. It will be reduced to exactly the kind of leisure that Pieper criticizes. It will thus become one more activity or pastime in an already deeply fragmented place. As such, it will add nothing to the harmony of an institutional

51. Benedict XVI, "Address." Benedict XVI notes that Saint Bernard of Clairvaux used "zone of dissimilarity" to describe the poor singing of the monks.

52. Harrison, "Augustine and the Art of Music," 31.

53. Benedict XVI, "Address." In "Liturgy and Sacred Music," Benedict XVI observes that ". . . Romano Guardini stressed emphatically that in the liturgy it is not a question of *doing* something but of *being* something." Benedict, *Unity*, 33.

54. Caldecott, *Beauty for Truth's Sake*, 53.

55. As cited, Caldecott, *Beauty for Truth's Sake,* 53. One of many examples that Caldecott gives of this ordered beauty is the "golden spiral," a geometric design that can be found in the galaxies as well as in small plants and shells.

culture, but rather simply reflect the fact that the institution itself does not believe there is such harmony. But this is exactly the point of retrieving the practice and grammar of liturgical singing. Such singing provides an external "objective condition," one that tunes ears to hear harmony and shapes mouths to sing of its cosmic reach.

The grammar of singing does not deny all that is discordant in the world: the harsh sounds of our sins, the cries of the suffering, and the often unbearable weeping in the face of death. The Psalms, of course, are filled with songs of lament as well as songs of praise. But in uniting one's voice to the great cloud of witnesses, one enters into the mystery of creation and one hears the discord of the fallen world within the wider harmony of hope in Christ.[56]

In this light, a more fruitful symbol for the academy than the kernel versus husk is the image of polyphony. This term refers to the playing of many sounds or notes, but in a way that harmonizes them in a single unity. Karl Barth writes that

> listening to the polyphony of creation as the external basis of the covenant . . . is listening to the symphony for which it was elected and determined from eternity and which the Creator alone has the power to evoke . . . . For when [God] speaks His one and total Word concerning the covenant which is the internal basis of creation, this symphony is in fact evoked, and even the self-witness

---

56. In "Liturgy and Sacred Music," Benedict XVI ends with a poignant reflection on a saying from Mahatma Gandhi where Ghandi refers to "the three living spaces of the cosmos and to the way in which each of these living spaces has its own mode of being. Fish live in the sea, and they are silent. Animals on the earth cry. But the birds, whose living space is the heavens, sing. Silence is proper to the sea, crying to the earth, and singing to the heavens. Man, however, has a share in all three. He bears within himself the depths of the sea, the burden of the earth, and the heights of heaven, and for that reason all three properties belong to him: silence, crying, and singing. Today—I should like to add—we see how the cry is all that remains for the man without transcendence because he wills to be only earth and also attempts to make heaven and the depths of the sea into his earth. The right liturgy, the liturgy of the communion of saints, restores his totality to him. It teaches him silence and singing again by opening up the depths of the sea to him and by teaching him to fly like the angels. By lifting up his heart, it brings the song buried in him to sound again. Indeed, we can even say the reverse: one recognizes right liturgy in that it frees us from general activity and restores to us again the depths and the heights, quiet and song. One recognizes right liturgy in that it has a cosmic not a group character. It sings with the angels. It is silent with the waiting depths of the universe. And thus it redeems the earth." Benedict, *Unity*, 42–43.

of creation in all the diversity of its voices can and will give its unanimous applause.[57]

For Barth the internal covenant—the internal communion between God and all creation—is the melody that frees creation to be itself, a grand symphony of praise to God. If we relate this image to the academy, then we can say that distinctive voices, different ways of knowing, and particular knowledges can be a polyphonous rather than a discordant diversity. Unlike the kernel versus husk image, in polyphony there is not an inconsequential periphery. What makes the different knowledges harmonious is that they are, in the final analysis, evoked by God. This is not to deny possible conflict and discord in various academic endeavors. But even these can become polyphonous when practiced in a way that acknowledges that human effort alone is completely insufficient. Polyphony captures the reality that a harmonious culture lives in gratitude and sees knowing as always a gift that enables participants to join the harmony of creation. It teaches the body how to practice true leisure.

Leisure and the grammar of feasting

Imagining leisure as the basis of the academy is, I have argued, not simply a pious concern; it is ontological. Pieper's description of leisure has to do with how we understand being. Is being "in the nude"[58] or is it inherently relational, as we discussed in chapter 2? Like singing, the practice and grammar of eucharistic feasting provides a way to renew leisure as the basis of academic culture.

Challenges to speaking of sacraments

Also like singing, however, sacramental feasting can seem peripheral to stereotypical academic concerns. Robert Jenson describes how "sacrament" was reinvented at least in some schools of modernity. For nineteenth and twentieth century liberal theology, he observes, the resurrection had become a value judgment rather than a fact. Since Jesus was regarded as a figure of past history, the question became, "How do we come into relation

57. Cited in Hauerwas, *With the Grain of the Universe*, 197.

58. The Cappadocians argued that no nature is "in the nude," but always has its "mode of existence." Zizioulas, *Being as Communion*, 88.

with the past Jesus, to be affected by him?" The response was to achieve contact as one would with any historical person: by reconstructing the figure through documentary evidence. Jenson states that for liberal theology historical scholarship "was something like a chief *sacrament*: We come into contact with Jesus by the historical study of Scripture, and in fellowship with him we are sanctified."[59] In this use, "sacrament" equals the historically verifiable.

Some Protestant traditions, by contrast, have dropped the use of sacrament altogether, preferring the language of "ordinance" or "symbol."[60] So understood, coming to the Lord's Table is a command of Jesus but not an actual means of grace (a position developed to some extent in contrast to the Catholic understanding of transubstantiation). While ecumenical discussions have recently shown some positive signs of these positions moving closer together, some Protestants worry that the language of sacrament distorts the nature of true grace by making it mechanical or quasi-magical.[61] As I discussed in chapter 2, sacramental language is crucial for understanding leisure as the basis of academic culture. Such language at its heart sees grace as embedded in nature as did the great Baptist theologian Walter Rauschenbusch when he prayed, "O God . . . grant us a heart wide open to all the beauty" so that we see how "even the common thornbush is aflame with Your glory."[62]

Pieper describes the first and ultimate sacrament as the incarnation.[63] Jesus is fully human and fully divine, the unique Son of the Father and thus not only a figure in the past, accessible through historical scholarship. An adequate Christology does not turn away from history, however, but sees the incarnation as the fulfillment of both history and creation. Jesus as

---

59. Jenson, "Karl Barth," 25, my emphasis.

60. My own Baptist tradition has tended, at least in the United States context, to describe the Lord's Supper as only an ordinance. But the language of sacrament was not uncommon in earlier Baptist confessions, and Baptist churches in other parts of the world (for example, in Jamaica and England) frequently use the language of "sacrament" today.

61. For a nuanced development of Baptist understandings of sacrament/ordinance (with representatives from the Baptist World Alliance) in international conversations with the Catholic Church, see Baptist World Alliance Delegation, "Baptists and Catholics Together," especially 61–67, 75–81.

62. This passage is from Rauschenbusch's prayer, "Thanks for Creation." Cited in Hauerwas, *A Better Hope,* 240.

63. Pieper, *Leisure,* 53.

sacrament is the complete union of nature and grace meaning that there is no contradiction between Jesus' humanity and his divinity.

Such christological convictions developed out of and along with practices of eucharistic feasting, both of which made possible a new ontology. John Zizioulas describes how theologians such as Ignatius and Irenaeus, reflecting in part on the Eucharist, came to interpret being and life in the same breath. For the Greek mind at this time, being preceded life, and life was (for Aristotle) "*a quality added to being*, and not being itself." But Irenaeus came to see Christ as "the truth not of the mind" (his fight against gnosticism leads him away from this) "but of the *incorruptibility* of being." Christ is not an intellectual principle that explains the universe but the "life and the universe of beings finds its meaning in its incorruptible existence in Christ, who takes up into Himself . . . the whole creation and history."[64] Being is identified with the incorruptibility of Christ who is abundant life. Irenaeus thus argues, against the gnostics ("the most rationalist movement of the period"), that since the Eucharist imparts life then it is *truly* Christ.[65] Christ as incorruptible being is related to the eucharist as imparting abundant life.

A crucial advance in this understanding (following Athanasius) of being is the idea "that *communion belongs not to the level of will and action but to that of substance*. Thus it establishes itself as an ontological category."[66] That is, communion is not something simply willed or generated but is inherent in being itself. God who is love creates an "immanent relationship of love *outside Himself*" such that "if [God] ceases to love what exists, nothing will be. Being depends on love."[67]

Sacramental feasting as communion

So understood, communion is not something added to being. Just as Jesus' being cannot be separate from his communion with the Father and with all humanity, so also our being as created cannot be entirely separated from communion with God. In our fallen state, we may not acknowledge

64. Zizioulas, *Being as Communion*, 80.

65. Thus we are not the source of life: "So we must never become puffed up, as if we had the source of life within ourselves . . ." Irenaeus, *Incarnation*, 91.

66. Zizioulas, *Being as Communion*, 86.

67. Zizioulas, *Being as Communion*, 91. Zizioulas is particularly describing the use of *ekstasis* in the theology of Dionysius and Maximus the Confessor.

this communion, just as a child may not acknowledge the love of a parent. Even so, it is an objective condition. A similar understanding applies to the Lord's Table. Some might imagine that the Lord's Table is ritual added to an otherwise real academic being. On this understanding, such "feasting," like leisure itself, might seem a waste of time, not relevant to the academic world. Such a view might concede that for those interested in this sort of feasting, a certain communion is possible, like the kind of community one finds at academic conferences and other such meetings.

With eucharistic feasting, however, the key point is that "though it always takes place in an actual human community, it isn't a feast that we create. It is something God offers and invites us to."[68] The Lord's Supper thus contradicts the idea that community in the academy or elsewhere is a human creation. Through reception of the divine gifts of the body and blood, participants learn to say something like, "We do not fully grasp all that we are."[69] This is because the mystery of God and of all creation is wider that one can say or even imagine. The self-knowledge that is received through this feasting is not reliant upon an indifferent world or a neutral human freedom in which we produce our own worth. The ontology of the Lord's Table rather says, "We receive, therefore all that we are is a gift from God." The grammar of feasting thus forms one to practice leisure in a way that acknowledges that, in the final analysis, we are not masters but recipients, created for communion.

Like singing, eucharistic feasting does not ignore sorrow, suffering, sin, and division. This is not a feast that pretends everything is fine. But sin, division, and so forth come to be seen in the selfsame moment that one sees the reality of God. Henri de Lubac notes how Origen, commenting on Isaiah, said "that the prophet began to see his wretchedness at the moment of beginning to glimpse the glory of God."[70] In other words, it is divine communion or rather the presence of God that humbles one in her own sinfulness even as that same presence extends the gift of healing. Divine communion as an overcoming of sin and separation reveals that an autonomous self, sphere, or subject is a fiction. It thus disallows a celebration of an independent secularity grounded in a scarce ontology. The feast of

68. Cited in Wainwright, *Faith, Hope, and Love*, 58.

69. This is a version of Jacques Paliard's quotation: "And I myself do not fully grasp all that I am." Cited in Lubac, *The Mystery of the Supernatural*, 214.

70. Lubac, *The Mystery of the Supernatural*, 214. Isaiah says both, "Woe is me! . . . for I am a man of unclean lips," and "Here am I. Send me!" (Isa 6:5, 8).

the Lord's Supper is rather for the life of the whole world. Thus Alexander Schmemann can say that original sin is not first of all about disobedience but about ceasing to see one's whole life "depending on the whole world as a sacrament of communion with God. The sin was not that man neglected his religious duties. The sin was that he thought of God in terms of religion, i.e., opposing Him to life. The only real fall of man is his non-eucharistic life in a non-eucharistic world."[71] Schmemann's ontology is eucharistic. Since gift and being are interchangeable, thanksgiving and gratitude are expressions of true being.

Moral versus ontological

One might concede that the Lord's Supper provides moral insights about feeding the poor or sharing with others. From this perspective, the Table is inspiring in the moral realm as a symbol of how one ought to behave, but it is not really relevant for the intellectual realm. This view is consistent with those theologians, philosophers, and historians who reject a Chalcedonian Christology, arguing instead that Jesus is a revolutionary figure preaching the kingdom of God, but one who never intended for his followers to worship him.[72] This Christology is moral rather than ontological. That is, it sees Jesus as a persuasive moral figure, but not the fully human and fully divine person who is the Son of God. As an essentially moral enterprise, the Lord's Supper too becomes a matter of human effort and remembering. The flip side of the Lord's Supper as mere symbol is interpreting it as a radical exception to the natural order of things. Whereas the symbolic view relegates the eucharist to a moral (versus factual) realm, the exceptional view interprets the eucharist as an intrusion into the natural order.

Yet the christological logic of eucharistic feasting speaks of the bread and wine becoming the body and blood of Christ from the inside. That is, Christ is neither a symbol leaving human nature as is. Nor is he simply a supernatural intrusion into an otherwise natural world. Zizioulas describes how in the eucharist God's Word reaches creation not from the outside, but as "'flesh'—from the inside our own existence, as part of creation."[73]

---

71. Schmemann, *For the Life of the World*, 7.

72. For a recent example of this approach, see the works of Bart D. Ehrman.

73. Zizioulas, *Being as Communion,* 114. This sacrament of love, as Augustine calls it, is intrinsic because Christ united himself with human flesh, with creation, not waving a magic wand but "emptied himself . . . being born in human likeness" (Phil 2:7).

Just as in the incarnation God comes to creation from within, so also in the eucharistic celebration God brings creation to fulfillment by means of creation. As Zizioulas puts it, "God does not dwell in the human mind as rational knowledge or in the human soul as mystical inner experience, but as communion within a community."[74] This is not simply a matter of human *willing* directed by the mind. That would be a moral understanding and as such easily relegated to the realm of personal choice. It is rather a reception in the Eucharist of a real gift—Christ's body and blood—which draws all being more fully into communion.

Feasting in the academy: irrelevant?

What does an academic culture look like that learns this particular grammar? Some will say that, in the final analysis, it makes no difference for the university at all, as my biology colleague said in reference to his work at a Catholic college. Relating the Eucharist to biology or any other discipline seems like a long stretch, if not simply impossible. Zizioulas briefly mentions how Einstein "showed that certain aspects of reality are intrinsically *relational*, rather than absolute . . . ."[75] Though expressing some reservations in regard to Einstein, Zizioulas nonetheless notes that a scientist relying on this ontology "will be able to recognize that he is carrying out a *para-eucharistic work*, and this may lead to the freeing of nature from its subjection beneath the hands of modern technological man."[76] Para-eucharistic means seeing that communion with divine life extends to all of creation, not just humanity, a view that thus frees one from the lust to manipulate and control. Zizioulas is not simply saying that a scientist or any other academic needs to approach his or her subject matter with only a desire not to manipulate or control knowledge. He is rather saying more radically that the Eucharist frees one to approach the world as it really is, i.e., that facts bear already a relational reality. So understood, values are not an imposed part of the nature of things. Analogously, the Eucharist is not a value attributed to the bread and wine, but divorced from the factual world. It is rather the way the world actually is.

74. Zizioulas, *Being as Communion*, 115.
75. Zizioulas, *Being as Communion*, 120.
76. Zizioulas, *Being as Communion*, 120.

In a similar vein, Zizioulas states, "A human being left to himself cannot be a person."[77] He relates this to Adam turning away from communion with God to be an "individual," and thus one for whom the other becomes an enemy. His true being is thereby reduced. Likewise, a university left to itself will distort its true being. To learn the grammar of authentic leisure through eucharistic feasting is to learn that academic being, like all being, is not neutral but inherently oriented toward communion: thus toward gift and reception.

One could object that this is too pure or too spiritual of an idea to be relevant in the real world of research, labs, learning, teaching, and so forth. But this is exactly the point at stake. How do we understand, see, and receive the real world? The grammar of eucharistic feasting enables truthful speech about the real world, that is, the world "aflame with the glory of God."

Babette's Feast

Leisure brings a Christian college or university into greater harmony and communion with Divine plenitude. The dominant academic mode, however, has become so habituated to scarcity (work versus worship, academy versus church) that it has become anemic. But such scarcity only reveals itself in light of an alternative.

Isak Dinesen's wonderful story "Babette's Feast" can serve as a parable of how leisure moves a community from scarcity to abundance. In this story, Babette, a famous Parisian chef, becomes a refugee after her husband and son are killed. Eventually, two poor Danish women allow Babette to live with them as their cook. The Danish women are part of a community, Dinesen writes, that has "renounced the pleasures of this world, for the earth and all that it held to them was but a kind of illusion and the true reality was the New Jerusalem toward which they were longing . . . ."[78] Despite this otherworldly focus, the community becomes caught in the memories of past injuries, quarrels, and destroyed friendships. Fourteen years pass. Babette comes into some money and decides to prepare a feast for her strict puritanical hosts (who have never discovered her background as a famous chef).

77. Zizioulas, *Being as Communion*, 107.
78. Cited in Mullins, "'Deeper Down in the Domain of Human Hearts,'" 29.

With her Danish hosts suspiciously looking on, Babette spends weeks preparing a meal for the poor community. Despite their misgivings over Babette's apparent waste, the community goes along with her plan, deciding ahead of time that it would be improper to react positively to such extravagance. Their reluctant participation in Babette's grand meal, however, draws them into a world of grace and forgiveness. Grudges and resentments melt away. In a final scene they are singing and dancing under the night stars, united by an extravagant meal of grace not only with each other but with all creation. Their song and dance in response to a Divine love heretofore unknown is an image of leisure.

While the academy is a very long distance from a small village in nineteenth-century Denmark, it is nonetheless true that all genuine being participates in Divine abundance, even when not acknowledged as such. It is also true in the academy, as elsewhere, that abundant being takes time. The heavenly meal that Babette fixed took weeks of preparation, or even longer, since as a former Parisian chef, she had spent years learning the art of excellent cooking. Similarly too, academic being with leisure as its basis is an art. If we were to engage the wider story of Babette, we would discover how over a period of many years, she had come to love the small village, and the particular sisters in that village who had welcomed her when she had nowhere else to turn. She had attended their worship services, been present at their small house meetings, and visited in their homes. Her feast was the culmination of years of learning to love, and love is ultimately what made sense of her feast.

True leisure rests on the assumption that the love of others as well as the love of learning and the desire for God are inseparable. Such leisure enables a community to move from a place of frugality to a place of abundance. While being in this place requires effort, it is not a human achievement but a Divine gift.

4

A PLACE OF PLENITUDE

Leisure and Academic Space

When one thinks about academic space, certain common divisions seem obvious, chief of which is a division between the academy and the church. One frequently hears, "The academy is not the church." At conferences on Christian identity and higher education, it is not uncommon to hear participants use "we" when speaking of the academy and "church" when referring to an entity that lies elsewhere in an entirely different space. The quandary is how to relate them.

This same division between the academy and the church is internal to the academy itself. Years ago, when teaching a class on "Catholic Social Thought," I decided it would be good for my students to read the US Bishops' Pastoral Letter, "Economic Justice for All" (1986). The letter situates economics within a broad gospel and social justice framework, one that attends strongly to concern for the poor as reflected in Scripture. My colleagues in the economics department, for their part, saw engagement with this kind of letter as outside of their disciplinary responsibility and expertise.[1] The fact that we read the letter only in a theology class, however, undermined the letter's content: namely that economics and theology are inextricably intertwined. I say this not to criticize my colleagues, whose

---

1. Students, consequently, are trained to think that real economics is what they learn in the economics department. Issues related to faith or "values" are add-ons and personal choices. This flat ontology easily leaves students to imagine that faith, theology, and church are in a sphere: extra-curricular choices, divorced from a whole way of being.

training no doubt shaped their understanding, but rather to show how deeply internalized the division is between church and academy, between faith and knowledge.

It will be tempting to fit leisure into this dominant spatial pattern. Leisure grounded in communion, contemplation, and ultimately Divine worship could easily seem to belong in the extra-curricular sphere, outside of the academic core of the institution. In this chapter, however, I challenge this assumption by arguing that leisure is not one *space* among others, but a *place* that pertains to the whole academy. In what follows, I first engage three distortions of academic space before developing how leisure is a place of academic plenitude.

"Seeing like a Walmart": compartmentalized space

Romand Coles uses the phrase "seeing like a Walmart" to describe how abstract spaces distort our lives.[2] Seeing like a Walmart is not only about Walmart. It is about how, as Wendell Berry puts it, the abstractions of science and industry lead to the belief that "everything is interchangeable." Seeing like a Walmart fosters what Berry calls a "rhetoric of nowhere." Such a depleted rhetoric "cannot speak of heaven and earth, but only of concepts."[3] A "rhetoric of nowhere" signals that one is living abstractly, divorced from concrete places and times. One place is as good as another.

Alasdair MacIntyre depicts this interchangeability in his well-known "disquieting suggestion" at the beginning of *After Virtue*. A grand-scale catastrophe creates havoc on earth resulting, eventually, in the loss of all scientific knowledge. All that is left are fragments disconnected from theories, experiments, and instruments. Without a wider context, use of the knowledge fragments seems arbitrary, one fragment interchangeable with another.[4]

MacIntyre relates this scenario to the moral fragmentation of our contemporary culture. There are no wider stories that help make sense of moral knowledge but only random fragments, hence a "rhetoric of nowhere." People imagine that they must simply choose their beliefs, values,

2. Coles and Hauerwas, *On Christianity, Democracy*, 341. "Seeing like a Walmart" is similar in many ways to Poteat's description of mall amnesia, discussed in chapter 1.

3. Berry, *Life is a Miracle*, 41–42. Cited in Hauerwas, *The State of the University*, 99.

4. MacIntyre, *After Virtue*. As some have noted, MacIntyre's scenario owes a debt to Walter M. Miller's *A Canticle for Leibowitz*.

and identities, a position that MacIntyre calls emotivism. This is a modern "doctrine that all evaluative judgments—specifically all moral judgments— are *nothing but* expressions of preference, expressions of attitude or feeling, insofar as they are moral or evaluative in character."[5] MacIntyre further observes that a focus on choice is in and of itself not new. An earlier conception of choice, however, placed it within a shared conception of human goods. Thus choices revealed character.

An example of MacIntrye's understanding is King Lear, who chooses to exile Cordelia, the only daughter who truly loves him. Such action reveals a profound character flaw: his inability to distinguish between those who grovel for gain and those whose love cannot be compromised. Shakespeare could rely on his audience to understand how kinship included honor and duty. Today, however, most of us would have little idea how to respond if we were asked, "What are the duties of an aunt?"[6] To an increasing extent, MacIntyre argues, relations with our kin are simply determined by choice. The dominant assumption is, "I am what my choices make me." Increasingly, "individuals understand themselves as not merely invited to but having *no alternative* to themselves choosing what is to come as good or bad, what is to come as better or worse. It is a matter of choice."[7] Whereas formerly a tradition of shared beliefs (how a father and daughter should express their love, for example) provided a wider context, now belief is an expression of personal choice.

Consequently, life becomes a series of episodes rather than something to be grasped as a whole. MacIntyre describes this compartmentalization:

> [I]ncreasingly all our lives are compartmentalized, so that as we move from the home to the workplace, to the meeting of the trade union branch, to the sports club, to some religious service in the parish, whatever it is, we move into and out of areas each of which has its own autonomous sets of norms, each of which requires of us that we adapt to those norms if we are to be effective in that situation and in such a way that we have to exchange one set of attitudes and norms for the other as we move between them. So it comes about that a new virtue is added to the list of

---

5. MacIntyre, *After Virtue*, 11–12.

6. MacIntyre takes this question from Marilyn Strathern's *After Nature*, which is about the history of kinship in England. MacIntrye, "A Culture of Choices."

7. MacIntrye, "A Culture of Choices."

the virtues, *adaptability*; and a new vice is added to the list of the vices, *inflexibility*.[8]

One could argue that a person acting differently in different contexts is to be expected, and even called for: a person who is both a surgeon and mother will not act the same in the respective settings. For MacIntyre, however, adaptability is a "virtue" from nowhere: the adaptable person adjusts to a compartmentalized world because there is no overall purpose or vocation to make sense of his or her fragmented life.

One can see compartmentalization and adaptability in the academy in at least two key ways. First, it is commonplace to legitimize Christian "identity" in the academy by pointing to campus ministry, service opportunities, or other such spaces. One seldom points to the business department, the psychology department, or the biology lab. A culture of choice and compartmentalization easily leads to the assumption that since beliefs are expressions of choice, they belong in the "belief sphere," now seen as a compartmentalized space in the academy. By failing to see how these areas are part of a larger whole, this view promotes "adaptability" and fragmentation. Stratford Caldecott rightly argues that such fragmentation in the academy is itself already a way of serving the market. "The fragmentation of education into disciplines teaches us that the world is made of bits we can use and consume as we choose. This fragmentation is a denial of ultimate meaning. Contemporary education therefore tends to the *elimination of meaning*—except in the sense of a meaning that we impose by force upon the world."[9]

A second common defense of the modern "virtue" of adaptability, in the academic world especially, has to do with technology. One frequently hears, for example, "the information age is changing everything."[10] Or "our kids learn within a system of education devised for a world that increasingly does not exist."[11] Typically the underlying conviction is, "You must adapt or you will not survive." Such appeals to adaptability play to human fear in a world seen as essentially competitive. Wendell Berry rightly notes that when you hear the words "more efficient," "you may expect soon to encounter 'inevitable,'" a word that obviates any need to consider an alter-

8. MacIntrye, "A Culture of Choices," my emphasis. See also MacIntyre, *After Virtue*, 105–6.

9. Caldecott, *Beauty for Truth's Sake*, 17.

10. Brumley, "After initial skepticism."

11. Cited in Scott, "High school teacher: I'm banning laptops in class."

native.[12] An institution mired in adaptability will have little sense of how compelling virtues, traditions, and stories can provide an alternative place of faithfulness in the midst of modern fragmentation.

In contrast to choice and adaptability, MacIntyre states that character is not something that one simply chooses; it rather chooses us.[13] Frodo from *The Lord of the Rings* exemplifies MacIntyre's point. Frodo "without willing it or wanting it came into possession of a ring whose own adventure changed everything in the path of his life."[14] Frodo does not simply choose his identity. Rather in the midst of events he does not choose, he seeks to respond to a more profound calling. Could he have chosen not to have taken the ring? As an abstract possibility, yes, but in so doing he would have ceased to be himself. Frodo's courage, while tested and at times fragile, is nonetheless not something that he can turn off and on at will. It has become part of who he is and how he sees the world, a display of his character formed in the context of adversity, tradition, friendship, and calling.

A focus on character rather than identity suggests the following: instead of discussing "Christian identity and higher education," what would it look like to focus on "Christian character and higher education"? This shift in language would at minimum make it difficult to relegate Christian convictions to a sphere since virtues, rightly understood, describe habits or ways of being that encompass a whole life. Virtues stand as an alternative to values. Institutions typically choose their core values but it is more difficult to choose virtues in the same way. Any reflection on virtues requires a rhetoric from somewhere since formation in virtue calls for particular practices embedded in stories about the good. One has little idea, for example, what the value of "diversity" looks like. Or, better stated, the value of

---

12. Berry, *Life is a Miracle*, 53. Berry describes this position as the "dogma of the survival of the wealthiest (i.e., mechanical efficiency)." Berry, *Life is a Miracle*, 52. The underlying message is: "The machine is coming. If you are small and in the way, you must lie down and be run over." Berry, *Life is a Miracle*, 53. One frequently hears this rationality in arguments for online education.

13. As Stanley Hauerwas observes about MacIntyre, "[T]he intelligibility of an action depends on the narrative continuities in an agent's life. Yet the ability to narrate my life depends on having narratives available that make my peculiar life fit within narratives of a community that direct me toward an end that is not of my own making. The intelligibility of my life, therefore, depends on the stock of descriptions at a particular time, place, and culture. I am, at best, no more than a co-author of my life." Hauerwas is referring specifically to MacIntyre's 1986 article, "The Intelligibility of Action." Hauerwas, "The Virtues of Alasdair MacIntyre."

14. Brownson et al., *StormFront*, vii.

diversity, dependent as it is on a "rhetoric of nowhere," looks like a modern individual who believes, "I am my choices." By contrast, a virtue only makes sense when narrated within the context of particular practices. I will return to a specifically academic virtue later in this chapter. For now, however, let us turn to a second way the academy is tempted to distort space.

Eruditio et Religio: how religious space becomes national space

Stanley Hauerwas recounts how Nan Keohane, in her inaugural address as the president at Duke University, confesses that only after she had agreed to become Duke's new president did she discover that Duke's motto was *Eruditio et Religio*. Initially, she states, the motto made her uneasy; "the emphasis on religion seemed hard to square with the restless yearning for discovery, the staunch and fearless commitment to seek for truth wherever truth may be found that is the hallmark of a great university."[15] Apparently only as she came to understand that religion is about the "burning passion for righteousness" and about the "moral impulse" was she able to see how *religio* could fit with *eruditio*: the unimpeded pursuit of truth.[16] Keohane's understanding reflects Immanuel Kant's well-known identification of religion with the moral law, a reality which for Kant implied the reward of a good God. For Kant, faith itself had no epistemic content. The supersensible realm was without meaning from the standpoint of knowledge though it had existential significance. Knowledge rather must be confined to the sensible world of time and space. Thus Kant believed that one needed to *deny* knowledge of God and immortality in order to find room for faith. Kant thus locates the foundation of faith (*religio*) in morality.

If we follow Keohane's trajectory, what does academic space look like? Keohane herself acknowledges that we have to have morality or academic space will become dry and barren; one needs the passion of religion/morality. One needs rational analysis, however, lest the passions get out of control. Reason keeps morality in check. Thus, as Keohane states, "There will always be a tension between the striving of objective knowledge and the subjective commitment to moral value . . . ."[17] Though we often try to keep these two in separate boxes so that they do not "contaminate" each

15. Hauerwas, "Missing from the Curriculum," 1.

16. Keohane, "Inaugural Address."

17. Keohane, "Inaugural Address," 228.

other, the goal should be to "make this tension productive . . . ."[18] Keohane herself does not elaborate which commitments or whose morality is best able to bring about such productivity, nor would she be able to on the basis of her assumptions. This is because by identifying religion as morality and morality as subjective commitment, she has left no way to adjudicate which moral commitments might allow for academic flourishing.

As such, the academy is easily assimilated to the dominant cultural ethos. To take one example, George Marsden cites the conclusion of a 1946 Report of the President's Commission on Education (appointed by Harry Truman): "religion is held to be a major force in creating the system of human values on which democracy is predicated . . . ."[19] The date of the report is significant. After World War II, serving American democracy became a major goal of American higher education. According to Marsden, religion as morality became morality as democratic ideals, "without directly resorting to Christianity" or any particular religion.[20] Moreover, Marsden states that religion as now private became "something that ought not interfere with the main business of the university."[21] The main business is rather to create successful citizens who serve their country well. While I would affirm that serving one's country is a laudable goal, the challenge remains to discern what "serving well" looks like. *Religio* as moral ideals leaves an institution unable to discern its purpose; it will rather be subject to fads of the time, whether nationalism, Marxism, or some other fashionable ideology.

Homogenized space: a culture of pluralism

In fact, Keohane's reference to truth as objective seems naïve today in the face of an emphasis on multiple voices and diverse rationalities, which points to our third way that the academy distorts space. As Marsden observes, in

18. Keohane, "Inaugural Address," 228.

19. Marsden, *The Soul of the American University*, 392. The document that Marsden cites is titled "Higher Education for American Democracy."

20. Marsden, *The Soul of the American University*, 389. Marsden is referring specifically to the Harvard Report of 1945, *General Education in a Free Society*.

21. Marsden, *The Soul of the American University*, 336. Thus, Marsden states, "Religious viewpoints, at least traditional ones, were considered both unscientific and socially disruptive." Instead, the university came to believe that a "universal science would provide an objective basis for a united society." Though "traditional Christian beliefs were unscientific, the Kingdom of God could be advanced through cultural development." Marsden, *The Soul of the American University*, 429.

the latter part of the twentieth century, belief in a neutral objective science was radically called into question as "most would admit that everyone's intellectual inquiry takes place in a framework of communities that shape prior commitments."[22] Pluralism arose out of the realization that there is no single moral or intellectual framework but a multiplicity of points of view. As we saw in discussing Marty's "Anticipating Pluralism" in chapter 1, *normative* pluralism is the belief that there is no way to discriminate between different convictions or frameworks.

Marsden observes, however, that pluralism has become almost a code word for its opposite as "persons from a wide variety of races and culture are welcomed into the university, but only on the condition that they think more-or-less alike. Though the leadership may no longer be all northern European male, the establishmentarian impulse toward homogenization still prevails."[23] In contrast to Marty's conviction that pluralism opposes homogeneity, Marsden claims the opposite. "Pluralism remains a basis for imposing uniformity."[24] Marsden points out that "religious viewpoints that do not blend into the multicultural melting pot are excluded."[25] Marsden goes on to argue that viewpoints such as "naturalism" are no less sectarian than other more explicitly religious understandings. He thus argues that all institutions for the sake of honesty ought to be more forthcoming about their convictions and boundaries. Furthermore, given the assumptions of pluralism, it is makes no logical sense to exclude whole classes of religious views: "religiously based perspectives need not be any more tendentious than other perspectives. Moreover, truth in advertising suggests that scholars and teachers should reveal their viewpoints."[26] Marsden thus advocates for a more genuine pluralism both *within* the university and *among* colleges and universities.

Stated differently, Marsden is arguing for a place at the table for all, especially for Christians, or better stated, for orthodox Christians. He still argues, however, that those at the table must follow certain rules, "the attendant features of a technological society, such as rules of procedural rationality and standards of professionalization guaranteeing such academic

22. Marsden, *The Soul of the American University*, 430.

23. Marsden, *The Soul of the American University*, 432.

24. Marsden, *The Soul of the American University*, 436.

25. Marsden, *The Soul of the American University*, 433.

26. Marsden, *The Soul of the American University*, 439.

practices as tenure and academic freedom within declared boundaries."[27] Not just anything can pass muster academically. Still required is procedural rationality that refers to basic rules of evidence and argument.

To summarize, then, Marsden argues that pluralism as it now exists in the academy *homogenizes* academic space. He maintains, however, that a genuine pluralism will not be intolerant toward a whole class of viewpoints (evangelical Christianity, for example). Those who hold Christian worldviews may have a place at the table as long as they follow the rules of the game. Elsewhere, Marsden compares Christians engaging academic pluralism to Christians playing a basketball game. When Christians enter the game, they do not require that the rules be changed, telling players to love their enemy, for example. In a similar way, Christians do not have to fully accept pluralism as normative in order to participate.[28]

The difficulty with Marsden's solution, however, is that he does not really offer an alternative to the homogenized space of pluralism. The "place at the Table" turns out to be an anonymous addition, more like passing through a large impersonal cafeteria than sharing a meal together. Stanley Fish, in his well-known essay, "Why We Can't All Get Just Along," argues that Marsden's position ultimately will not work. He turns to the portrayal of Satan and Adam in Milton's *Paradise Lost*: "There is no opposition here between knowledge by reason and knowledge by faith because Satan and Adam are committed to both simultaneously. Each performs an act of faith—the one in God and the other in materialism—and then each begins to reason in ways dictated by the content of his faith."[29] Marsden's position, it would seem, agrees with this point. Is it not in fact a key reason to extend pluralism? But Fish uses this point—no opposition between faith and knowledge—to go in an entirely different direction. The problem with liberalism (or we could say pluralism)[30] is not that it is "not liberal enough." Thus, he states: "If you persuade liberalism that its dismissive marginalizing of religious discourse is a violation of its own chief principle, all you will gain is the right to sit down at liberalism's table where before you were

27. Marsden, *The Soul of the American University*, 440.

28. Marsden, *The Outrageous Idea*, 56.

29. Fish, "Why We Can't." Fish delivered an earlier version of this essay in a lecture honoring George Marsden's installation on the faculty at the University of Notre Dame.

30. For my purposes, liberalism and pluralism are variations of the same position. Both relegate "faith" to personal choice; both assume proceduralism determines the rational; and both inherit from Cartesianism the belief that being is inherently neutral.

denied an invitation; but it will still be liberalism's table that you are sitting at, and the etiquette of the conversation will still be hers."[31]

To develop his argument, Fish engages the logic of liberalism's table through one of its chief architects: John Stuart Mill, for whom the chief duty of "the reasonable man is to be tolerant of all views . . . ." Mill specifically identified intolerance with religion.[32] Fish notes that for Mill, the trouble with Christianity, and with any religion grounded in firm convictions, "is that it lacks the generosity necessary to the marketplace's full functioning." It is "one-sided" since it insists on "the rightness of its perspective while being deaf to positions that might challenge it.[33]

While liberalism and pluralism appear to be neutral, Fish argues that they rest rather on

> the substantive judgment that the public sphere must be insulated from viewpoints that owe their allegiance not to its procedures— to the unfettered operation of the marketplace of ideas—but to the truths they work to establish. That is what neutrality means in the context of liberalism—a continual pushing away of ortho- doxies, of beliefs not open to inquiry and correction—and that is why, in the name of neutrality, religious propositions must either be excluded from the marketplace or admitted only in ceremonial forms, in the form, for example, of a prayer that opens a session of Congress in which the proposals of religion will not be given a serious hearing.[34]

Fish describes pluralism as a specific orthodoxy with rules of play that will inevitably exclude claims that contradict it. He thus argues that Marsden's desire to enter the game of pluralism under its procedural rules can only in the end marginalize religion by turning it into one more non-threatening viewpoint among others. "Marsden wants to argue against that marginal- ization, but his suggestion for removing it is in fact a way of reinforcing it."[35] Pluralism's commitment to procedural rationality turns proceduralism

31. Fish, "Why We Can't."

32. Thus Mill states "in the minds of almost all religious persons . . . the duty of toleration is admitted with tacit reserves . . . ." Cited in Fish, "Why We Can't."

33. Fish, "Why We Can't."

34. Fish, "Why We Can't."

35. Fish, "Why We Can't." Fish adds, "To invoke the criterion of intellectual validity and seek shelter under its umbrella is to surrender in advance to the enemy, to that liberal rationality whose inability even to recognize the claims of faith has been responsible for religion's marginalization in the first place."

itself into the common good before which all other goods and convictions must give way.

As Fish implies, pluralism dovetails with being in a market society, one completely dominated by market forces. In such a society, values are interchangeable and monetary value homogenizes everything. Kenneth Surin, in "A 'Politics of Speech': Religious Pluralism in an Age of McDonald's Hamburgers," argues in fact that religious pluralism is embedded in and formed by a global economy. Under pluralism's "global gaze," difference becomes *merely* different, a position that ends up domesticating and assimilating the other. Pluralism is not possible without "global media and information networks, international agencies and multinational corporations . . . [which] declare that nations, cultures, religions and so forth, are simply obsolete if they are maintained in their old forms as fixed and intractable particularities."[36] So understood, pluralism (a tacit objectivism) produces the other as merely different in the same way that the market assimilates everything it touches into one more option and one more commodity.[37]

As such, pluralism is a game, as Marsden rightly notes, but it is one that celebrates an endless exchange and an infinite difference. There can be no winning (that would be hegemonic) but only playing. This playing is aesthetic in the Kierkegaardian sense: it is non-committal, i.e., there is no real reason to prefer one difference over another. Being, in other words, is not a sign of something beyond itself; things in this world are not "tokens of a reality that exceeds them infinitely."[38] Playing this game does not lead one toward delight in wonder before the mystery of being but rather pulls one into being as always equivocal and disordered. It destroys the soul.

36. Surin, "A 'Politics of Speech,'" 200 and 201. Surin concludes that "to resist the cultural encroachment represented by the McDonald's hamburger, therefore, is of a piece with resisting the similar depredation constituted by this world ecumenism," Surin, "A 'Politics of Speech,'" 200–1.

37. Fish himself famously refers to this as "boutique multiculturalism," in Fish, "Boutique Multiculturalism."

38. Caldecott, *The Radiance of Being*, 60. To see the world as a token or sign is to see being as created, as inherently a sign of something else. A rejection of this way of seeing, as discussed in chapter 2, had its source in fourteenth-century Christian philosophy that separated science from faith, and God from nature in what came to be known as the "*via moderna* of the nominalist philosophers . . ." Caldecott, *The Radiance of Being*, 29. Increasingly, priority has been given to the empirical over the metaphysical, to quantities, external aspects, and experimental evidence over subjective qualities. Caldecott, *The Radiance of Being*, 31.

In this section, I have looked at how academic space is distorted in at least three ways: it is compartmentalized, it is separated from morality, and it is homogenized. None of these spaces, divorced as they are from being as *telos*, goodness, and orientation, allows for true leisure, communion, or gift exchange. The communion and friendships that do develop (and they certainly do) happen in spite of this compartmentalized, mechanistic way of being. I return to leisure and the practice of friendship in my final chapter.

Leisure: a place of abundance

For now, however, I want to consider what it means to describe the academy as a place of plenitude. As noted in previous chapters, I ground my analysis in the conviction that the whole cosmos is in fact oriented to God. To say that all of creation is oriented toward God is to say that nature and grace are not and never can be spatially outside of each other. This would be an extrinsicist assumption.[39] One cannot compartmentalize grace, place it in sphere, or reduce it to personal preference, all of which make of grace a scarce commodity. The places where we live and move and have our being are places of abundance. This includes the academy; it too is a place of plenitude dependent upon being as gift. Of course, as we have seen in our discussion of space, this academic place of plenitude is easily distorted. To recover a renewed sense of place, I look at how Scripture, virtue, and leisure working in tandem make reception of Divine plentitude more possible.

Scripture: the academy as gift

At the North Carolina Baptist State Convention in 1834, Agent J. Culpepper, Chairman of the Committee on the Wake Forest Institute, gave a report about the new institute, later to be called Wake Forest College. "There are," he said, "more than thirteen thousand dollars subscribed, and a part of it paid, for the purpose of erecting suitable buildings for the accommodation of the teachers, and students at the Wake Forest Institute." He continued:

> We have therefore abundant reason to thank God and take courage. Probably no person who was present at the formation of the

---

39. Milbank, *The Suspended Middle*, 46. Milbank notes that if nature and grace are outside of each other, then grace will either depend on our agreement to receive it, or it will entirely coerce our wills.

Convention [in 1830], or our first annual meeting, expected to see, at this early period, what we now witness . . . a manual labor School established, possessing the confidence of the community,—offering instruction to seventy promising, and many of them, we hope, truly pious youth; and also affording gratuitous instruction to several of our young brethren in the ministry . . . . We may truly say that the Lord has done great things for us, whereof we are glad.[40]

Culpepper's fellow Baptists would have known that he was drawing from Scripture, specifically from the Psalms: "The Lord hath done great things for us, whereof we are glad" (Psalm 126:3 KJV). Culpepper is not here using Scripture to prove a point, but rather allowing it to serve as an ecclesial *lens* through which he interprets the birth of the college, a birth he attributes ultimately to the providence of God.[41] Through this scriptural lens, Culpepper sees something specific: he sees the college as a gift from God. This is remarkable for two reasons. While Southern Baptists will eventually found fifty colleges and universities, many Baptists in the South at this time were suspicious of such endeavors because they saw higher education as moving away from Bible simplicity.[42] Secondly, the scriptural vision that Culpepper shares with his audience is one that still affirms the Bible as an interpretative lens through which to understand the world. It has not yet become what Jonathan Sheehan calls "The Enlightenment Bible," authoritative "by virtue of its connection and relevance to human morality, aesthetics, and history."[43] It has not yet become, along with an institution's denominational connection, a piece of heritage.

40 "Proceedings of the Fourth Annual Meeting," 11. The manual labor School referred to the fact that the institute aimed to unite "manual labor with study." One to two hours of labor each day for students had the "salutary effect of . . . giving strength and health to their bodies, and vigor to their minds." "Report on the Institute," in the "Proceedings of the Fourth Annual Meeting," 17

41. In this sense, Culpepper and his audience are like the early church fathers, such as Origen, who were "less intent on explaining Scripture than on illuminating everything by it." Lubac, *Scripture in the Tradition*, 46.

42. See Burtchaell, *The Dying of the Light*, 360–64. As Samuel Wait, first president of Wake Forest, put it in his first baccalaureate address: "Keep in mind the fact, that not all, even of your own brethren, are yet convinced of the wisdom of this design [founding the college]. A portion of them yet fear, that by educating young ministers, we shall lead them off from the simplicity of the gospel, and corrupt the word of God." Wait, "Baccalaureate Address."

43. Sheehan, *The Enlightenment Bible*, xiv. Sheehan notes that this shift in the nineteenth century became *Bildungskultur*, "the culture of education that helped shape European nations and institutions for two hundred years." This culture, as Sheehan describes

In Culpepper's understanding, there is no separation between church and academy. The college is a child of the church. In the words of David Thompson, then Vice President of the Baptist State Convention and Chairman of the Committee of Education, the college is "the legitimate offspring of the Convention."[44] Culpepper, Thompson, and others, looking through Scripture, see a natural and organic unity between church and college. The pattern that dominates their imagination is one of Divine provision, a pattern that leads them to profound gratitude.

This is not to say that this scriptural lens was not murky at times or even deeply distorted. Most tragically, Southern Baptists in the academy and elsewhere defended the practice of slavery. Burtchaell describes, for example, how trustees at Wake Forest banned a textbook, *Moral Science* (1835), written by Francis Wayland, the Baptist president of Brown University, because of its condemnation of slavery. In 1849, John Brown White, the third president of Wake Forest, himself a slave owner, nonetheless proposed that "Negroes" be admitted to the Lord's Supper at the Wake Forest Baptist Church, a proposal that was predictably rejected and probably contributed to White's short tenure as president of the school. The conviction that Scripture provided a lens through which to see all of life remained embedded, however, even though it could be mired in blindness and sin.[45]

James McClendon describes this way of seeing Scriptural patterns as a "baptist vision" that has persisted across time, a vision he emphasizes that is not unique to Baptists but has been exemplified in the life of others, such as Dietrich Bonhoeffer (Lutheran) and Dorothy Day (Catholic). The vision turns on a particular way of understanding the logic of Scripture. McClendon uses the phrases "this is that," and "then is now" to describe this scriptural vision. "This is that" comes from Acts 2:16 (KJV) where Peter, on the day of Pentecost, reads from the prophet Joel, and says to his listeners, "This [what you see here today] is that." The "that" is the word of the prophet Joel: "God declares . . . I will pour out my Spirit upon all flesh, and your sons and your daughters shall prophesy, and your young men shall see visions, and

---

it, was one that shifted from a biblical to a neohumanist paradigm. As such it was a paradigm in which "Jews were increasingly excluded from the patrimony of Western nations." Sheehan, *The Enlightenment Bible*, xiv.

44. "Proceedings of the Fourth Annual Meeting," 17.

45. Years later, Wake Forest would become one of the first colleges in the South to admit an African American; in 1962, the school admitted Ed Reynolds from Ghana. A key rationale was that since Baptists send missionaries to Africa, then why not let Africans study at a Baptist university?

your old men shall dream dreams" (2:17). Peter is saying to the early church that the outpouring that Joel ("that") describes is what you see here today ("this"). Scripture is not only a record of the past or a set of moral instructions, but "a disclosure of the meaning and significance of the present."[46] So understood, the "baptist vision" is a way of discerning how providential patterns can mold both space and time.

As noted, this kind of reading is by no means exclusively Baptist or even Protestant.[47] This kind of scriptural vision would have shaped the self-understanding of many colleges and universities across different Christian traditions. College seals still communicate its remnants. The Oxford seal relates "the Lord is my Light" (Ps 27) to academic knowledge and wisdom.[48] On the Wake Forest seal, one sees the Greek letters for Christ (chi and rho) between the alpha and omega, above *pro humanitate* (for humanity), indicating the beginning and end of the college belongs within a cosmic and christological framework. Princeton University's seal displays the Latin for Old and New Testament, signifying that Scripture provides the pattern for the institution's self-understanding. Many college and university seals display an image of the Trinity, the abundant communion of Father, Son, and Holy Spirit. Agent Culpepper, then, in giving his report is relying upon Scriptural patterns of divine provision well-embedded in Scripture and in the tradition of hundreds of colleges and universities.

A modern audience might be tempted to hear this kind of Scripture talk as an antiquated form of piety, no longer relevant to the modern academy. What would it look like, however, to see the academy as a providential place of abundance? In asking this question, I am not seeking a nostalgic return to an earlier period. Rather, I am asking how certain providential patterns can shed light on our current context. How might a scriptural pattern of abundance enable the academy to say "this"—a college or university—is "that," a place of Divine plenitude?

First, it is important to see how Divine abundance is a pattern throughout Scripture: Abraham receives three divine guests who assure him of Yahweh's abundant promise; God provides daily manna in the wilderness for

46. McClendon, "Embodying the 'Great Story.'"

47. McClendon's description can be related to Henri de Lubac's analysis of the four senses of Scripture in Christian tradition. The four senses—the literal, moral, figurative, and eschatological—were layered ways of reading Scripture for and with the church, and thus for the world. In *Hope Among the Fragments*, Ephraim Radner describes how these scriptural patterns providentially mold lives and institutions.

48. The Latin is *Domina nustio illumea.*

the Hebrew people; Jesus multiplies the fish and loaves to feed thousands; the Last Supper is already the messianic banquet. One sees the pattern of God providing life and rescue over and again. While this abundance is always present, it is not always accepted. The Hebrew people, for example, turn to worship an idol, choosing the impoverishment of false worship over the abundance of covenant and communion with God.

Given the dominant pattern of placing church and academy in different spheres, one might assume scriptural patterns apply to the church but not to the academy. But divine abundance, rightly understood, pertains to *all* that is. All of creation is in communion with God, a relation given and sustained by God. David Schindler develops this scriptural pattern by emphasizing, as we saw, that "the creature's relation to God is such that the creature is never, in the 'logic' of its being, or in any of its thoughts or actions, neutral toward God. No abstraction toward God, be it only for methodological or strategic reasons, is without implications with respect to the existence and meaning of God."[49] That is, no college or university is ever neutral toward God.[50] To bring in God after one has determined methodologies, research programs, and so forth is to assume an extrinsic relation to God. God as "an addition" distorts the pattern of Divine abundance.

But what about academic inquiry? What about the modern requirement to bracket God in order for knowledge or research to be legitimate? The questions gain traction in part because academics fear their disciplinary knowledge will seem less credible. In response to such concerns, Stanley Hauerwas states that "the challenge before Christians today is not whether a Christian university is possible, but whether the kind of knowledge and practices that characterize such a university would be an alternative to what is taught in non-Christian universities . . . the question remains whether Christian universities could produce a historiography in which God appears as something more than a God belief by some people—that is, a god of the gaps."[51] A god of the gaps is a god brought in after the fact of knowledge: to account for morality, the inexplicable, or spirituality. If Divine abundance pertains to all that is, however, the challenge is to see what

49. As David Schindler states, "Simple neutrality toward God . . . even a moment of methodological abstraction—implies that the relation between God and the creature is just so far a relation between two entities . . . it implies the external relation that is properly termed a relation of addition." Schindler, "The Significance of Hans Urs von Balthasar," 21.

50. MacIntyre makes a similar point in his lecture, "Catholic instead of what?"

51. Hauerwas, "Missing from the Curriculum," 5.

difference God makes—what difference the pattern of Divine abundance makes—for how knowledge is pursued and imagined, and what practices best enable such pursuit.

One might worry, given the assumptions of modernity, about imposing a particular theology or "worldview" on those who do not share it. From this perspective, it seems inhospitable to promote a scriptural pattern when an institution has members who do not accept it. But, as I have emphasized, a so-called neutral institution is not really neutral; it is rather gnostic, naturalistic, and so forth. Since the scriptural pattern of Divine abundance rests on the conviction that all being is created for communion, it opens space to acknowledge the other as creature, and therefore as gift. This ontology of communion does not homogenize space into a neutral zone, an empty space onto which we are free to construct our own identities. Rather it makes room to recognize and receive the gift of the other, particularly the Divine Other, and to discover how Divine generosity is folded into all disciplines and knowledges. To see the academy itself as a gift from God is to see it as a place of communion with God and others in all spheres. What does this look like? It hopefully goes without saying that this does not look like pious phrases simply tacked on to projects or university events.[52] Rethinking the deep fragmentation that characterizes the academy calls for renewed habits of thought, key of which is a reconsideration of academic virtue.

Studiousness: a habit that requires leisure and makes it possible

Earlier I discussed how compartmentalization and adaptability have led to a false formation, one that easily leads to a kind of academic amnesia, a forgetfulness of being as communion. What then is a virtue that moves one toward the truth of being, a virtue especially needful in the academy today? Paul Griffiths offers a response by calling attention to a distinction between *curiositas* and *studiositas*. He notes that Christians actually coined a word for study: the Latin *studiositas*, which literally means "studiousness."

52. Years ago, at my first end of the year faculty dinner at Saint Mary's College, I remember being caught off guard by the President's concluding comments in which he thanked "our mother Mary." My surprise was not so much that as a Protestant I was unused to such a conclusion. My disorientation was rather that it seemed to me to come out of nowhere, as a kind of Catholic "add-on" to an otherwise standard curriculum and intellectual program where any reflection or thought about Mary was almost completely absent.

Griffiths writes, "Christians felt the need, it seems, of a new word to label their understanding of the desire to know, and this can serve as a sign of the newness of the Christian understanding of study."[53] The early church fathers (Ambrose and Augustine) and Christians up through the early Renaissance wanted to distinguish between different kinds of intellectual appetites. Studiousness pointed to a virtuous appetite for knowledge whereas *curiositas* pointed to a vicious one, damaging to our true nature.[54]

Curiositas is thus something different than our modern "curiosity." While both *curiositas* and *studiositas* seek knowledge, they do so for different purposes. "Curiosity . . . is appetite for nothing other than the ownership of new knowledge."[55] Whereas curiosity seeks possession,

> studiousness seeks participation . . . . Curiosity is concerned . . . with novelty: curious people want to know what they do not yet know, and ideally what no one knows. Studious people seek knowledge with the awareness that novelty is not what counts, that, indeed, novelty is finally impossible because anything that can be known by any one of us is already known to God and has been given to us as unmerited gift.[56]

To say that God already knows anything that can be known to us is not to say that God hoards knowledge, doling it out in some arbitrary way across time. It is rather to emphasize that all knowing is first of all not human achievement but Divine gift. *Studiositas* is the virtue that trains us, and the academy more broadly, to see that all knowledge is ultimately given by God and therefore that our knowing is embedded in a larger whole, a

---

53. Griffiths, Lecture, personal correspondence.

54. Griffiths adds that "one of the more remarkable transformations in the history of European intellectual life was the removal of curiosity from the table of the vices and its inscription into the table of the virtues. From the beginnings of Latin Christianity in the second century (Tertullian, Cyprian, Ambrose, Augustine), *curiositas* was defined as a vice; but by the fifteenth century it had begun to be considered a virtue, and by the eighteenth century it was simply assumed by most European thinkers to be virtuous, and the earlier understanding of the term was largely lost." Griffiths, "The Vice of Curiosity," 48.

55. Griffiths, "The Vice of Curiosity," 50. Griffiths is referring to Augustine. Our modern phrase "idle curiosity" still carries some of the meaning that Griffiths describes (as does "curiosity kills the cat"). Before Paul gave his Mars Hill sermon in the Book of Acts, Luke states that "the Athenians and foreigners living there would spend their time in nothing but telling or hearing something new" (Acts 17:21). The NRSV notes, "The Athenians at this time were famous for their curiosity." They simply wanted to possess knowledge, not to be transformed by it.

56. Griffiths, Lecture, 3.

harmony that coincides with the goodness of creation. As Michael Foley states, *studiositas* is a virtue that enables "the mind to delight in the right reading of reality, while [*curiositas*] render[s] the mind myopic and fettered by the will's own self-imposed shadow."[57]

As Griffiths indicates, both curiosity and studiousness are rooted in the affections and desires. The vice of *curiositas*, however, leads one to desire to master and possess knowing: to sequester it as one's own. In relation to my discussion of ontology in chapter 2, I would say that a person suffering from the vice of *curiositas* lives in a flattened world. In such a flattened world, knowing is the means through which one seeks to control or construct a universe that is essentially closed. Thus, as Griffiths states, the "advocate of curiosity occupies a world of ownership and mastery to which the proper response is the gesture of *control*." The virtue of studiousness, by contrast, leads one to receive knowing as gift and in so doing to participate in communion with God. *Studiositas* enables a person to live in a "world of gift and participation to which the proper response is one of *gratitude* and *delight*."[58] Whereas the person practicing *curiositas* seeks knowledge in a fragmented and opaque world, the person practicing studiousness cannot help but see being and knowing as gestures of Divine generosity.

Studiousness, it is important to note, is not the same as being diligent or studious. *Studious* means studying well and being focused (certainly in themselves good activities). If a studious person, however, is diligent primarily in order to garner good grades, a high reputation, or financial reward, then *curiositas* prevails. Studiousness is not simply mastering an area of knowledge, but learning how to receive knowing as gift that draws one more fully into the truth of his or her being: a creature created for communion with God. The dynamic is toward Divine plenitude. Studiousness thus places one before a Divine generosity that a person dominated by *curiositas* cannot see or even imagine.

In contrast to the commonsense assumption that values are personal choices, virtues are collective. That is, one has virtues as part of a larger body. Firefighters, for example, are trained to have the courage it takes to enter a burning building. Such courage is collective in the sense that it requires the training of a wider firefighter community. A firefighter might lose courage, or become a firefighter for purposes extrinsic to being a good

---

57. Foley, "Thomas Aquinas' Novel Modesty," 410. Foley argues that Aquinas's treatment of *humilitas* and *superbia* lines up nicely with *studiositas* and *curiositas*.

58. Griffiths, lecture, 4, my emphasis.

firefighter (prestige, for example), and so succumb to the vice of foolhardiness. For firefighters collectively, however, courage is inherent for good work and cannot be reduced to an individual option.[59] In what sense or how is *studiositas* a collective academic virtue?

George Grant provides a helpful starting place in his discussion of the "primal" in North American experience. By "primal," Grant means the experience of coming to a new land, of conquest, and of seeing nature itself as something to be conquered. "If the will to mastery is essential to the modern, our wills were burnished in that battle with the land. We were made ready to be leaders of the civilization which was incubating in Europe."[60] Grant is thus relating the pursuit of mastery and of the search for the new to the concrete experience of North America with the land, with the experience of leaving one country and coming to a new place in order to take hold of it. Grant's use of "primal" points to convictions that form a collective identity so deeply that they are often more tacit than explicit. He continues: "The conquering relation to place has left its mark within us. When we go into the Rockies we may have the sense that gods are there. But if so, they cannot manifest themselves to us as ours . . . . There can be nothing immemorial for us except the environment as object."[61] The "primal" that Grant is describing thus objectifies the world, inhibiting one from seeing beyond that which can be mastered or controlled. The language of "values" and "freedom" is bound up with this narrative of novelty and with the will for technological advancement. Grant does not deny "Western technical achievement," but, for my purposes, illustrates how habits are woven into the very flesh of a collective identity: the will to master and to discover the novel is woven into a certain collective understanding of the American way of life.[62]

59. For a helpful reflection on virtues as collective, I am indebted to Byerly, "The Virtuous Community."

60. Grant, *Technology and Empire*, 17–18.

61. Grant, *Technology and Empire*, 17.

62. As we also saw in chapter 3, Grant describes how technology and modern moral discourse are deeply intertwined: "the moral discourse of 'values' and 'freedom' is not independent of the will to technology, but a language fashioned in the same forge together with the will to technology. To try to think them separately is to move more deeply into their common origin." Grant, *Technology and Empire*, 32.

In a similar vein, Benedict Anderson argues that the newness of the American nation—through rupture and death—parallels the sense of time that makes possible the self-creating individual. The individual, like the nation, is always free to leave the past behind. Indeed, the individual must do so to become free. Anderson, *Imagined*

This identity extends into the academy. Knowing as owning and possessing the new (*curiositas*) is woven into the fabric of the academy. The language of "values" and "freedom"—understood as freedom from the past or from natural constraints—typically prevails in academic discourse. As such, knowing is a human achievement with little sense of being and knowing as gift. This is not to say that "bad" people in the academy are being selfish and competitive. It is rather to emphasize how habits of being can malform a collective identity in such a way that aspects of creation disappear. As Grant puts it, the "gods cannot manifest themselves." In light of this formation, is there an *institutional* way to foster the virtue of studiousness as integral to a collective academic identity? In asking this question, I am not seeking an abdication of personal responsibility but a way of describing the academy as a place that takes seriously knowing and being as gift.

To give at least a partial response to my question, it is important to see that studiousness is, in reality, a form of prayer. As we know, there are many different kinds of prayer: petition, confession, thanksgiving, and so forth. If prayer—broadly understood—is communion with God, then studiousness is the habit of study in communion with God. It is the habit of learning to take delight in Divine wisdom and to practice gratitude for the gift of creation in all of its manifold richness. In effect, studiousness forms one to see study as prayer. As a collective virtue, it enables an institution to *resist* divorcing study from prayer, or the academy from the church.

Some might hear the call for *studiositas* as a kind of sentimental gesture. A sentimental, pietistic perspective might interpret studiousness to mean that inward disposition matters more than the work of study, learning, and research. But this is to undermine how virtues are both embodied and collective habits. Studiousness is not simply an inner pious attitude but a collective way of being and thinking. Those who practice studiousness see the world differently than those who live by *curiositas*, not unlike how the courageous see a different world than the fearful. Those who are unformed in *studiositas* can certainly know things, but they will know them "without reference to the God who called [them] into being and sustains [them] in being."[63] They will thus know them in a limited sense.

A "realist," on the other hand, might say that studiousness is too idealistic or too rose-colored for the real academic world of knowledge, argument, and research. Pray if you want but it makes no difference when

Communities.

63. Griffiths, Lecture, personal correspondence, 14.

it comes to the acquisition of new knowledge or the publication of new information. After all, the university has thrived and continues to thrive without such a virtue. Yet, what does it mean to thrive? As I have argued, the academy today is fragmented, divided, and compartmentalized. This is not to deny that good comes from the university. But as we have seen, contemporary academic realism is deeply formed by a mechanistic ontology devoid of purpose. To the extent this is true, extrinsic goods such as financial success or prestige will determine what it means to thrive. Studiousness, by contrast, forms the academy to pursue goods intrinsic to its calling, which is to embody and seek Divine wisdom.

Finally, describing studiousness as an alternative place, patterned on Divine generosity, might seem to some too specifically Christian and thus inaccessible to those who are not Christians. And yet, studiousness embodies the conviction that knowledge is not a possession but a gift. The academy is not about possessing knowledge in competition, but about receiving knowledge as well as other persons in gratitude. Whereas *curiositas* fosters competition and rivalry, *studiositas* acknowledges God is not our rival but desires to give abundantly (John 10:10). Just as *curiositas* excludes or fails to see any relation between knowing and Divine abundance, so also does *studiositas* exclude or, more fully, offer an alternative to that "roaming unrest of spirit"[64] untethered to its true end.

Leisure as a complex place

As we saw in chapter 3, Pieper described leisure as the true basis of culture. Culture is not simply what humans do or create; it is most fully what humans receive as the gift of being from God, not only their own but that of the whole cosmos. Peter Kreeft argues that the relegation of the contemplative (constitutive of leisure) to only monks is a sign of a decayed culture.[65] I have argued that leisure, rightly understood, is not one space among many in an academic institution. It is rather a place: a way of being. Leisure pertains to all spheres of the academy. It is not as if one leaves a sphere of leisure and then enters the space of the classroom, research, or a faculty meeting. It is better to think of different kinds of leisure, just as one would think of different forms of prayer.

---

64. Pieper cited in Foley, "Thomas Aquinas' Novel Modesty," 410.

65. Kreeft, "What Judgement Means."

Some have used the term *complex space* to describe how different places can overlap. William Cavanaugh, for example, uses "complex space" to say that the church is "doing more than [only] resisting or participating in the dominant society."[66] Complex space refers to the fact that ecclesial space is not isolated from other spaces. For my purposes, complex space, or I prefer complex place, names the fact that the church and the academy are not simply two separate spaces. As I cited earlier, one often hears that "the academy is not the church." True, the church is distinct from the academy in the sense that the church baptizes disciples into the body of Christ. But at the same time, being the body of Christ is not relegated to a location; it pertains to a whole way of life. It is a complex place in the sense that it cannot be reduced to either academic space or church space. One might well respond differently in different contexts, but the responses will not result from modern "adaptability" but from such virtues as faithfulness, studiousness, and, above all, love.

So also, leisure is complex in the sense that it moves beyond a work versus worship, or knowledge versus faith, dualism and toward a participation in Divine plenitude in all places. To practice leisure and acquire studiousness is to see that one is always participating in divine generosity, albeit in different ways. If we apply this to the church and academy, then we can say that both are ways of participating in God. The place is complex in the sense that these entities are not two spheres, but one manifold way of being that delights in the goodness of God.

To see the academy as participating in this kind of complex space is to "leave the imagination of a dominant society behind."[67] The complex space of leisure is thus an alternative to "'seeing like a state,' or like a Walmart."[68] This is because the place of leisure is about first receiving from others, and ultimately from God, in the particular and ordinary places where we are. It is the antithesis of seeing in the abstract or using a "rhetoric of nowhere."

Leisure can only become a collective way of being when the academy itself seeks ways to embody it. This could take the form of an institutionalized liturgy of the daily office or of some other form of worship, a practice I discuss more fully in the next chapter. Of course, any practice of communal prayer could become a form of "hoop jumping," disconnected from the liturgy of the classroom or the laboratory. This would reflect our dominant

66. Cavanaugh, "A Politics of Vulnerability," 106.

67. Cavanaugh, "A Politics of Vulnerability," 106.

68. Coles and Hauerwas, *Christianity, Democracy*, 341.

culture where "going to church" is easily divorced from a whole way of being. There is, then, a need to reflect on *how* leisure is the basis of academic culture in the classroom, in the laboratory, or in a faculty meeting. For example, are there ways that "boundaries" might be crossed so that leisure as a complex place becomes more visible?

Let's return to my opening scenario about the division between economics and theology. To practice leisure as a complex place is to reimagine the boundaries so that while the disciplinary fields remain distinct, they are not closed to each other. For example, then, how might a college or university teach economics so that being as oriented toward a Divine abundance is taken seriously? How might it challenge a dominant understanding of economics based on the rational profit-maximizing individual? How might economic theory engage the well-being of the whole where, as Wendell Berry argues, people matter?[69] That there might not be clear answers at the beginning of such a process is part of what it means to be willing to dwell in the complex place of leisure, the first step of which is being able to name the ways such modern divisions easily distorts our lives. If it is true that being has both its source and *telos* in God's excessive abundance, then leisure as resting in that truth can only draw an institution more fully toward its true destination, even if only in fits and starts.

A virtue, as Aquinas emphasized, is a good habit in the sense that it "perfects a given power." Any particular habit is determined to be good or evil because creatures have ends given by God. A good habit helps move one toward her end; a bad habit does the opposite.[70] More broadly, as I have emphasized, virtues can move an institution towards its true end. A person does not acquire virtues on his or her own; they are always ultimately gifts of grace. Even the desire to receive them is itself a gift of grace, a sign of God's desire for love and communion as well as of our true purpose. While it might be true that the academy is far from being a place of leisure, it is

---

69. Berry discusses this topic in a number of different essays. See, for example, "Christianity and the Survival of Creation," in *Sex, Economy, Freedom and Community*, 93–116. For further discussion of this point, see Newman, "Hospitality and Christian Higher Education."

70. Kimbriel states that for Aquinas virtues also always involve the gift of grace that comes, in this instance, in two forms. The first is the Divine activity of moving the creature "either to some new knowledge or to a particular activity." The second is one that imparts a quality to the soul "enabling it to move itself." Kimbriel, *Friendship as Sacred Knowing*, 141.

also true that any longing for a faithful academic culture is already a Divine gift drawing persons toward a more authentic alternative.

To summarize, I have discussed three dominant (and overlapping) configurations of academic space: 1) the fragmentation of academic space into different disciplines that often have little to do with one another, 2) the relegation of non-academic space such as leisure and faith to an entirely separate sphere and 3) the reduction of all spaces to mere difference with the subsequent loss of place. I argue that leisure, rightly understood, overcomes these ways of conceiving academic space. The virtue of *studiositas*—understood as the pursuit of knowledge in the context of participating in the love and wisdom of God—makes leisure integral to all academic pursuits. By contrast, it is the nature of *curiositas* to negate leisure. Since *curiositas* is marked by an inordinate seeking after knowledge, a key symptom is a roaming unrest of the spirit (*evagatio mentis*), the extreme form of which is "complete rootlessness."[71] It is thus the opposite of teaching, learning, and being from a place of rest, a rest, as we have seen that is not passive but an active participation in Divine abundance. The virtue of *studiositas* as a way of practicing leisure thus overcomes the separation between church and academy since resting in God pertains to both. In the place of true leisure, the academy does not exist separate from the church, but rather extends the leisure/worship of the church in the pursuit of particular kinds of knowledge. Rightly understood, leisure is a shared *place* that makes both church and academy possible.

71. Hibbs, "In the Wake of the Enlightenment," 101. Hibbs is discussing Aquinas's understanding of *curiositas*.

5

A DIFFERENT RHYTHM

Leisure and Academic Time

Modern constraints on time easily diminish leisure. In the academy, as elsewhere in contemporary culture, time seems scarce. Tenure is a battle against the ticking clock. Students and faculty fight to meet deadlines and to complete work. Aware of this pressure, some colleges and universities have even created stress-free zones where students, for example, can spend time playing with puppies. Such efforts, while possibly helpful, nonetheless underscore how time as stressful and scarce remains the norm. The burden of this chapter is to give a different account of time, one in which time is not scarce but essentially abundant. Rightly understood, leisure is not in competition with academic time but constitutive of it. For an institution to imagine otherwise is to live in warped time. In what follows, I engage three stories of distorted time in the modern academy. I then turn to a renewed understanding of time and to rituals of plenitude that might yet sustain leisure in the academy today.

Story one: academic time as market time

When my daughter was applying to college, she received a glossy invitation from a school affiliated with the United Methodist church. The college was inviting her to a special event for accepted students to be held at a local Italian restaurant. The invitation announced that special guests from the college, i.e., administrators and faculty, would be attending. My daughter was excited since this would be an opportunity for her to find out more about the college. The event, however, was scheduled for 7 PM on Holy Thursday. This conflicted with the Holy Thursday service at our church, where my husband (also United Methodist) pastors. The school apparently had no qualms with scheduling an admissions event at this time. Were those who planned the event aware that it was Holy Thursday? They assured me they were. But this did not prevent them from offering their own alternative meeting.

One could possibly dismiss this conflict as merely a sign of a college admissions' busy schedule. Perhaps there was no other time for their gathering. In any case, this particular evening was most convenient for them. The fact that the college, however, decided to market the school on Holy Thursday reflects how deeply implicated they are in market time.

We could also call such time liberal capitalism which has as its most basic feature *individualism*. According to Murray Jardine, liberal capitalism is characterized by "attempts to establish a political, economic, and social system that is *neutral*" toward individuals, ways of life and religious or philosophical worldviews.[1] As displayed in our story, the college was neutral toward its own religious time. It rather allowed the market to determine its calendar. To survive in market time one needs to compete with others in a way that weakens any relations or bonds that might inhibit success. In this instance, Holy Thursday stood in the way of the college's competition for prospective students who could add to the college's "value." So understood, market time frees (or rather destroys) an institution's bonds to liturgical ways of being in time.

Who can blame the college, however, for making their time a priority over ecclesial time? In fact, does not the academy need to play by market time in order to survive? Yes and no. Murray Jardine calls attention to a helpful distinction between a market society and a market economy. A *market society* (versus a market economy) is one in which "all human relations are reduced to contract," resulting in a disintegration of the "longer-term

---

1. Jardine, *The Making and Unmaking*, 33. As Adrian Pabst similarly states, "capitalism is predicated on an ontology that makes philosophical and theological claims about the nature of the shared world we inhabit. More than any other economic system, free-market capitalism weakens real relations among actually existing things because it privileges discrete, individual objects at the expense of the social, cultural, and religious structures and arrangements that bind them together . . . ." Pabst, "Introduction," 4.

bonds needed to sustain human society."[2] In a *market economy*, by contrast, the market is not *the* overriding force. Jardine notes that in some cultures, for example, various communal bonds or concerns might override market values. In such an economy, people might

> buy from a merchant who charges higher prices out of a sense of personal loyalty . . . . More efficient producers may refrain from putting less efficient producers out of business by limiting their own production. They may do this because they feel it would be uncharitable to destroy the livelihood of others or simply because they feel that they already have enough wealth and don't need any more, preferring instead greater leisure time. This type of behavior was quite common in Europe before liberalism became dominant . . . .[3]

In a market economy, we could add, an academy would not allow the market to determine all time; other communal or ecclesial bonds would shape its life.

Liberal capitalism, however, takes the market as the model for all of society. Having enough wealth is an alien concept in a *market society*, where the market dominates, producing a ruthlessly fierce competition. Such ruthless competition grows "only in a culture that is both highly individualistic and highly concerned with creating material wealth—that is, the bourgeois culture with its secularized Protestant ethic."[4] As Jardine indicates, however, participating in a market economy rather than a market society enables a person or institution to make wise use of the market rather than allow it to determine all relations. In other words, communal bonds shape market time and practice.

Our college admissions story indicates how easily academic institutions become market societies rather than places relying upon a market economy in discerning ways. The disintegration of bonds rightly describes the way that this particular college (like so many others) has come to think of its "religious" identity. The college's mission statement holds that it "retains a relationship with the United Methodist church." Significantly, the language of "retaining a relationship" reflects legal contract terminology more than it does a description of long-term bonds embedded in a shared understanding of life. As such, it communicates how market time has

---

2. Jardine, *The Making and Unmaking*, 132.
3. Jardine, *The Making and Unmaking*, 132.
4. Jardine, *The Making and Unmaking*, 132.

turned such bonds into matters of personal choice. It is not surprising then that the institution sees Holy Thursday (or any holy day) as irrelevant to its own self-understanding.

Story two: academic work versus leisure

James K. A. Smith describes Frosh Week, the orientation week for first year students at many colleges and universities, as a "consummate ritual of initiation." As such, it is a retreat from the world of summer jobs and anticipated class drudgery. Implicit in the practices of Frosh Week "is a vision of the good life that valorizes egoistic pursuit of personal pleasure, a passionate commitment to the tribe (expressed in 'team spirit' at the football stadium or intensified in the 'brotherhood' of fraternities), and an instrumental relation to learning that values it only insofar as it makes it possible to achieve the goods of prosperity, accumulation, status, and power."[5] While Smith notes the widespread criticism of this kind of ritual, or at least aspects of it, he observes that it nonetheless turns out to be good preparation for the kind of person the university hopes to produce: "productive, successful consumers who will be leaders in society." The students are initiated into loyalty to school and to a way of life. Smith thus notes how in the Frosh Week scenario both leisure and work are placed in service to specific ends: being successful which is equated with productivity and consumption. As such, "the university is simply an outpost of the earthly city, an extension and training ground for the arenas of the market and the state . . . ."[6]

So understood, leisure and work share a distorted end. Frosh Week embodies the assumption, highly criticized by Pieper, that leisure is good because it helps a person or institution be more productive. To see this distortion more fully, let's return to the secularized Protestant work ethic mentioned above. As is well known, Max Weber argued that a certain Puritan understanding of salvation and predestination contributed to the rise of capitalism. According to Weber, while the Puritans believed that salvation was a free gift, they nonetheless had to work long and hard to show that they were in fact saved. Productivity was a sign of God's favor, and leisure, by contrast, a waste of time. The Puritans were far from ostentatious, preferring instead an ascetical frugality akin to monasticism (but without leisure). According to Weber, as this intense work ethic became secularized

5. Smith, *Desiring the Kingdom*, 116.
6. Smith, *Desiring the Kingdom*, 116.

it created great wealth, eventually unleashing market forces across society. Jardine describes how the secularized version of this work ethic also sought signs of salvation. Just as the Puritans worked in order to produce signs of being saved, so also "in a secularized Calvinist consumer culture the fear of appearing to be a failure—the residual fear of damnation in the secularized Calvinist psyche—is exploited to sell things."[7] In the secularized version, monetary wealth and consumption become "signs" of salvific success.

One sees in Frosh Week, then, an extension of this secularized Calvinist consumer culture. Good time is productive time that can be measured by the signs of success: good jobs, prestigious graduate schools, research grants, publications, and so forth. But, one might ask, is it not good to work hard, to get good grades, to produce books, and so forth? None of these activities are in themselves a problem. The distortion, however, lies in the loss of true leisure and the reduction of time to either utilitarian effort or pure waste. To the extent that the academy gives itself over to this time, it distorts the abundance of true leisure.

Story three: academic time as rational and inclusive

A final story of time in the modern academy has to do with a contentious exchange, in which I was involved, about the mission statement at Saint Mary's College (Notre Dame). This particular debate came about when the Vice President for Mission, in consultation with some students, staff and faculty, attempted to change the current statement, arguing that it needed to be shorter and reflect more fully the vision of the Holy Cross sisters who founded the institution. Many of the faculty strongly opposed her efforts. Their opposition, among other things, centered on the use of two phrases that were regarded as offensive: "Gospel values" and "justice" (interpreted to mean biblical justice).[8] The original statement maintained that "Saint Mary's promotes a life of intellectual vigor, aesthetic appreciation, religious sensibility, and social responsibility . . . ." A key revision in the newer statement read: "Through commitment to Gospel values, the College provides an environment that nurtures lives of faith, justice and service, challenging

---

7. Jardine, *The Making and Unmaking*, 208. Jardine maintains that this culture of compulsive work (and later consumption) can be attributed not only to a Calvinist conception of predestination but also to a secularized work ethic developed by early liberalism in which the basic moral imperative for humans is to work hard.

8. Some faculty related "biblical justice" to a harsh punitive justice.

women to make a difference in the diverse world in which they live." Some faculty argued that the terms "religious sensibility" and "social responsibility," in the original statement, were phrases more conducive to openness and diversity. Some faculty charged that the vice president's invocation of the phrase "Gospel values" had the effect of "dumbing down" the current statement, and thus "disassociating Saint Mary's with well-respected liberal arts colleges."[9]

If we look at this debate through the lens of how one perceives academic time, what might we discover? First, the assumption that "Gospel values" betray an understanding of the academy—one that dumbs down the college in relation to its peers—displays the relegation of Christianity, and particularly Catholicism, to a time of naïve, irrational myth. On this view, one assumes that particular religions, in order to enter real academic space-time, must translate their narrow particularity into supposedly more generic, rational, and therefore acceptable language. From this perspective, any invocation of specifically Christian language, i.e., "Gospel values," will sound unenlightened and exclusive.[10]

Secondly, we see an intensification of academic time equated with modern rational time in the conviction that religion is primarily a sensibility rather than a rationality. The earlier mission statement assumes that rational institutions will study religion as a sensibility but not as itself a rationality. Reason is set over against the "religious," in effect placing religion outside of real academic time. It is rather to be studied objectively as a historical phenomenon, a motivation, a set of beliefs, etc. Such academic time ends up extending modernity's invention of religion, discussed in chapter 1. The European Enlightenment assumed that "the 'historical' religions, Judaism and Christianity, were hopelessly corrupt, ridden by superstition and Priestcraft and inherently incredible because they were grounded on the belief that God had actually entered into human history [time] in the Exodus and the Incarnation."[11] This means that Christianity and Judaism as well as other religions now require a rational foundation in order to enter real time.

9. Saint Mary's College, Minutes.

10. While "Gospel values" is better than the abstract "religious sensibility," equating the Gospel with values also shows the influence of modern rationalism. To equate the Gospel with values underwrites a modern fact/value dichotomy.

11. Poteat, "Interpretation of Religion in Modern Western Culture."

The reduction of a faith to a sensibility, however, is as problematic for its adherents as a reduction of chemistry to a sensibility would be to chemists. Rational time ends up relegating all that is not rational (in the sense defined) to the irrational sphere. On this view, religious myth is just that. It belongs in imaginary time, not real academic time. Translating religion in this way, however, ends up destroying it. As Stanley Hauerwas pointedly states, the academy is "often comprised of people who are willing to study a religion on the condition either that it is dead or that they can teach it in such way as to kill it."[12]

Scarcity: the emptying of time

These stories—the Holy Week admissions event, Frosh Week ,and the Mission statement conflict—are representative of how academic time relies on scarcity rather than abundance. By scarcity, I mean time depleted of true leisure and interpreting leisure instead as useless or useful only for entertainment. Time ceases to be a participation in the heights and depths of Divine plenitude.

To even talk about time in terms of such plenitude sounds odd and unrealistic. It makes more sense, on the dominant view, to describe time as limited and measured by the calendar. This is due in part to the fact that we live in an age, as Anthony Giddens observes, that is characterized by an emptying of time. Giddens argues that in modernity time has become disconnected from space (place); "the uniformity of time measurement by the mechanical clock was matched by uniformity in social organization of time."[13] This emptying of time was "in large part the precondition for the 'emptying of space' and thus had causal priority over it."[14] That is, the emptying of time leads to a separation from a particular locale and set of relations. Giddens describes this emptying or "disembedding" as a shift in social relation from "local contexts of interaction" to their "restructuring

---

12. Hauerwas, *Sanctify Them*, 211. Hauerwas is referring specifically to religious studies departments. He states, for example, that biblical scholars and church historians "can no longer study the Resurrection as if Jesus might have actually been raised, but now they study the beliefs and behaviors of people who believed in the Resurrection." Hauerwas, *Sanctify Them*, 211.

13. Giddens, *The Consequences of Modernity*, 18.

14. Giddens, *The Consequences of Modernity*, 18.

across indefinite spans of time-space."[15] Key examples of such disembedding are 1) money which is a way of bracketing time, 2) expert systems such as technical systems that organize large social areas, and related to these 3) capitalist markets.[16] The globalized market with its time of exchange and commerce overruns the time of a particular locale or the economy of a given community. Giddens emphasizes that high modernity is a period cut loose from its moorings in what he calls "the reassurance of tradition."[17] Consequently, "Although [modernity's] originators looked for certainties to replace preestablished dogmas, modernity effectively involves the institutionalization of doubt."[18]

Giddens's analysis indicates the emptying to time can lead to anxiety: apart from the "reassurance of tradition" time can seem uncertain. While this can lead to pessimism, optimism is just as likely. Modernity believes in progress through technology and education. Christopher Lasch notes that more extravagant versions of progressive faith such as the "perfectibility of man" collapsed a long time ago. But the idea of progress lives on "by postulating an indefinite expansion of desires, a steady rise in the general standard of comfort, and the incorporation of the masses into the culture of abundance."[19] Most Americans when presented with a choice between more free time or more work will chose more work, which means more money and more consumption. Over twenty-five years ago, Juliet Schor remarked on this exponential growth in consumption: "In 1990, the average American owns and consumes more than twice as much as he or she did in 1948, but also has less free time."[20] Jardine further observes that the "unrestricted market forces [of capitalism] tend to make everyone in the society conform to the standard of the hardest-working people as a matter of sheer survival."[21] That such is the case exemplifies how time, disembedded from traditioned places, becomes unceasing competition and forever expanding desires. One must continually work to keep up with the hardest

15. Giddens, *The Consequences of Modernity*, 21.

16. Giddens, *The Consequences of Modernity*, 26, 27.

17. Giddens, *The Consequences of Modernity*, 176.

18. Giddens, *The Consequences of Modernity*, 176.

19. Lasch, *The True and Only Heaven*, 78.

20. Schor, *The Overworked American*, 2.

21. Jardine, *The Making and Unmaking*, 263. Jardine engages the thought of Jeremy Rifkin, Juliet Schor, and Arlie Russell Hochschild in arguing for a way to restructure work so as to allow for people to spend more time with family and in neighborhoods and community.

workers or risk losing out. The irony is the time that frees us from tradition for the sake of progress (optimism) easily binds us to market forces beyond our control (pessimism).

What is time?

One might argue that any alternative understanding of time in the academy today is a mere pipe dream. Alfred N. Whitehead's description of the "the bifurcation of nature" surely includes time: nature (time) as it is in itself and nature (time) as perceived by us "adorned, festooned—and falsified—by the secondary qualities supplied by our senses."[22] Real time makes planes run on time. Any other understanding of time is secondary. As a public place, an academic institution must run by real time, not adorned time. Most of us—at least those who are Westerners—see this real time as linear. In this sense, we are inheritors of a biblical versus cyclical view of time.[23]

Matthew Levering argues, however, that a linear view of time is not itself fully biblical in the sense of reflecting a Trinitarian understanding of time. In his book *Participatory Biblical Exegesis: A Theology of Biblical Interpretation*, Levering argues that while the Bible should be studied in its original ancient contexts, this study should not stand on its own. He calls also for a participatory biblical exegesis: "while temporal reality is a 'linear' unfolding of moments, it is so precisely as participating in the triune God."[24] The Trinity's creative and redemptive "vertical" presence suffuses all "horizontal" time. "This metaphysical and christological-pneumatological participation in God joins past, present, and future realities in a unified whole, so that through God's presence each moment is related intrinsically, not merely extrinsically, to every other moment."[25] To say that all moments are intrinsically related is to see the triune God's creating and redeeming presence as integral to all time. Far from diminishing history, a "fully historical biblical exegesis depends on reinstating the participatory dimension

22. Poteat, *Recovering the Ground*, 162.

23 The early Greeks had a circular understanding of time based in the cycles of the natural world. In their time, the radically contingent event that brought about a new reality was not fully possible. Michael B. Foster and Stanley L. Jaki, OSB, among others, show how a biblical understanding of time as truly contingent helped make modern science possible.

24. Levering, *Participatory Biblical Exegesis*, 1.

25. Levering, *Participatory Biblical Exegesis*, 1.

of historical realities."[26] In other words, history as linear can only fully be read in light of God's creating and redeeming presence in all time.

Levering acknowledges various arguments against his position, not the least of which is the conviction that history refers to a realm of human autonomy, one in which theological realities are extrinsic. Levering traces this view of history to late medieval thought and (following such thinkers as Catherine Pickstock and Olivier Boulnois) particularly the nominalist thought of Dons Scotus. Levering relates Scotus's philosophy particularly to time, stating that Scotus rejects a strong teleological and participatory understanding of nature/creation, replacing it instead with a strictly linear understanding of time. Some have argued that this linear understanding allows humans the freedom to reason out their own paths, thus finding truly humanitarian ethical norms.[27] But Levering states that nominalism "paved the way for the Enlightenment to set eternal life in opposition to history . . . . From this loss of a grasp of the simultaneous totality of time in God's presence, there was a dissolution of time itself into a continuum of isolated moments."[28] God's presence in time makes possible a providential purpose apart from which linear time becomes meaningless. An opposition between eternity and history leads to an understanding of Divine action as "as external, interruptive, and bearing no real relations to creaturely realities. God, in effect, becomes causal will, intervening in creaturely reality from outside but unconnected to the creation."[29] When linear time becomes isolated from participatory time, then understandings of Divine action become distorted, in turn reducing the nature of human action.[30]

---

26. Levering, *Participatory Biblical Exegesis*, 3. At a number of points, Levering engages those who see his approach as one of *eisigesis*, and thus see his method as one of reading into Scripture the teachings of the church rather than one based on sound historical scholarship. Levering's response, as indicated, is that at stake is whether "the reduction of Scripture to the linear-historical dimension does not itself distort, even historically, the exegesis of biblical texts." Levering, *Participatory Biblical Exegesis*, 184.

27. Levering, *Participatory Biblical Exegesis*, 20. Levering is referring particularly to the historian Anthony Levi.

28. Matthew Lamb as cited in Levering, *Participatory Biblical Exegesis*, 21. My emphasis.

29. John Webster as cited in Levering, *Participatory Biblical Exegesis*, 24. While Levering cites Webster approvingly, he also criticizes him for avoiding metaphysical discourse. Levering, *Participatory Biblical Exegesis*, 179–80.

30. If Divine action is seen as the intrusion of an arbitrary will, then human action becomes reduced either to a form of quietism or to a Pelagian assertion of the will as salvific.

What difference does understanding time as participatory make for the life of the academy? First, Levering's analysis makes clear that time is a *theological* category. A strictly linear understanding of time relies upon a nominalist theology, one that sees time as essentially autonomous and freedom in time as auto-deterministic. By contrast, a Trinitarian theology makes possible an understanding of time as intrinsically participatory, and freedom as gift and response. Secondly, an understanding of time as both linear and participatory opens a way for the academy to attune itself to the true rhythms of reality. The rhythms include Divine abundance, reception and gift: all ways of speaking of creation as oriented toward communion with God.

Before considering this attunement more fully, however, it will be helpful to revisit the thought of William H. Poteat to see how he arrives at a conclusion similar to Levering's but by a different route. Poteat shows how historical memory alone is not enough to preserve identity or to understand being. As we saw in chapter 2, Poteat discusses how Hannah Arendt in *The Human Condition* turns to the *vita activa* as the place where human uniqueness is preserved. As she argues, "In acting and speaking, men show who they are, reveal actively their unique personal identities and thus make their appearance in the human world . . . ."[31] She continues that "this space does not always exist, and although men are capable of deed and word, most of them . . . [like the] jobholder or businessman in our world—do not live in it . . . . To be deprived of it means to be deprived of reality . . . ."[32] In contrast to this deprivation, as we saw, Arendt locates reality in the polis where the "revelatory quality of speech and action comes to the fore where people are *with* others and neither for nor against them—that is, in sheer human togetherness."[33]

Let's consider Poteat's response to Arendt from the perspective of time. He argues that one's "who-ness" can only be preserved in an "ongoingly contemporaneous 'history' in which a living and personal being is always actually appearing in the fabric of my actual activity of acting and speaking. . . . Only a living, personal God can guarantee my eternal significance."[34] Thus, Poteat concludes that Arendt's commendable turn to speaking and acting before others in order to maintain our "whoness" requires the presence

31. Arendt, *The Human Condition*, 179.
32. Arendt, *The Human Condition*, 199.
33. Arendt, *The Human Condition*, 180.
34. Poteat, "A Skeleton Key," 3.

of a personal God who guarantees one's eternal significance. "Historical memory, which for Arendt takes the place of divine providence, cannot afford such a guarantee . . . ."[35] Arendt briefly alludes to Augustine early in her book—particularly Augustine's question to God, "What am I?"—but does not incorporate this into her analysis. Poteat returns to Augustine's *Confessions* where Augustine "transcends from the world and establishes his eternal validity as incarnate spirit in covenant with him who gives as his name 'I will be that I will be.'"[36] Poteat argues that on Arendt's own premise, Augustine's response is the logical one. Like Levering, Poteat is relying upon an understanding of time that cannot be reduced to memory or history. While Arendt turns to the Greek polis to secure one's personal whoness, Poteat shows the necessity of an eternal and faithful Presence in time. So understood, time is intrinsically covenantal.

One might argue, however, that while *some* people might share this belief, it is not a legitimate one for the academy. Rather something like Arendt's essentially Greek view is more adequate: the academy itself a kind of polis where professors or administrators, after their death, are remembered fondly through memorial funds, scholarships, paintings, and so forth. If one chooses to believe in covenantal time, they may but the "new kind of 'polis' that is first brought into being when Abraham makes covenant with Yahweh"[37] seems out of place in the academy. It collides with time as measured, historical, and progressive. Any alternative to this time easily seems an imposition. What would covenantal time in the academy look like?[38]

---

35. Poteat, "A Skeleton Key," 3.

36. Poteat, *Recovering the Ground*, 135.

37. Poteat, *Recovering the Ground*, 135.

38. One response to this question would be to say that covenantal time looks like the time in which Poteat himself engaged his students as faithful teacher, mentor, and friend. Poteat had a unique way of holding students accountable to *who* they were and were called to be. As his colleague E. Maynard Adams (UNC Chapel Hill) said at the time of his death, Poteat's personal connections with his students came about because of "the way in which he interpreted life for them." Cited in "William H. Poteat." See also Berkman, "Poteat Changed My Life."

Poteat reflected on his teaching as follows: "I, and my students in the measure to which they have truly joined the colloquy, have from the outset aspired to be radically critical of the Critical tradition of modernity, which is to say, we have undertaken to become postcritical. Like any parasite, this essentially polemical convivium has battened on its host, hoping, not to weaken and eventually bring down, but, rather, modestly to change the universities in which it was formed and by whose sufferance it has lived. At least those of us who have sustained this colloquy have hoped to be and have changed." Poteat, *Polanyian Mediations*, ix. Poteat sought to dwell and teach in time postcritically,

What difference would it make in how an academic institution understands itself? Would it even be possible for the academy to survive in this alternative time?

Too late to make a difference?

Stanley Fish, among others, would say no to this last question. In his response to George Marsden, discussed in the previous chapter, Fish states, "'We already had the Enlightenment' and religion lost." While Fish is sympathetic with those who seek to restore The Soul of the American University, as Marsden does, he thinks their efforts are in the long run futile. Poignantly, he states that those who set out to "restore the priority of the good over the right . . . find the protocols of the right—of liberal proceduralism—written in the fleshly tables of their hearts." The loss of the modern university's soul is "not simply a matter of historical fact: It is inscribed in the very consciousness of those who live in its wake."[39] Fish's words are indeed sobering in that they point to the difficulty if not impossibility of a genuine academic renewal. But are they true? Fish rightly observes that any genuine renewal in the academy will entail more than making observations or even telling a different story; it will involve the fleshly tables of our hearts. Any genuine academic reform will be more than a mental exercise; it will need to be written in our flesh, which is to say that it will call for different practices and habits than those that have predominantly formed the modern academy.

But is it too late for this kind of reform? Both Fish and Marsden, while ending in different places, nonetheless agree that the marginalization of Christian identity from the academy has had to do with how Christians themselves have internalized certain features of the liberal academic story. While Marsden optimistically hopes that Christians can be legitimate players in the pluralistic game, Fish pessimistically maintains that it is too late to make a difference. Fish's analysis resonates with the ending of MacIntyre's *After Virtue*; MacIntyre describes living in a new dark ages where

---

meaning among other things that time is more than past, present, and future. Time is a covenantal dwelling place. Poteat once said to me, "God has called you to place where there are no foundations," his words in part a call to me to remember the fullness of time. For further reflection on Poteat's teaching, see Canon, "Haven't You Noticed."

39. Fish, "Why We Can't."

the barbarians "have already been governing us for quite some time."[40] Ma-cIntyre's well-known opening scenario, as we saw, indicates that the darkness is so great that those living in it do not even realize they are speaking incoherent, fragmented languages. As I have argued, the modern academy is not unlike this scenario: fragmented and formed by distorted stories. If the darkness is so pronounced, is Fish correct to believe that it is too late to make a difference?

The words "too late," however, depend upon an understanding of time as scarce. To describe time as covenantal or participatory, however, is to say that "too late" can never really describe time. God's abundance in time is not early or late, but always present. This is not to deny that the fullness of God's kingdom, while present, is not yet fully manifest. But it is to say that we have all the time we need; we cannot run out of time. This seems absurd from a certain perspective. Time is limited because we all die; we only have a certain amount of time. "Too late" makes perfect sense within the logic of the limit of death. But to see time as a gift is to acknowledge that time is part of God's good creation, renewed and redeemed through Christ. The resurrection is the ultimate sign of Divine abundance; time is not limited or bound by death but transformed now into communion with God. So understood, it is never too late for Divine abundance. I was vividly reminded of this during my last semester of teaching at Saint Mary's College. One of the sisters stopped by my office, gave me a picture of Jesus washing the disciples' feet, and said, "God does not abandon us." In the face of a devastating decline in the number of sisters at the college and what this meant not only for her own life but for the life of the institution, was she being naïve? Within the framework of time as gift, she was being completely clear-eyed. Even in times of apparent and real darkness or discouragement, time remains what it actually is: the occasion to live being as gift.

But how does time as abundance relate to the loss that marks time? Fish and Marsden, among others, register this loss as it relates to a separation if not outright divorce between the academy and its founding church. James Burtchaell describes this loss as a dying of the light: the light in which one sees education as a vocation of the church. Certainly there are individuals as well as some colleges and universities that have sought and continue to seek to keep the light going. But by far the typical story is one of alienation between church and academy.

40. MacIntyre, *After Virtue*, 263.

In the face of such alienation, describing an abundant "now" could seem like a mere illusion. It is instructive to recall, however, that *saeculum*, from which we derive "secular," originally referred to a time rather than a space. *Saeculum* described the interval between the fall and the eschaton. The significance of this usage lies in the fact that there was no secular sphere or space over against a spiritual one, no earthly realm entirely separate from a heavenly one. Rather, as I discussed in chapter 1, the modern secular had to be invented, and nature, human action, and society reimagined "as a *sphere* of autonomous, sheerly formal power."[41] If *saeculum*, however, refers not to a space cordoned off from religion but to the interval of time between fall and eschaton, then a different space/time image emerges. The *saeculum* is the now and not-yet of God's abundant time, and as such pertains to all of creation. The *saeculum* as time is inherently teleological.

So understood, the challenge is not negotiating between secular versus spiritual time. The challenge is rather how to be in created time faithfully. In addressing this challenge, Karl Barth asks, "Have we ever done more than make a toilsome and pitiable beginning, which on close inspection is perhaps no more than a false start?" A negative response to this question supports Fish's sense that it is indeed too late to make a difference in the modern university; we can only make false starts. Barth continues, however, "If we were concerned with an end in itself and as such, then there would be good cause indeed to fear that only this bitter Too Late awaits even the Christian."[42] The basis of hope, Barth argues, is not ourselves but the One in whom we hope who is already present as hope's basis. Since the God in whom one hopes is already present, we owe "Him this active witness."[43] Barth rightly directs the aim of hope away from securing an outcome to receiving the presence of Christ in all of the particular times and places in which a person or institution finds itself.

Vaclav Havel, the Czech poet and president, captured the proper sense of hope when he said, "it transcends the world that is immediately experienced, and is anchored somewhere beyond its horizons . . . . It is an ability to work for something because it is good, not just because it stands a chance to succeed . . . . It is not the conviction that something will turn out well, but the certainty that something makes sense, regardless of how it turns out."[44]

41. Milbank, *Theology and Social Theory*, 9. My emphasis.

42. Barth, *Church Dogmatics IV*, 929.

43. Barth, *Church Dogmatics IV*, 929

44. Cited in Bockmuehl, "Hope and Optimism," 24.

Pessimism, or its twin optimism, make sense when the focus is progress and securing an outcome through human effort alone. By contrast, Christian hope makes sense because God has not abandoned our time but is even now the source of abundance and communion. One is thus freed to live being as gift, even if the difference it makes is not readily apparent. God's abundance in the *saeculum* is manifest in *both* the now and not-yet of God's kingdom.

The contemplative life/the active life

A key challenge to living in time as abundance is the contrast, often made, between the contemplative and active life. Arendt discusses how contemplation was elevated over any kind of activity as early as Plato, particularly in his political philosophy. In this early context, the Greek *skholé* (σχολή) meant not just leisure time but also freedom from labor and work as well as political activity,[45] a usage that highlights the opposition between contemplation and action. Arendt identifies two key components of this Greek understanding of contemplation. First, it reflects Plato's contention that the beginning of philosophy had to do with "shocked wonder at the miracle of Being."[46] Secondly, this Socratic understanding of contemplation results in a state of purified speechlessness: " the essentially speechless state of contemplation, [which] was the end of philosophy."[47] Arendt goes on to suggest that this kind of speechless wonder entered into ordinary experience through craftsmanship and fabrication (contemplating the beauty of the craft, for example). Such contemplation eventually dropped out, however, with a shift away from the craft or product to the process, as can be seen in the contrast between the work of a local craftsman and the mass production of items in the modern age. Arendt observes: "contemplation was no longer believed to yield truth and . . . it had lost its position in the *vita activa* itself and hence within the range of ordinary human experience."[48] The result was the "elimination of contemplation from the range of meaningful human capacities . . . [as] almost a matter of course."[49]

45. Arendt, *The Human Condition*, 14.

46. Arendt, *The Human Condition*, 302. According to Arendt, Aristotle attributes this understanding to Plato.

47. Arendt, *The Human Condition*, 302.

48. Arendt, *The Human Condition*, 304.

49. Arendt, *The Human Condition*, 305.

I lift up these points from Arendt's more extended analysis to show how contemplation and action have been separated from each other. As Schindler describes this Greek view, "action is understood to be related to contemplation only as it were by way of *succession*, as something that occurs either *before* or *after* but in any case never *coincident with* contemplation. And action at the same time is something that becomes devalued . . . a necessary concession to, our 'immanence' in time."[50] Contemplation is defined over against action.

If leisure is to become a vital practice and way of being in time, is there a way to move beyond this either/or dichotomy? Is there a way to understand the *vita activa* and *vita contempletiva* as more integrally related? This will require turning again to the nature of time. If time is participatory and covenantal, then contemplation and action will be more that serial efforts or sequences placed in opposition to one another. In Schindler's essay "Time in Eternity, Eternity in Time: On the Contemplative-Active Life," he discusses how time is at once active and contemplative. Relying upon Hans Urs von Balthasar's Trinitarian understanding of time in eternity, he states:

> the Father's "*active* action" is conditioned by the "*passive* action" of the Son and of the Spirit—and vice versa. Activity and passivity in God are thus always-already different *because of their relation to each other*: activity is not "merely" active, nor is passivity "merely" passive. On the contrary, "mere activity" now takes on an inherently generous character, and "mere passivity" an inherently receptive character.[51]

So understood, God's "time" is not simply an infinite continuation. Rather God's own triune being is full, dynamic, and abundant. The Son rests fully in the Father and this rest or receiving involves the Son's total giving, and vice versa. Following von Balthasar, Schindler describes how this Trinitarian understanding opens time up: "expectation, fulfillment, newness, surprise—and the movement implied by these—and passivity, all of which characterize time, are not mere negatives that are to be eliminated in eternity."[52] According to Balthasar, God places surprise and fulfillment in finite time to provide an image of God's infinite time.

But in what sense is Balthasar saying that within the Trinity there is surprise and newness? Would this not subject God to time rather than the

---

50. Schindler, "Time in Eternity, Eternity in Time," 53.

51. Schindler, "Time in Eternity, Eternity in Time," 58.

52. Schindler, "Time in Eternity, Eternity in Time," 59.

other way around? Balthasar places words like *become, change, surprise,* and so forth not in a linear time frame, but within a Trinitarian framework. He thus describes the Trinitarian life as a "communion of surprise" in the sense of the Trinity being "an infinite ever-overflowing fulfillment."[53] So, for example, the "Father's handing-over of himself to the Son is seen by the Son as 'the object of infinite amazement, wonderment and gratitude.'"[54] The surprise that Balthasar attributes to the Trinity is not quantitative (something left yet to be given), or chronological (something to be given in the future), or gnoseiological (an unshared secret).[55] Rather, the language of surprise, as well as excess or ever-greatness, indicates a "linguistic form of amazement." It is a way to understand God as "an ever-greater event of love," and the divine persons as being "in grateful wonderment at each other."[56] This language does not then signify a lack. As Antonio López describes Balthasar's position:

> Surprise in God does not mean that one of the persons unexpectedly discloses to the others what was previously, avariciously, kept secret. Rather, it has to do first of all with the fact that the hypostases are eternally other (person), and, second, with the mysterious nature of the reciprocal gift that the eternal happening of God is: the ever-greater, personal, gratuitous love that generates gratitude both for the gift that is eternally given and received and for the 'expectation' that is always already 'fulfilled.'[57]

So understood, Trinitarian "time" in eternity is surprise, delight, wonder, and love, a time revealed most fully in the person of Jesus. From this Trinitarian understanding, contemplation and action are not opposed but

---

53. Schindler, "Time in Eternity, Eternity in Time," 58. As Schindler notes, Hans Urs von Balthasar describes the Trinity as inclusive of time. Thus, for Balthasar "rather than saying that there is no becoming (*Werden*) in God, one should speak instead of the 'super-becoming of the innerly-divine event' . . ." Schindler, "Time in Eternity, Eternity in Time," 57. Such a statement could sound as if Balthasar is denying Divine immutability or impassibility. Yet Schindler cautions against this interpretation. Balthasar's desire, rather, is to move from a more "monopolar" context for understanding God to a Trinitarian and personalist one. Balthasar's point "is that it is precisely the *personal—love*—which reveals the primary meaning of ontology, *of* being." Schindler, "Time in Eternity, Eternity in Time," 59–60. On this understanding, God does not change or become other than who God *is*. But the "is" is to be understood as personal and therefore always dynamic.

54. Lopez citing Balthasar in "Eternal Happening," 96.

55. Lopez, "Eternal Happening," 97.

56. Lopez, "Eternal Happening," 98

57. Lopez, "Eternal Happening," 101.

one calls for the other. As Schindler states, "What is revealed to us in and by the God of Jesus Christ is how contemplation and action reveal their true meaning to us from the beginning only in relation: in the relation called love."[58] Receptivity unfolds into true self-giving even as self-giving requires receiving from another.

In Schindler as well as Balthasar, time is not primarily linear in the sense of time as a receding past and a distant future. Time is rather the extension of God's abundant triune love. As such, it is filled with wonder and surprise. One enters this time through receptivity and generosity, through contemplation and action, which are always intrinsically related. What is important to see in Schindler's analysis of the contemplative and active life is an overcoming of temporal/active *versus* the eternal/contemplative. Separated from each other, action easily becomes superficial doing and busyness; and contemplation turns into a barren theorizing.[59]

As previously discussed, Pieper diagnoses busyness and constant work as symptoms of sloth. As we saw, sloth or *acedia* is the inability or refusal to be who one or what one is created to be. When institutional time is perceived as strictly linear and therefore scarce, it will produce a slothful culture. By contrast, living in time as open to divine plenitude will produce a culture of leisure and a people capable of taking wonder and delight in the world, whether the world of colleagues and friends or the natural world of stars and atoms. Generosity toward others and creation becomes a way of actively acknowledging and extending a contemplative receptivity. Leisure names an integration of the contemplative/receptive and the active/generative, and thus a way of living in time faithfully.

Rituals of plenitude

How does an academic institution, however, practice or make more possible this way of being in time that is at once contemplative and active? The question indicates already that a full response requires more than individual effort. Academic institutions, like political or economic institutions in which the academy is embedded, can encourage or hinder the requisite virtues and practices for active/contemplative living. MacIntyre describes

---

58. Schindler, "Time in Eternity, Eternity in Time," 65. Schindler states, "paradoxically, the same passion of *compete self-giving* is what gives the true meaning to action." Schindler, "Time in Eternity, Eternity in Time," 65.

59. Schindler, "Time in Eternity, Eternity in Time," 67.

how *pleonexia*, the drive to have more and more, was considered a vice in the Middle Ages, but, under the institution of capitalism, has become a virtue. Thus capitalism "provides systematic incentives to develop a type of character that has propensity to injustice."[60] MacIntyre's point about *pleonexia* helps us see how deeply institutions shape cultures. The virtue (vice) of wanting more than necessary is not something that people simply choose; they are rather inculcated into an institutional way of being. If it is true that a Christian university needs to be "supported by a community with practices that force us to reshape our imagination and our knowledges,"[61] then what kinds of practices can reshape how the academy imagines time?

In order for the academy to live out of a renewed understanding of time, it will need to embrace a different rhythm. Institutions can live into the rhythm of Christian time in a variety of ways. One of the key ways that Christians across the centuries have been attuned to abundant time is through the practice of daily, communal prayer, sometimes known of the Daily Office. R. R. Reno discusses how daily prayer, a tradition traced back to ancient Judaism, took on a more formal structure in Western monasticism where prayer was ordered by seven hours, a rhythm inspired by the Psalter, specifically Psalm 119:164, "Seven times a day I praise you." The cycle has shifted over time. Reno notes that *The Book of Common Prayer* focuses mostly on Morning and Evening Prayer. In whatever form, the prayer has typically cycled through reading the Psalms. Reno states, following Dietrich Bonhoeffer, that this rhythm of prayer is more than a human tradition. It is rather acknowledging and receiving the gift of time, thus giving praise to God. Reno emphasizes that the psalms are words that Christ enunciated in his own voice and, as such, "they are [the Lord's] praise given to us for our use."[62]

Some might object that there is not enough time for this kind of practice or that faculty or administrators will see it as irrelevant to the real work of the institution. Another concern, mentioned above, has to do with those in the institution who are not Christian, or, even if they are, will feel uncomfortable with this sort of practice. One might also wonder, if these were

---

60. Cited in Hauerwas, *Sanctify Them*, 224.

61. Hauerwas, *Sanctify Them*, 225. Hauerwas gives as an example how knowledge taught in the university reinforces the conviction, from the perspective of realism, that violence in inevitable. Thus we teach American history as if America is the main character rather than God.

62. Reno, *In the Ruins*, 154. Bonhoeffer describes the Psalms as the "prayerbook of the Bible."

required, whether they would not violate academic freedom. Consider, however, a professor who chooses not to read, write, research, or teach. In so doing, he would eventually cease to be a professor. Certain activities are intrinsic to the role. Similarly, time as intrinsically participatory leads to practices of prayer, and vice versa. One might argue that a person can pray on their own time. But to do so would be to lapse into the very thing that abundant time challenges: participatory time is not simply a personal choice but the way created time is.

While the practice might well vary, praying some form of communal prayer is a door through which to enter more fully into abundant, participatory time. Such rhythmic praying is not simply a pious gesture. Trained as many are to interpret faith as private, it might be easy to consider such prayer as an intrusion into the public academic sphere. From this perspective, it will appear to be someone's faith, but not everyone's. As James K. A. Smith emphasizes, however, the question is not "whether or not liturgy?" but rather "which liturgy?" There will always be liturgies guiding the academy, even if only implicitly. If some liturgy is always at play, then the question deeper down is which liturgy is an institution enacting? So understood, time is not a neutral category ("everyone's") but an ontological and theological category (inherently convictional). If there are no institutional practices that participate in time as communion, as abundance, indeed as delightful surprise, then some other time will ultimately dominate, distorting the life of the mind. The power of the Daily Office, or daily communal prayer, is that it draws an institution into time as watchfulness, receptivity, and doxology. It enables an institution to remember and to participate in God's memory. It might sound odd to attribute memory analogously to God, but to do so is to point to God's re-membering and reforming a people, and through them, all of creation. Such a practice is a way of forming an institution to see how a contemplative receiving from God and others is also at the same time about being enabled to participate generously in God's creative and redeeming abundance in time.

If cyclical, communal prayer is an ancient practice of being in abundant time, a more recent practice might be interdisciplinary teaching or research. Such efforts can take place with little attention to Divine abundance, mired rather in liturgies of productivity and success. As discussed earlier in the context of economics and theology, however, interdisciplinary practices can also be liturgies of attention to the whole, to an abundant being in time that transcends the fragmentation of the disciplines. As such, they can become ways of being, at once contemplative and active.

Christopher Alexander's discussion of "intensifying centers" provides insight into how a grasp of wholeness (or transcendence) overcomes fragmentation while not erasing distinction. Alexander, an architect, argues that space and matter (we could add time) are not simply dead mechanistic entities but "possess *degrees of life*, because the elements of which they are made relate to each other not as mere parts but as mutually supporting 'centers.'"[63] Thus, different features—such as boundaries, good shape, ambiguity, and so forth—each describe "one of the possible ways in which centers can intensify each other."[64] Alexander thus uses the language of "intensifying centers" to describe how in the natural world separate components enrich each other making possible a life-giving whole, heretofore unrealized. "The 'wholeness' to which such centers contribute is a field-like structure (gestalt) that is somehow ontologically prior to the features of which it appears to be composed."[65] Implicit in Alexander's understanding is an ontology of relation and communion: various components in relation to one another form a whole greater than its separate parts, making the whole both life-giving and beautiful.

Caldecott observes that Alexander's same features (strong centers, boundaries, echoes, etc.) could be applicable in economics "where a more intensely 'living' economy is one—like that described by G. K. Chesterton, E. F. Schumacher, *et al.*—in which strong centers, such as small businesses and the various elements of civil society, act to support each other in a whole that is more than the sum of its parts."[66] Such an understanding, notes Caldecott, stands in contrast to a monolithic, growth-addicted economy that is essentially mechanistic.

What if different disciplines saw themselves as intensifying, mutually supporting centers rather than as separate, often isolated departments? Or, more broadly, what if the academy and the church interpreted themselves in this light? On Alexander's view, coherence, intensity of life, beauty, and

63. Caldecott, *The Radiance of Being*, 62. Caldecott is here describing Alexander's architectural philosophy.

64. Alexander, *The Nature of Order*, 241. For example, a garden in which the light falls exactly right, in which the spaces to walk have beautiful boundaries, and in which benches are well placed in relation to other aspects will have a gestalt or wholeness where the different features bring the others to life.

65. Caldecott is describing Alexander; *The Radiance of Being*, 63.

66. Caldecott, *The Radiance of Being*, 64.

depth of structure are all related. And a "center" is a focus of attention that makes one aware of relations within a wider pattern. To imagine each discipline or institution as an intensifying center is to become open to ways that it might become more fully itself (and thus more whole) *through* juxtaposition and engagement. Such a process moves the academy away from a mechanistic ontology and toward an ontology grounded in communion and in the goodness and beauty of created being. This is not to say that such an approach is without confusion, conflict, or tension, but practiced in the context of leisure and abundant time it rests in the hope that such ways of being are ultimately generative.

Time as freedom

Years ago, a friend and I were sitting outside Duke Chapel when we overheard a student tour guide point to the chapel while adding, "Don't worry. You don't have to believe anything to come here." The implication was that belief is your personal choice, and one of your options is to believe nothing. Many assume that the only alternative to this position is the imposition of belief. I once told this story to a colleague, and was met with stony silence. Did she assume that my point in telling the story was that every student should be required to be Christian? Is the alternative the freedom to choose your beliefs?

More recently, Duke University decided to allow the Duke Muslim Students' Association to chant a weekly call-to-prayer from the Duke Chapel bell tower. The chant (called the "adhan"), which lasts about three minutes, was to be moderately amplified. According to the Association, the proposal for this practice had three aims: 1) to set forth an "interreligious reimagining of a university icon," 2) to communicate welcome to the Muslim community, and 3) to challenge media stereotypes of Muslims.[67] The decision on Duke's part met with strong reaction, some accusing Duke of being anti-American and of supporting Muslim violence (the timing of the proposal was in the wake of the Charlie Hebdo killings). The opposing side argued that the chapel was a neutral space available to all, and that freedom of expression should extend to all in the university. It therefore was unfair not to allow all religious groups to use this space. The university ended up reversing its decision.[68]

---

67. Bretherton reports these aims in "Religious Vandalism or Interfaith Hospitality?"

68. For a response that did not support the logic of either of these sides, see the letter

For my purposes, it is instructive that both of the dominant sides of the debate appealed to American freedom. On the one hand, the university ought to defend America's borders and not implicitly, so they imagined, support terrorism associated with Islam. On the other hand, the university ought to support freedom of expression. Both sides, however, relied upon the preservation of freedom to bolster their position. Whether nationalism takes the form of fear and protection of borders for the sake of freedom, or the protection of freedom of expression, a reliance upon the nation determines the range of the argument.[69] To the extent that this is true, the memory of the nation-state trumps any other memory.

In an often-cited argument, Benedict Anderson states that a change in understanding time made possible the imagined community called the nation.[70] "It is difficult today to recreate in the imagination a condition of life in which the nation was felt to be something utterly new . . . . The Declaration of Independence of 1776 makes absolutely no reference to Christopher Columbus, Roanoke, or the Pilgrim Fathers, nor are the grounds put forward to justify independence in any way 'historical,' in the sense of highlighting the antiquity of the American people."[71] The creation of the nation signals a break with the past. The newness of the nation—through rupture—parallels the sense of time that makes possible the self-creating individual. According to Anderson, it is the novelty of time that makes both the nation and the individual possible. Within this understanding of time, freedom has to do with self-creation and self-determination. To the extent that students, faculty, campus groups, and the university embrace freedom as self-determination they are living in the time of the imagined community called the nation.

David Burrell, however, describes another way to understand freedom. Following Aquinas, he states that freedom is less a question of self-determination than "one of attuning oneself to one's ultimate end."[72] Thus

---

by Richard B. Hays, then Dean of Duke Divinity School, to the Duke Divinity School community.

69. As Abdullah Antepli, the first Muslim chaplain at Duke, stated, "At the end of the day, this is not an Islam conversation. It's an America conversation. It's a 'who do we want to be and how do we want to arrange and accommodate diversity?' conversation. Are we a zero-sum society? Are you less of who you are if I am who I am?" Cited by Graham, "For Whom the Muezzim Calls."

70. Anderson, *Imagined Communities*, 6.

71. Anderson, *Imagined Communities*, 193.

72. Burrell, *Faith and Freedom*, 110.

any good choice implies an orientation to an end. Such direction is not itself a choice but a consent to one's being: "any good choice will presuppose an orientation to the end, where the orientation itself is not a choice but a consent to the orientation of one's very being."[73] Aquinas's understanding "links us with the Augustinian restlessness by attending to existence and to its source."[74] Freedom is thus attending and attuning ourselves to our true end. When this "end is enhanced beyond our imagining, as in the ways revealed by God to Jewish, Christian, or Muslim believers, the consent becomes a *response* of faith."[75]

If one moves from the time of the imagined community called the nation—in which time is novel and freedom is self-determination—then how might we reframe the kind of argument surrounding the use of the Duke Chapel tower? First, a resolution will not be found in an embrace of freedom as choice, dependent ultimately upon the "neutral" violence of the nation-state. Secondly, we can note that while Jews, Christians, and Muslims reason differently with Scripture (both among themselves and with each other), they share the conviction that time is participatory though interpretations of this differ. To live in this time as communion is to see that true freedom has to do with consent to an end given by God. Such consent is a response of faith to the One who is ever-faithful. I do not know what the result of reasoning in light of this memory would be in terms of sharing or not sharing holy space. But the response would be one in which participants took time to be in communion with each other in the presence of Scripture, and ultimately of God.[76] Christians, for their part, would need to engage how space and time are sacramental, an understanding rooted in the conviction that in the sacraments God *gives* us saving and healing signs.[77] Such an understanding contradicts a flattened ontology in which one space is just like any other, a basketball court no different than an altar. It also contradicts a secularized Protestant work ethic, discussed earlier, that sees salvific signs in human work and productivity.

73. Burrell, *Faith and Freedom*, 110. Burrell shares with Augustine, Aquinas, and the Christian tradition more broadly that "creatures cannot be their own end."

74. Burrell, *Faith and Freedom*, 111.

75. Burrell, *Faith and Freedom*, 110.

76. I have in mind here something like scriptural reasoning: the practice in which Christians, Jews, and Muslims read Scripture together not in spite of but out of their unique commitments.

77. For the contrast between producing signs and receiving the sacraments as signs from God, see Schindler, "2011 11 30 Face to Face."

Some might object that an understanding of time as communion and freedom as consent is itself an imposition since not all in the university share this understanding. But here again it is important to remember that there is no neutral time; as Anderson notes, it is always imagined. The dominant way to imagine time in most universities is time as the place of self-creation and novelty. In the global market, significant time is now measured in milliseconds.[78] Years ago, Robert Coles related the increased speed of time to the loss of timeful rituals:

> Wars can take a moment, and the world can be destroyed . . . . [Maybe we can] wonder whether there isn't a breakdown affecting the artist, the writer, the warrior, the political leader, the psychiatrist, anyone, affecting the educator with his computer, which he's told he must use, and affecting some essential aspects of humanity, having to do with words and experiences like "distance" and "respect" . . . . And the word "craft," which means *time* and thought and leisure—whether that, too, isn't so fatally collapsing that there is a breakdown in what you call ritualization.[79]

Coles is sounding a similar note as Arendt: time as novel, even instantaneous, disallows any room for contemplative receptivity. The modern academy still has its public rituals: getting tenure, publishing, teaching, meetings, graduation, and so forth. But Coles's description of timeful rituals comes from a memory of time as more than human effort and self-determination.

Living in the abundant time of receptivity and generosity will move the academy closer to the harmony that resounds with *all* of creation. The "love that moves the sun and other stars" is the same love that moves our being as communion and is the source of genuine freedom, academic or otherwise.

---

78. For example, high-speed computers using automated trading systems rely on tightly measured time to turn a profit. "Latency" is a term used to refer to the delay between the transmission of information from its source to its reception at destination. Latency is determined by the speed of light, corresponding to around 3.3 milliseconds per 1,000 kilometers of optical fiber.

79. Cited in Poteat, *The Primacy of Persons*, 36.

6

MAKING LEISURE MORE POSSIBLE

In the latter half of the nineteenth century, Noah Porter, president of Yale University (1871–1886), wrote sympathetically about the relation between Athens and Jerusalem. Porter was able to embrace Milton's words describing the end of learning as a "repair" to the

> ruins of our first parents, by regaining to know God aright, and out of that knowledge to love him, to imitate him, be like him . . . . But because our understanding cannot in this body found itself but on sensible things, nor arrive so clearly to the knowledge of God and invisible things, as by orderly conning over the visible and inferior creatures, the same method is to be followed in all discreet teaching.[1]

While Porter appears to acknowledge that the end of education is to know and love God, he concludes that since we are "sensible beings" we cannot clearly arrive at such knowledge. In all teaching, the same method of attending to sensible things (what we can know) applies. Porter concludes that the college is not designed for "spiritual edification" but for "study and intellectual discipline."[2] Even so, the college should nurture the Christian commitments of its members. Overall, the academy should be dedicated to the pursuit of truth and sensitive to those with Christian conscience. Henry

---

1. Cited in Johnson, "Down the Mountain," 573. Johnson is quoting from Porter's *The American Colleges and the American Public*. Johnson also wrote *The Christian College*. The quotation is from Milton's *On Education*.

2. Cited in Johnson, "Down the Mountain," 574.

Johnson describes Porter's understanding as, at the time, bold, strong, and inspiring. He was "digging in against an open, active and increasingly secular culture."[3] His books were widely read. Johnson poignantly adds however, "But shortly is would also disappear, unlamented in its passing—a little longer at Yale than at most institutions, but not very. Porter's words were a homily not at the matins of a new academic day but at the vespers of a fading tradition . . . ."[4]

I would say that Johnson's description is partially true. Porter is struggling not simply to shore up a "fading tradition," but to synthesize two competing traditions: one that allows him to talk about the end of learning as knowing and loving God and another Kantian tradition that separates faith and knowledge. The latter prevails to the extent that Porter allows a quasi-gnostic faith to shape his understanding of the spiritual as separate from the intellectual. To the extent that Porter can talk about the spiritual over against the academic, his imagination has been enchanted by the kinds of academic stories discussed in chapter 1, their common thread a closed ontology in which love is extrinsic to being.

Making leisure more possible, I have argued, calls for naming the stories that form and malform us. As Stanley Hauerwas has said, "You can only live in the world you can see, and you can only see the world you have learned to say."[5] But how do we learn to say? What language can we borrow, as the hymnist writes? Further, as we see in Porter's story, it is possible to use words—about the end of learning, for example—in such a way that the words do not fully resonate or form a way of life. Other habits of speech prevail. This reality suggests that learning to speak in renewed ways about the academy requires renewed habits that resist the tight boundaries between the spiritual and the intellectual, between knowledge and love of God, or between study and prayer. In this concluding chapter, then, I turn to two practices that make leisure more possible: the habit of paying attention as described by Simone Weil and the practice of friendship. First, however, I turn again to *acedia* as an academic vice that obscures true lei-

3. Johnson, "Down the Mountain," 571.

4. Johnson, "Down the Mountain," 574.

5. This theme appears throughout Hauerwas's writings. Both Iris Murdoch and Ludwig Wittgenstein have influenced Hauerwas on this point. Wittgenstein, for example, emphasizes that learning a language is learning a form of life. Hauerwas cites Murdoch in *The Sovereignty of the Good*: "I can only choose within the world I can *see*, in the moral sense of 'see' which implies that clear vision is a result of moral imagination and moral effort." Hauerwas, "Murdochian Muddles," 190.

sure. I look particularly at how this vice is present in the academy through the symptoms of boredom and neglect.

Diagnosing acedia in the modern academy

As we saw chapter 3, Pieper identifies the opposite of *acedia* or sloth as "a man's happy and cheerful affirmation of his own being, his acquiescence in the world and in God—which is to say love."[6] While a symptom of *acedia* may be laziness, I argued that more relevant to the modern academy are the symptoms of busyness and nonstop work. Pieper emphasizes that "to be bound to the working process is to be bound to the whole process of usefulness, and moreover, to be bound in such a way that the whole life of the working human being is consumed."[7] A person suffering from *acedia* is unable to rest in his or her being and knowing as gift, ultimately from God. *Acedia* thus blocks the ability to have wonder and delight, both of which rely on surprise and the reception of gift.

R. J. Snell, in *Acedia and its Discontents: Metaphysical Boredom and an Empire of Desire*, emphasizes that *acedia*, not simply an individual vice, is manifest today especially through the symptom of boredom. A whole culture can be characterized as slothful: one can anticipate such a culture "to be very busy . . . to be ever more distracted, exhausted, and bitter in the unending attempt to express and display freedom without humility before the yokes of place, limits, order."[8] A slothful culture chaffs against the limits of its created being within the order of God's good creation. Distraction and exhaustion seems the opposite of boredom. Snell continues, however, "No longer a vice afflicting individuals only, *acedia* has become a cultural reality; nestled deep in the roots of our ways of acting and living, sloth seeps into our loves and lives in virtually every domain, before finally transforming itself into boredom and nihilism."[9] The kind of boredom that Snell describes is not about having little to do. A culture can be caught up in unceasing activity and still be bored. Snell makes a distinction between "situative boredom"—a preacher drones on and on, or a date brags about his video game prowess—and ontological boredom.[10] The latter kind of boredom has

6. Pieper, *Leisure*, 25.

7. Pieper, *Leisure*, 38.

8. Snell, *Acedia and Its Discontents*, 66.

9. Snell, *Acedia and Its Discontents*, 61.

10. Snell, *Acedia and Its Discontents*, 66–72.

to do with lacking adequate desire. One has only the freedom to choose in a disinterested world. Ontological boredom thus prevents a person or a culture from desiring a higher end. Snell uses the word *malaise* to describe this cultural malady: in "our indifference to the vast array of numbingly indifferent choices" such a culture denies "transcendental beauty, goodness and truth in the mediation of particular finite forms."[11] That is, the ontologically bored sense that "there is nothing worth desiring . . . goodness no longer delights."[12] In the absence of such desire, a culture mired in *acedia* births nihilism "as the noughting of the world and ourselves."[13] Boredom and nihilism are thus always co-symptoms, a lack of desire for goodness and beauty feeding and being fed by a denial that these even exist.

To Snell's insightful diagnosis of boredom as a collective symptom of modern *acedia*, we can add another one that is especially endemic to the modern academy: neglect. The Egyptian monk, Evagrius Ponticus (b. 346), one of the first Christians to write about *acedia,* famously describes it as the "noonday demon" because it tended to strike monks in the middle of the day as they were overcome with spiritual weariness.[14] Especially relevant to his understanding was Psalm 118: "My soul slumbers on account of ἀκηδία." Very probably, says one commentator, "this verse reminded the monks of the danger they experienced in being tempted to grow listless and to give up."[15] Slumber came to refer to "the loss of knowing what man's nature and his goals in this life are."[16] That is, *acedia* produces a weariness about the status of the self before God. As Origen stated, such slumber is "the *neglect* on the part of the rational soul of the virtues and of the knowledge of God."[17] Aquinas, too, relates *acedia*, which he calls an "oppressive sorrow," to a sluggishness that neglects the Divine good.[18]

How might these symptoms of boredom and neglect relate to the academy? A single example will serve. As George Grant observes, if "the teacher of literature, however much he is steeped in the poets, has not

---

11. Michael Hanby as cited in Snell, *Acedia and Its Discontents*, 71.

12. Snell, *Acedia and Its Discontents*, 77.

13. Snell, *Acedia and Its Discontents*, 73.

14. Wenzel, *The Sin of Sloth*, 17. According to Wenzel, Anthanasius's commentary on *Selecta in Psalmos* is the first identification of the noonday devil with *acedia*.

15. Wenzel, *The Sin of Sloth*, 17. The Psalm cited is from the Septuagint.

16. Wenzel, *The Sin of Sloth*, 19.

17. Wenzel, *The Sin of Sloth*, 19. Cited from the *Selecta in Psalmos*, 17. My emphasis.

18. Aquinas, *ST* 2.2.35.

thought about the relation of poetic beauty to the final beauty, his teaching is liable to end up in a rather insipid aestheticism . . . if the teacher of science does not see that the reality of nature must be seen in its relation and dependence upon other realities, the teaching of science can lead youngsters to the cheapest kind of materialism."[19] In this instance, the teacher is neglecting the final beauty or fuller reality and thus, in Kierkegaard's words, displaying a despairing refusal to be before God. In so doing, in failing to attend to the heights and depths of created being, the teacher is creating a context for ontological boredom. The figure of Don Juan, as described by Kierkegaard, exemplifies this boredom: since he lives in the world "aesthetically" (noncommittally), he quickly becomes bored with his lover and moves on to another. To be struck by the "noonday demon" is to become listless, unable to live in light of a final good.[20] Like all vices, *acedia* is a privation dependent on the goodness of being. As such, it deprives a person or an institution from attending to the virtues and knowledge of God.

Paying attention with a view to the love of God

Simone Weil's "Reflections on the Right Use of School Studies with a View to the Love of God" offers a rich alternative to *acedia*, especially in its manifestation as boredom and neglect. Weil argues that study can be a road to sanctity. In light of our example above, she would say that studying poetic beauty can be a path to discovering final beauty. Weil begins by focusing on paying attention. "Students must therefore work," she writes, "without any wish to gain good marks, to pass examinations, to win school successes; without any reference to their natural abilities and tastes; applying themselves equally to all their tasks, with the idea that each one will help to form in them the habit of that attention which is the substance of prayer."[21] Attention, as Weil understands it, has to do with waiting and receiving. It is

---

19. Grant, "The Paradox of Democratic Education," 179. Grant emphasizes that he does not mean the teacher must have picked up a few "pleasant aphorisms" on the side. Rather, he or she "must strive to think things as a whole not only as a student but throughout his [or her] life." Grant, "The Paradox of Democratic Education," 179.

20. As is well known, Kant also sought to awake himself from his dogmatic slumbers by turning to nature (starry skies) and to the moral law within. One sees in this turn an impulse toward nature as purposeful. Kant undercuts this, however, by developing an account of rationality based on human effort alone. As such, he allows no rational place for true leisure. See chapter 3 for a discussion of Pieper and Kant.

21. Weil, *Waiting on God*, 53.

the "substance of prayer" because prayer places one in a position of waiting before God.

Weil thus criticizes any purely utilitarian understanding of education. In her essay "Reflections on Quantum Theory," she describes how utility has become the cultural norm:

> In the present crisis there is something compromised which is infinitely more precious even than science; it is the idea of truth . . . . So soon as truth disappears, utility at once takes its place, because man always directs his effort toward some good or other. Thus utility becomes something which the intelligence is no longer entitled to define or to judge, but only to serve . . . . That is where we are today. Everything is oriented towards utility, which nobody thinks of defining; public opinion reigns supreme, in the village of scientists as in the great nations. It is as though we had returned to the age of Protagoras and the Sophists, the age when the art of persuasion—whose modern equivalent is advertising slogans, publicity, propaganda meetings, the press, the cinema, the radio—took the place of thought.[22]

To reduce the pursuit of knowledge to pure usefulness is to fail to engage larger questions of truth. Such utility thus leads a person or an institution to serve false masters. Weil asks, "When someone exposes himself as a slave in the market place, what wonder if he finds a master?"[23] Writing on the brink of World War II, Weil's words about propaganda, spiritual neglect, and an intelligence "enslaved by the power of arms" take on, in retrospect, a sense of poignant urgency.

Paying attention to school studies in the face of such obstacles might seem a trivial gesture; it is far removed from the world's problems. On the other hand, paying attention in the context of school might seem obvious. Who has not heard a teacher demand attention from her students? For Weil, however, paying attention is not about mustering willpower, contracting

22. Weil, *On Science*, 63–64. More recently, Brad Gregory describes how the academy justifies its existence against the bar of usefulness. One hears, "Your degree will help you go to graduate school or get a job," or "education helps citizens (and the nation-state) be competitive players in the global market." Thus most American students including those at elite institutions of higher education "tend to be nonchalant if not cynical about the pursuit of truth, and view undergraduate education primarily as grade-getting, pre-professional training en route to gaining admissions to professional schools on the path to becoming doctors, lawyers, business-people—or the next generation of academics." Gregory, *Unintended Reformation*, 303.

23. Weil, *On Science*, 64.

one's brows, holding one's breath or stiffening one's muscles, as when an adult tells a child, "Pay attention!"[24] Weil describes the habit of attention rather as a "negative effort"; it is not about human control or mastery but "consists of suspending our thought, leaving it detached, empty and ready to be penetrated by the object. It means holding in our minds, within reach of this thought, but on a lower level and not in contact with it, the diverse knowledge we have acquired which we are forced to make use of."[25] Weil describes this attention as a kind of waiting, not a passive waiting but an active waiting as when we are waiting "for the right word to come of itself at the end of our pen . . . ." She concludes, "We do not obtain the most precious gifts by going in search of them but by waiting for them."[26] By using the language of "gift" and "love," Weil is radically reversing a utilitarian approach to study. One does not study merely to secure an extrinsic goal; one studies to become a particular kind of person. In this instance, one becomes a person capable of waiting and of receiving knowledge as gift which, she states, is the substance of prayer. While this might seem to some a small gesture, Weil is offering an alternative to being enslaved to the utility of the marketplace.

Weil extends the habit of paying attention to include attention to failure. In a passage challenging to modern ears, she tells her readers to "take great pains to examine squarely and to contemplate attentively and slowly each school task in which we have failed, seeing how unpleasing and second-rate it is, without seeking any excuse or overlooking any mistake or any of our tutor's corrections, trying to get down to the origin of each fault." She continues, "There is a great temptation to do the opposite, to give a sideways glance at the corrected exercise if it is bad, and to hide it forthwith."[27] Paying attention to failure is good in that it allows one to become more fully receptive to others and more aware of being and knowing as gift. As such, it allows for growth in humility. As Weil states, "Above all it is thus that we can acquire the virtue of humility, and that is a far more precious treasure than all academic progress." Growth in humility is a treasure because it is growth in truth.

But what does Weil mean by truth? It is not simply a block of knowledge. As I have indicated, Weil finds it impossible to separate holiness,

24. Weil, *Waiting on God*, 54.
25. Weil, *Waiting on God*, 54.
26. Weil, *Waiting on God*, 56–57.
27. Weil, *Waiting on God*, 53–54.

study, and knowledge. That this is so underscores how for Weil the habits of attention and humility are requisite for receiving the gift of truth. Weil writes the following about geometry: "The solution in a geometry problem does not in itself constitute a precious gift, but . . . being a little fragment of particular truth, it is a pure image of the unique, eternal and living Truth, the very Truth which once in a human voice declared 'I am the Truth.'"[28] One may know geometry by itself but such isolated knowing fails to engage the fullness of being. To know a geometry solution as a precious gift is to receive it as a sign or image of something greater: living Truth. To call geometry a sign of Truth is to acknowledge its ordered relation to all of creation; it is a sign of living Truth because it points ultimately to the Divine Source of all that is.

Weil can thus make the surprising claim, "Every school exercise, thought of in this way, is like a sacrament."[29] If a sacrament, broadly defined, is a visible means of an invisible grace, then Weil is arguing that study can be a visible means of grace. By training the habit of attention, study can draw one towards the love of God. Not only can study draw one toward God, it also at the same time draws one toward love of neighbor. Weil observes, "Not only does the love of God have attention for its substance; the love of our neighbour, which we know to be the same love, is made of this same substance." Becoming a person with the habit of attention forms one to seek and be open to the love of God in all persons and places, both in the academy and elsewhere.

Weil's argument relates most fully to leisure and the academy in the following way. Similar to our discussion of *studiositas*, Weil sees no firm boundary between study and prayer. Her analysis implies that just as prayer and study cannot be separated so neither can leisure and the academy. Both are ways of becoming a certain kind of person or institution. Apart from certain virtues—humility and love—our study will disfigure our being. In our study and learning, we are not masters of a machine, or of a cosmos that is dumb and blind. We are rather "humble slaves," waiting on Another.

Leisure and the necessity of friendship

The loss of leisure in the academy cannot be understood apart from what Chad Pecknold describes as a modern crisis in friendship. Pecknold argues

28. Weil, *Waiting on God*, 57.
29. Weil, *Waiting on God*, 57.

that this crisis has led to a detachment from the common goods of family, polity, and religion. Apart from friendship, he states, such goods are unrealizable. Pecknold calls attention to how goods held in common require friendship, and that a breakdown in a shared, higher good leads to a loss of friendship.[30]

To engage the practice of friendship more fully, especially in relation to the academy, I turn to Samuel Kimbriel. In *Friendship as Sacred Knowing: Overcoming Isolation*, Kimbriel argues that wisdom requires friendship. His analysis follows a "particularly Christian philosophical habit—'the befriending of wisdom'—in which understanding [is] taken to be a kind of communion."[31] As we will see, for Kimbriel, friendship is far more than personal preference. It has the widest possible scope: it is a "cosmic phenomenon."[32]

In order to develop how friendship is sacred knowing, Kimbriel extends Charles Taylor's use of the "porous" self in contrast to the "disengaged" self.[33] The disengaged self is not simply purely rational but occupies a certain "stance" in relation to reality. At the heart of this stance, says Kimbriel, is the way that "meaning" or "reason" has "migrated from its prior residence in the furniture or the cosmos to reside almost exclusively *within* the human person."[34] For Descartes, and Cartesianism more broadly, this inwardness "becomes radically severed from the cosmic ontic logos."[35] By "cosmic ontic logos," Kimbriel means that order and communion are constitutive of all being. The disengaged self imagines that one can sever bonds with others and with the cosmos in order to be truly rational. As such, the "longings of friendship can no longer be seen as sharing in a broader reality."[36] The porous self, by contrast, sees bonds to others and to the cosmos not as restrictions but as ways of knowing and of befriending wisdom.

---

30. Pecknold, "Political by Nature."

31. Kimbriel, *Friendship as Sacred Knowing*, 1.

32. Kimbriel, *Friendship as Sacred Knowing*, 4.

33. Taylor uses these terms to characterize the modern self's assumption that genuine knowledge and meaning are no longer part of the furniture of the cosmos in which one participates; these come rather through disengagement.

34. Kimbriel, *Friendship as Sacred Knowing*, 11.

35. Kimbriel, *Friendship as Sacred Knowing*, 16. Describing Taylor's analysis, Kimbriel states that "the Cartesian rational philosopher must rather reject natural spontaneous connection outside the mind by disengaging from all external physical objects including, most importantly, one's own body." Kimbriel, *Friendship as Sacred Knowing*, 15.

36. Kimbriel, *Friendship as Sacred Knowing*, 22.

Kimbriel particularly engages the thought of John the Evangelist, Augustine, and Aquinas to develop an understanding of being as porous, a reality he ultimately relates to the triune God. "In the Son's befriending love, the community is caught up into the love of the Father and Son, a love which then shines forth in one's own activity of love." To be caught up into such friendship is to be "caught up ever more deeply into Truth."[37] Whereas the disengaged self believes he can acquire knowledge on his own through self-mastery, the porous self receives knowing as always a gift of communion (friendship) with God and others. According to Kimbriel, the deficiency of the disengaged self is that its rationality undermines its own true being, a being embedded in a cosmic love. The porous enquirer, by contrast, takes up a "stance" of learning that acknowledges that being itself is already a reception of Divine Love. "Loving and knowing become identified precisely because the deepest contours of reality are those defined by divine love, whether that be within God himself or as displayed in creation."[38] To see the difference between a porous and a disengaged stance is to see the necessity of friendship as sacred knowing.

Following in the tradition of Aristotle, Kimbriel emphasizes that such friendship is a political project.[39] True friendships establish "an ever truer form of human community." This form depends on the fact that the "loving action of Christ, who is the first friend, is shared with human community more broadly; befriending love begets ever more love."[40] The politics of this friendship shaped ultimately by the economy of Divine love is an alternative to the politics of the disengaged self that severs friendship from knowing. Kimbriel states about this latter politics, that "contrary to its own story about itself, it is, in fact, fundamentally *irrational* in constitution."[41]

Some might object that Kimbriel's understanding of friendship as a political project is too explicitly Christian and therefore exclusive. Yet to see being as porous is to see that communion lies at the heart of knowing. As such, friendship as sacred knowing overcomes the deep isolation and fragmentation that easily mark the modern academy. From this understanding,

37. Kimbriel, *Friendship as Sacred Knowing*, 171.

38. Kimbriel, *Friendship as Sacred Knowing*, 5.

39. Similarly, MacIntyre discusses how from an Aristotelian understanding of friendship "a modern liberal political society can appear only as a collection of citizens of nowhere who have banded together for their common protection." MacIntyre, *After Virtue*, 156.

40. Kimbriel, *Friendship as Sacred Knowing*, 172.

41. Kimbriel, *Friendship as Sacred Knowing*, 169.

it is the stance of disengagement that is exclusive in that it requires detachment from others and from the world.

Kimbriel engages an imaginary interlocutor who challenges him to offer evidence that knowing does not begin from a place of isolation. The challenge, Kimbriel notes, is not innocent but rather reveals the deep contrast between the two stances. For the "disengaged self" who assumes isolation is more fundamental, the "specificity of one's basic disposition to reality is a major problem . . . since it undoes its claim to impartiality . . . ."[42] In other words, for the disengaged self, partiality is a problem as it undermines one's assumptions of knowing and reasoning. This lack of full rationality thus brings the fear of relativism. Kimbriel notes that for the "porous self," however, the lack of full rationality "brings instead a longing for deeper participation in that which is most real."[43] Seen in the light of this cosmic longing,

> [r]elativism is thereby revealed to be not a universal problem afflicting all sensibilities, but rather a local difficulty threatening those who pin their notion of rationality to the standards of the thinking subject in this fashion. The porous stance, at this point, looks where it always has, namely to gift, since inasmuch as the soul is properly ordered to reality, it is always so ordered as a result of the donation of the broader economy of order in which it is embedded.[44]

According to Kimbriel, one can never actually slip the bonds of this broader economy since the "logic of cosmic love" is constitutive of all created being. This love reaches even into the depth of our being where, as Augustine emphasizes, the Inner Teacher (Friend) is present. As Kimbriel observes, Augustine thinks is it impossible for humanity to exist in any kind of "autonomous or 'self-constituted' fashion apart from God."[45] More fully, "the 'love with which we love' is a manifestation of God's own presence with us."[46] Thus Augustine's analysis of the operation of human understanding "relies heavily on the idea that *not all that is interior is one's own*."[47] To say

42. Kimbriel, *Friendship as Sacred Knowing*, 165.

43. Kimbriel, *Friendship as Sacred Knowing*, 165–66.

44. Kimbriel, *Friendship as Sacred Knowing*, 166.

45. Kimbriel, *Friendship as Sacred Knowing*, 81.

46. Kimbriel, *Friendship as Sacred Knowing*, 83.

47. Kimbriel, *Friendship as Sacred Knowing*, 81. Emphasis in original. Henry helpfully notes how Kimbriel at this point departs from Taylor in his interpretation of Augustine.

not all that is interior is one's own is to acknowledge that one has received even what is interior as gift. That this is true makes friendship essential to knowing and being.

I have only briefly engaged Kimbriel's wide-ranging analysis. Even so, we can note at this point how his argument sheds light on leisure in the academy. The modern disengaged academy is in many ways an image of the isolated self writ large. Kimbriel describes how such disengagement undermines the truth of the community of knowers as porous toward love and wisdom. Even in the their ignorance, however, the Inner Teacher haunts human souls for whom to "exist at all is to exist as a moment in a broader movement of love . . . ."[48] To live into this movement through friendship is to become porous to a Divine Wisdom that desires to befriend us. So understood, Kimbriel's account of friendship as sacred knowing is an extension of leisure. As we saw, Pieper identifies the deepest springs by which leisure is fed as divine worship. These springs make leisure possible by enabling a person or an institution to receive its being as gift and communion (friendship) with God. To say leisure is the basis of academic culture is to see the necessity of friendship as the way to Wisdom.

Broken friendship: ecclesial disunity and the loss of academic leisure

Kimbriel's account of friendship as a political project helps make sense of the connection between ecclesial disunity and the academy's loss of leisure. Both Brad Gregory and James Burtchaell give some attention to how division in the church—what I am calling a loss of ecclesial friendship—has contributed to the disengaged academy. Stated differently, a crisis in friendship (the term Pecknold uses to describe modernity) has made it more difficult for the academy to see how leisure is the basis of its culture. This reality suggests that recovering ecclesial friendship is crucial for a renewal of academic leisure.

In his discussion of "secularizing knowledge," Gregory argues that following the reformation Catholic and Protestant theologians turned their

---

Taylor "identifies Augustine's inward turn as anticipatory of Descartes' hyper-isolated *cogito ergo sum*," while for Kimbriel, Augustine's enquiry undermines such disengagement, in Henry, "Review," 414. I am deeply appreciative to Henry for bringing Kimbriel's book to my attention.

48. Kimbriel, *Friendship as Sacred Knowing*, 168.

time and attention to doctrinal controversies in order to refute their opponents. Such efforts, he argues, had the effect of isolating scholars from engaging new kinds of research and knowledge. Thus "in expounding orthodoxy, safeguarding souls, battling opponents and essentially abandoning theology's aspiration to integrate any and all truth about God and creation, Lutheran, Reformed, and Catholic theologians were living in an ever more vulnerable refuge."[49] The vulnerability had to do with a growing separation between theology and the rest of knowledge. "The longer that rulers championed rival doctrines in their universities and shielded theologians, the less prepared would the latter eventually be to answer questions about how their respective Christian truth claims might fit together with the ever-growing mass of new knowledge being made elsewhere."[50] By the nineteenth century, theology either became one more discipline among others in the marketplace of ideas, or it became irrelevant in the modern research university. Gregory thus states, "With theology banished from knowledge-making in research universities on both sides of the Atlantic, no successor enterprise sought to understand how knowledge in all disciplines might fit together."[51] According to Gregory, then, a key cause of secularized knowledge in the university today had to do with how ecclesial division distracted the academy from attending to how various knowledges might relate to a wider whole.

Gregory embeds his analysis in a wider thesis that is as controversial as it is intriguing: the Reformation had untended consequences, chief of which is a secularization in which the turn to reason alone (following Scripture alone) gave way to an irresolvable pluralism, a reality that shapes both Protestants and Catholics today. Gregory does trace secularized

---

49. Gregory, *The Unintended Reformation*, 332. Gregory is here describing the sixteenth to seventeenth centuries.

50. Gregory, *The Unintended Reformation*, 339.

51. Gregory, *The Unintended Reformation*, 358. Gregory notes how the academic disciplines' secularized and specialized knowledge "catered to the self-determined desire of dechristianized, Humean individuals . . . [and to] the political protection of the individual right of autonomous consumer to construct themselves as they please amid wall-to-Walmart, post-Fordist capitalism . . . ." Gregory, *The Unintended Reformation*, 364. Gregory concludes that such compartmentalized lives "not only are idolatrously antithetical to Catholicism but are bound to erode the experiential knowledge acquired in its communities of faith, and thereby to render Catholicism's truth claims implausible, objectionable, and/or seemingly irrelevant . . . ." Gregory, *The Unintended Reformation*, 363–64.

knowledge to pre-Reformation time.[52] He acknowledges, for example, that "the assumptions of metaphysical univocity and Occam's razor" shaped the "methodological naturalism and evidentiary empiricism" of secular knowledge.[53] Gregory argues, however, that Reformation figures exacerbated this theological mistake.[54] Whether or not it is entirely fair to attribute secularized knowledge mostly to the Protestant Reformation is beyond the scope of my analysis.[55] Significant, for my purposes, is Gregory's attention to how the church's disunity coincides with academic fragmentation.

While Burtchaell's analysis of the academy differs in significant ways from Gregory, Burtchaell too sees ecclesial disunity as crippling in its impact. Burtchaell, for his part, focuses on pietism, stating that while pietism began as a renewal movement in response to a dry orthodoxy, it ultimately lacked the resources to sustain the life of the mind. As Burtchaell puts it, pietism came to propound "the primacy of spirit over letter, commitment over institution, affect over intellect, laity over clergy, invisible church over visible . . . ." Burtchaell acknowledges that the Pietists' return to origins indicated a strong ecumenism, however it "could not maintain itself; in a second generation, its adherents often knew nothing or little of tradition."[56]

52. William Cavanaugh observes that Gregory's thesis is controversial not because he argues that the Reformation birthed modernity or that pluralism in Christianity led to Western pluralism, all of which he notes is widely recognized. It is controversial, says Cavanaugh, because for Gregory this trajectory is "on the whole, a bad thing." Cavanaugh, "The Modest Claim," 409.

53. Gregory, *The Unintended Reformation*, 358.

54. Gregory, *The Unintended Reformation*, 358. He criticizes, for example, Zwingli's "spatial dichotomizing of Jesus's divine and human natures . . . ." Gregory, *The Unintended Reformation*, 42–43.

55. In my view, Gregory's analysis at times lays too much at the feet of the Reformation, as if Protestants, for example, in contrast to Catholics had no conception of being a moral community (340), or as if it is in "Reformation-era fashion" simply to resort to power (342). In Cavanaugh's largely positive review of *The Unintended Reformation*, he observes that "in emphasizing the doctrinal origins of the problems of modernity, Gregory sometimes overplays his hand." Cavanaugh, "The Modest Claim," 409.

56. Burtchaell, *The Dying of the Light*, 841. Burtchaell briefly relates this pietism to the Reformation by describing "the radical disjunction between divine knowledge and human knowledge [which] had been central to classical Reformation thinking . . . . The older, pre-Reformation view, that faith was goaded by revelation to seek further understanding, and that learning itself could be an act of piety—indeed, the form of piety proper to a college or university—succumbed to the view that worship and moral behavior were to be the defining acts of a Christian academic fellowship. Later, worship and moral behavior were easily set aside because no one could imagine they had anything to do with learning." Burtchaell, *The Dying of the Light*, 842.

According to Burtchaell, pietism devolved in two different but related ways: liberal piety and rationalism. On the one hand, those "determined to persevere as Christians developed a liberal piety whose wisdom had to be framed so broadly as to lack all depth . . . ." On the other hand, in the face of irresolvable theological quarrels, pietism devolved into rationalism: "fast on the tracks of Pietism came rationalism . . . . [The] direct disciples of the Pietists were the liberals, whose reductive pieties were a midway stage between Pietism and Rationalism."[57] The kinship between pietism and rationalism can be found in the turn away from confessional particularities, now interpreted as "sectarian" and "dogmatic."[58]

Burtchaell observes that the effects of pietism and rationalism have been as evident in Catholic colleges and universities as they have in Protestant ones. For example, Burtchaell cites Sr. Alice Galling, OSU, former executive secretary of the Association of Catholic Colleges and Universities, who argued that "faith has no business sponsoring education." She explained, "My theological understanding of faith . . . is that it is a gift from the Lord which enables us to say 'I believe.' . . . I do not see how it can be the ground for the institution's existence. I think, on the contrary, that the only legitimate goal of a college or university is an 'educational' purpose . . . ."[59] The division between belief and knowledge replicates a pietistic separation between inner faith and outward tradition. For such Catholic pietism, as Burtchaell notes, the church cannot "rightly sponsor—or even endure—disciplined, principled inquiry."[60]

Significantly, for my purposes, Burtchaell emphasizes that this devolution from pietism (turning inward) to rationalism (abandoning the church) "arose first within the churches [both Catholic and Protestant], not within the colleges."[61] Nowhere was this more evident, notes Burtchaell, than in the inability of church leaders to move beyond a dichotomy between faith and knowledge. Many either distrusted scholarship and advanced learning *or* uncritically accepted modern naturalism. Like Gregory, then, Burtchaell argues that ecclesial division has contributed to the "secularizing" of knowledge and the academy.

57. Burtchaell, *The Dying of the Light*, 463.

58. Burtchaell, *The Dying of the Light*, 463.

59. Cited in Burtchaell, *The Dying of the Light*, 831–832, and 713.

60. Burtchaell, *The Dying of the Light*, 832.

61. Burtchaell, *The Dying of the Light*, 847.

If Burtchaell and Gregory are at least partly right in relating a diminished academic being and knowing to pietism (for Burtchaell) or to the Reformation (for Gregory), then is their solution somehow to go back to pre-Reformation ways of being and thinking? Both scholars reject this. In his conclusion "Against Nostalgia," Gregory argues against a supercessionist reading of history. He acknowledges the many goods that have come with modernity but challenges the standard narrative that moves from the medieval darkness of dogma and tradition to the modern light of freedom and pluralism. Gregory's turn away from nostalgia, however, appears most fully when he attends specifically to metaphysical assumptions: "Unsecularizing the academy would require, of course, an intellectual openness on the part of scholars and scientists sufficient to end the long-standing modern charade in which naturalism has been assumed to be demonstrated, evident, self-evident, ideologically neutral . . . . It would require all academics . . . to acknowledge their metaphysical beliefs as beliefs . . . ."[62] Seeing the secularization of knowledge as an "historically contingent process" frees one to imagine more truthful alternatives.

Burtchaell, for his part, claims to offer no remedy for a disengaged academy but he does turn, if only briefly, in an ecumenical direction. Thus authentic ecumenism, he states, "discovers wholesome elements of Christian faith or piety in another communion, admits their authenticity, and takes them as incentives to emulation and self-renewal. Authentic reform is the rediscovery of wholesome elements in a church's past which have been lost, and takes them as cues for renewal."[63] For Burtchaell, academic renewal calls for an ecumenical effort by discovering how healing elements within different traditions might renew the whole.

As helpful as Burtchaell's recovery of wholesome elements is, this renewal, I would emphasize, needs to be embedded in a rich political and theological understanding of friendship, such as the one Kimbriel offers. That is, such renewal is not only about discovering elements in another

---

62. Gregory, *Unintended Reformation*, 386. Gregory acknowledges that any challenge to current academic socialization is sure to be resisted. "Subversive ideas and unsettling research that threaten seemingly settled foundational assumptions are just as likely to be welcomed now as they were in the late Middle Ages—that is, not at all." While I appreciate Gregory's diagnosis, it is not clear to me how honesty about one's own convictions and metaphysical beliefs is able to resolve what Gregory sees as the key problem. Honesty about metaphysical beliefs could easily be absorbed into the normativity of pluralism and thus be subject to the same kind of "consumeristic" ways of being that Gregory criticizes in his book.

63. Burtchaell, *The Dying of Light*, 847.

communion and taking them as incentives for self-renewal; it is also more fully about being open to being drawn into communion with others through Divine Wisdom even in the midst of brokenness. Through our failure and brokenness, as Weil emphasizes, we learn humility and love. And humility and love are virtues that restore academic leisure, both as a specific practice (prayer) and way of being (contemplative receptivity and generous activity). And the renewal of leisure strengthens friendship by rooting it more fully in a shared reception of the gifts that God desires to give and that are, in a sense, already present.[64] If love and knowledge reciprocally nourish one another, as Kimbriel along with Augustine, Aquinas, and St. John the Evangelist claim, then friendship across ecclesial division becomes a key way of realizing divine abundance in the academy and moving toward leisure as its true basis.[65]

The love of learning and the desire for God

To say leisure is the basis of academic culture is another way of saying that the love of learning and the desire for God cannot be separated. In Jean Leclercq's classical study of monastic culture, he describes how "education is not separated from spiritual effort."[66] "There is no Benedictine life without literature,"[67] and "the monastery is truly a 'school for the service of the Lord'—*dominici schola servitii*."[68] Thus, he states that "the knowledge of

64. As Brian Daley, SJ, notes, though unity "is hindered or clouded by our sinfulness and 'slowness of heart' (Luke 24:25)," it nonetheless "already exists among us as God's gift." Daley, "Rebuilding," 74.

65. Benedict XVI likewise describes a "wonderful circle in which love and knowledge reciprocally nourish one another." Benedict XVI, *A Reason Open*, 95. The context of this quotation is Benedict's reflection on Teresa of Avila whose writings (particularly about her experience before a crucifix) seem to ask us: "How can we remain indifferent to such love? How can we ignore him who has loved us with such great mercy?" Benedict XVI, *A Reason Open*, 95. The love of God merits the attention of our hearts and minds and thus can activate this "wonderful circle" of knowledge and love. Benedict's position implies that failures in loving are also failures in knowing. One cannot therefore say, for example, "we do not *need* the 'weaker' sister." Such a posture relies on a view of the self or academy as disengaged rather than porous.

66. Leclercq, *The Love of Learning*, 18.

67. Leclercq, *The Love of Learning*, 17

68. Leclercq, *The Love of Learning*, 18. Leclercq summarizes: "The whole organization of monastic life is dominated by the solicitude for safeguarding a certain spiritual *leisure*, a certain freedom in the interest of prayer in all its forms, and, above all, authentic

letters and the search for God"[69] are two fundamental elements of the same quest. This quest gave birth to the university, a fact that amplifies how their quest for God drew them *toward* learning, study, and teaching.

But of what relevance is this monastic culture today? One can hardly expect a turning back the clock or a retreat to some pre-modern sphere. In a talk given in 2008 at the Collège des Bernardins, Pope Benedict XVI specifically engages the question of whether or not monasticism still has "something to say to us today, or are we merely encountering the world of the past?"[70] He responds by saying that it was not the monastic intention "to create a culture nor even to preserve a culture from the past. Their motivation was much more basic. Their goal was: *quaerere Deum* [to seek God]."[71] In seeking God, they were not left in the dark. Even in the midst of the confusion of the times, Benedict states, they had "signposts" to follow disclosed in the book of sacred Scriptures. They understood that the "word must not only be pondered but also correctly read." This was no individualistic task but required the communion of others, and ultimately of God. The Word, Benedict emphasizes, thus brings one into conversation with others and most fully with God. Significant for my purposes, Benedict states that "by inner necessity, the search for God demands a culture of the word . . ." As a part of this culture, the monks built libraries and schools and searched for God in "secular sciences."[72]

Benedict describes this as ultimately a christological understanding of culture. Citing John 1:14 ("the word became flesh"), he states that "amid what is made (factum) there is now Logos, Logos is among us." Education became a way of learning "to perceive, in the midst of words, the Word itself."[73] Benedict concludes, "A purely positivistic culture which tried to drive the question concerning God into the subjective realm, as being unscientific, would be the capitulation of reason, the renunciation of its highest possibilities, and hence a disaster for humanity, with very grave

---

contemplative peace." Leclercq, *The Love of Learning*, 19. My emphasis.

69. Leclercq, *The Love of Learning*, 13. Leclercq is referring specifically to St. Benedict.

70. Benedict XVI, "Address of His Holiness." Benedict begins his talk by reminding his audience (many of whom were cultural leaders of France) that they are in an historic place tied to monastic culture, built by "the spiritual sons" of Saint Bernard of Clairvaux.

71. Benedict XVI, "Address of His Holiness."

72. Benedict XVI, "Address of His Holiness."

73. Benedict XVI, "Address of His Holiness." The Pope uses the Latin: *Verbum caro factum est* (John 1:14).

consequences. What gave Europe's culture its foundation—the search for God and the readiness to listen to him—remains today the basis of any genuine culture."[74] According to Benedict, monasticism helps one see that sequestering the Divine Logos to a subjective realm is irrational. True rationality entails a willingness to listen and receive the Logos present in one's place and time, and indeed in all creation. This seeking is eschatological but not in the sense of being otherworldly. Rather the Logos is already present even as one recognizes a mysterious fullness yet to come.

Leclercq rightly emphasizes that the love of learning and the desire for God have "no one simple solution which has been devised once and for all and need only be applied in conformity with a legislative rule." The seamlessness between the love of learning and the desire for God "must be continually rediscovered, re-invented, rejuvenated in a living and spontaneous manner, for each period and each milieu . . . ."[75] Leclercq thus describes a fluidity associated with the *ratio studiorum* or plan of studies; it could take different shapes and diverse forms. While Leclercq is describing a monastic culture, his words speak to our context as well. In any place and time, the love of learning and the desire for God must continually be rediscovered and rejuvenated. As I have argued, it will be characterized by certain flexible virtues and practices: "paying attention" as a way to overcome a separation between prayer and study, and friendship as a political project oriented toward a shared good. Above all, the love of learning and desire for God will rest in leisure as a practice and way of being that reconfigures time and space.

Rightly understood, the challenge today is not how to get God back into the academy. It is rather how to become persons capable of seeking and listening to God in all places. This would be an impossible task if it were not for the gift of friendship, most fully the Friendship of God. Such Divine Friendship, as we have seen, is not intended to reduce God to a buddy or a pastime. Rather Divine Friendship identifies how God, the source of all that is, desires communion with all of creation. It is only in light of this cosmic logic that leisure as the basis of academic culture makes sense. Such Divine Abundance opens the academy up to a Mystery so rich, so illuminating, and so profound that it exceeds human understanding even as it is the beginning of wisdom.

---

74. Benedict XVI, "Address of His Holiness."
75. Leclercq, *The Love of Learning*, 22.

BIBLIOGRAPHY

Alexander, Christopher. *The Nature of Order: An Essay on the Art of Building and the Nature of the Universe*, Vol. 1. NY: Routledge, 2004.

Anderson, Benedict. *Imagined Communities: Reflections on the Origin and Spread of Nationalism*. New York: Verso, 1983.

Arendt, Hannah. *The Human Condition*. Chicago: University of Chicago Press, 1958.

Aquinas, Thomas. *Summa Theologica*. Translated by the Fathers of the English Dominican Province. Benziger Bros. ed. Westminster: Christian Classics, 1947. http://www.ccel.org/ccel/aquinas/summa.html.

Asad, Talal. *Formations of the Secular: Christianity, Islam, Modernity*. Stanford, CA: Stanford University Press, 2003.

——. *Genealogies of Religion: Discipline and Reasons of Power in Christianity and Islam*. Baltimore: John Hopkins University Press, 1993.

Augustine. *The Confessions*. Translated by Maria Boulding. Hyde Park, NY: New York City Press, 1997.

Balthasar, Hans Urs von. "Introduction." In *The Scandal of the Incarnation, Irenaeus Against the Heresies,* by Irenaeus, 1–11. San Francisco: Ignatius, 1990.

Baptist World Alliance Delegation for Theological Conversations with the Pontifical Council for Promoting Christian Unity. "Baptists and Catholics Together: The Word of God in the Life of the Church." *American Baptist Quarterly* 31 (2012) 28–122.

Barron, Robert. *The Priority of Christ: Toward a Postliberal Catholicism*. Grand Rapids: Brazos, 2007.

Barth, Karl. *The Doctrine of Reconciliation*. Vol. 4 of *Church Dogmatics*. Edited by G. W. Bromiley and T. F. Torrance. New York: T & T Clark, 1956.

——. "Fifteen Answers to Professor von Harnack." In *The Beginnings of Dialectic Theology,* edited by James M. Robinson, 167–70. Richmond, VA: John Knox, 1968.

Battersby, Christine. *The Phenomenal Woman: Feminist Metaphysics and the Patterns of Identity*. New York: John Wiley and Sons, 2016.

Bauerschmidt, Frederick C. *Holy Teaching: Introducing the Summa Theologiae of St. Thomas Aquinas*. Grand Rapids: Brazos, 2005.

Baxter, Michael J. "Review Symposium, Dennis M. Doyle's *Communion Ecclesiology*." *Horizons* 29 (2002) 331–34.

Benedict XVI. "Address of His Holiness Benedict XVI." Collège des Bernardins. September 12, 2008. https://w2.vatican.va/content/benedict-xvi/en/speeches/2008/september/documents/hf_ben-xvi_spe_20080912_parigi-cultura.html.

————. *A Reason Open to God: On Universities, Education and Culture.* Washington, DC: The Catholic University of America, 2013.

————. *The Unity of the Church.* Grand Rapids, MI: Eerdmans, 2010.

Berkman, John. "Poteat Changed My Life." *Tradition and Discovery* 36 (2009–2010) 64–66.

Berry, Wendell. *Life is a Miracle: An Essay Against Modern Superstition.* Washington, DC: Counterpoint, 2001.

————. *Sex, Economy, Freedom and Community.* New York: Pantheon, 1994.

Bockmuehl, Markus. "Hope and Optimism in Straitened Times." *Pro Ecclesia* 21 (2012) 7–24.

Bretherton, Luke. "Religious Vandalism or Interfaith Hospitality? Reflections on the Non-Proclamation of the 'Adhan' from Duke Chapel." January 17, 2015. http://www.abc.net.au/religion/articles/2015/01/17/4163809.htm.

Brownson, James V., et al. *StormFront: The Good News of God.* Grand Rapids: Eerdmans, 2003.

Brumley, Jeff. "After initial skepticism, online theological education growing." *Baptist News Global.* January 31, 2014. https://baptistnews.com/article/online-theological-education-growing-4.

Burrell, David B. *Faith and Freedom: An Interfaith Perspective.* Malden, MA: Blackwell, 2004.

————. *Freedom and Creation in Three Traditions.* Notre Dame, IN: University of Notre Dame Press, 1993

Burtchaell, James T. *The Dying of the Light: The Disengagement of Colleges and Universities from Their Christian Churches.* Grand Rapids: Eerdmans, 1998.

Byerly, Meghan. "The Virtuous Community: Collective Virtue and the Christian Community." MDiv thesis, Baptist Theological Seminary at Richmond, 2015.

Caldecott, Stratford. *Beauty for Truth's Sake: The Re-enchantment of Education.* Grand Rapids: Brazos, 2009.

————. *The Radiance of Being: Dimensions of Cosmic Christianity.* Tacoma, WA: Angelico, 2013.

Canon, Dale. "Haven't You Noticed that Modernity Is Bankrupt? Ruminations on the Teaching Career of William H. Poteat." *Tradition and Discovery* 21 (1994–95) 20–32.

Carroll, Anthony J. "Disenchantment, Rationality and the Modernity of Max Weber." *Forum Philosophicum* 16 (2011) 117–37.

Cavanaugh, William T. "The Modest Claim of an Immodest Book." *Pro Ecclesia* 22 (2013) 406–12.

————. *The Myth of Religious Violence.* New York: Oxford University Press, 2009.

————. "A Politics of Vulnerability: Hauerwas and Democracy." In *Unsettling Arguments*, edited by Charles R. Pinches et al., 89–111. Eugene, OR: Cascade, 2010.

Cayley, David. *George Grant in Conversation.* Ontario: Anansi, 1995.

Coles, Romand, and Stanley Hauerwas. *Christianity, Democracy, and the Radical Ordinary: Conversations Between a Radical Democrat and a Christian.* Eugene, OR: Cascade, 2008.

Coughlan, Neil. Review of *The Dying of the Light*, by James Burtchaell. *Commonweal* 126 (1999) 19–21.

Daley, Brian. "Rebuilding the Structure of Love: The Quest for Visible Unity Among the Churches." In *The Ecumenical Future,* edited by Carl E. Braaten and Robert W. Jenson, 73–105. Grand Rapids: Eerdmans, 2004.

Bibliography

Dosen, Anthony. *Catholic Higher Education in the 1960s: Issues of Identity, Issues of Governance*. Charlotte, NC: Information Age, 2009.

English, Adam. "The New Academic Freedom and the Changing Face of Baptist Higher Education." In *The Scholarly Vocation and the Baptist Academy*, edited by Roger Ward and David Gushee, 68–86. Macon, GA: Mercer University, 2008.

Evans, Gillian Rosemary. *The Medieval Theologians*. Oxford: Blackwell, 2008.

Farley, Edward. *Theologia: The Fragmentation and Unity of Theological Education*. Eugene, OR: Wipf & Stock, 2001.

Fish, Stanley. "Boutique Multiculturalism, or Why Liberals Are Incapable of Thinking about Hate Speech." *Critical Inquiry* 23 (1997) 378–95.

———. "Why We Can't All Just Get Along." *First Things*, February 1996. https://www.firstthings.com/article/1996/02/001-why-we-cant-all-just-get-along.

Fitzgerald, Timothy. *Discourse on Civility and Barbarity: A Critical History of Religion and Related Categories*. New York: Oxford University Press, 2007.

———. *The Ideology of Religious Studies*. New York: Oxford University Press, 2000.

Foley, Michael P. "Thomas Aquinas' Novel Modesty." *History of Political Thought* 25 (2004) 402–23.

Frei, Hans. *Types of Christian Theology*. Edited by George Hunsinger and William C. Placher. New Haven, CT: Yale University Press, 2001.

Giddens, Anthony. *The Consequences of Modernity*. Stanford, CA: Stanford University, 1990.

Giussani, Luigi. *The Risk of Education: Discovering Our Ultimate Destiny*. Spring Valley, NY: Crossroad, 2001.

Gleason, Philip. *Contending with Modernity: Catholic Higher Education in the Twentieth Century*. New York: Oxford University Press, 1995.

Graham, David A. "For Whom the Muezzim Calls." *The Atlantic*, January 15, 2015. http://www.theatlantic.com/politics/archive/2015/01/for-whom-the-muezzim-calls-duke-muslim-call-prayer/384562/.

Grant, George. "The Paradox of Democratic Education." In *Collected Works of George Grant: Volume 2 (1951–1959)*, edited by Davis Arthur, 166–81. Toronto: University of Toronto Press, 2002.

———. *Technology and Empire: Perspective on North America*. Toronto: House of Anasi, 1969.

———. *Technology and Justice*. Notre Dame, IN: University of Notre Dame Press, 1986.

Green, Clifford J., ed. *Karl Barth: Theologian of Freedom*. Minneapolis: Fortress, 1989.

Gregory, Brad S. *The Unintended Reformation: How a Religious Revolution Secularized Society*. Cambridge, MA: Belknap Press of Harvard University Press, 2012.

Griffiths, Paul. *Intellectual Appetites: A Theological Grammar*. Washington, DC: The Catholic University of America Press, 2009.

———. Lecture, personal correspondence.

———. "The Vice of Curiosity." *Pro Ecclesia* 15 (2006) 47–63.

Hall, Randal L. *William Louis Poteat: A Leader of the Progressive-Era South*. Lexington, KY: University of Kentucky, 2000.

Hanby, Michael. "Creation and Aesthetic Analogy." In *The Analogy of Being: Invention of the Antichrist or the Wisdom of God?*, edited by Thomas Joseph White, 341–78. Grand Rapids: Eerdmans, 2011.

Harnack, Adolf von. "Fifteen Questions to Those Among the Theologians Who Are Contemptuous of the Scientific Theology." In *The Beginnings of Dialectic Theology*, edited by James M. Robinson, 165–66. Richmond, VA: John Knox, 1968.

———. *What is Christianity? Lectures Delivered in the University of Berlin during the Winter-Terms, 1899–1900*. New York: G. P. Putnam's Sons, 1903.

Harrison, Carol. "Augustine and the Art of Music." In *Resonant Witness: Conversations between Music and Theology*, edited by Jeremy S. Begbie and Steven R. Guthrie, 27–45. Grand Rapids: Eerdmans, 2011.

Hart, David Bentley. *Atheist Delusions: The Christian Revolution and Its Fashionable Enemies*. New Haven, CT: Yale University Press, 2009.

———. *The Beauty of the Infinite: The Aesthetics of Christian Faith*. Grand Rapids: Eerdmans, 2004.

———. "The Destiny of Christian Metaphysics." In *The Analogy of Being: Invention of the Antichrist or the Wisdom of God?*, edited by Thomas Joseph White, 395–410. Grand Rapids: Eerdmans, 2011.

———. "Review Essay of Catherine Pickstock, *After Writing: On the Liturgical Consummation of Philosophy*." *Pro Ecclesia* 9 (2000) 367–72.

Hauerwas, Stanley. *A Better Hope: Resources for a Church Confronting Capitalism, Democracy, and Modernity*. Grand Rapids: Baker Academic, 2000.

———. "Missing from the Curriculum." *Commonweal* (September, 1994) 1–5.

———. "Murdochian Muddles: Can We Get Through Them If God Does Not Exist?" In *Iris Murdoch and the Search for Human Goodness*, edited by Maria Antonaccio and William Schweiker, 190–208. Chicago: University of Chicago Press, 1996.

———. *Sanctify Them in the Truth: Holiness Exemplified*. Nashville: Abingdon, 1998.

———. *The State of the University: Academic Knowledges and the Knowledge of God*. Malden, MA: Blackwell, 2007.

———. "The Virtues of Alasdair MacIntyre." *First Things*, October 2007. http://www.first things.com/article/2007/10/004-the-virtues-of-alasdair-macintyre.

———. *With the Grain of the Universe: The Church's Witness and Natural Theology: Being the Gifford Lectures Delivered at the University of St. Andrews in 2001*. Grand Rapids: Brazos, 2001.

Hays, Richard B. "Letter to Members and Friends of the Duke Divinity School Community." January 15, 2015. https://www.washingtonpost.com/news/grade-point/wp-content/uploads/sites/42/2015/01/Duke-Chapel-Decision-1.15.15.pdf.

Hearn, Thomas. "To Dream with One Eye Open, A Ten-Year Report to the University: 1983–1993." Winston-Salem, NC: Wake Forest University, 1993.

———. Unpublished Speech. North Carolina Baptist State Convention, November 14, 1989. Archived in WFU Presidents' Papers, Thomas K. Hearn, Jr. Z. Smith Reynolds Library, Special Collection and Archives, Wake Forest University, Winston-Salem, NC.

Hearne, Vicki. *Adam's Task: Calling Animals by Name*. New York: Skyhorse, 2007.

Hebert, L. Joseph., Jr. "Be Still and See: Leisure, Labor, and Human Dignity in Josef Pieper and Blessed John Paul II." *Logos* 16 (2013) 144–59.

Henry, Douglas V. Review of *Friendship as Sacred Knowing: Overcoming Isolation* by Samuel Kimbriel. *Christian Scholar's Review* 44 (2015) 412–14.

Hesburgh, Theodore M., ed. *The Challenge and Promise of a Catholic University*. Notre Dame, IN: University of Notre Dame Press, 1994.

———. *God, Country, Notre Dame.* Notre Dame, IN: University of Notre Dame Press, 1999.

Hibbs, Thomas S. "In the Wake of the Enlightenment: The Catholic Church and Political Theory." In *Gladly to Learn and Gladly to Teach: Essays on Religion and Political Philosophy in Honor of Ernest L. Fortin, A.A.*, edited by Michael P. Foley and Douglas Kries, 95–108. New York: Lexington, 2002.

Inazu, John D. *Confident Pluralism: Surviving and Thriving Through Deep Difference.* Chicago: University of Chicago Press, 2016.

———. "How Confident is Our Pluralism? A Conversation with Professor John Inazu." Interview with Al Mohler. *Thinking in Public* podcast, October 17, 2016.

Ingham, Mary Beth, and Mechthild Dreyer. *The Philosophical Vision of John Duns Scotus.* Washington, DC: Catholic University of America Press, 2004.

Irenaeus. *The Scandal of the Incarnation: Irenaeus Against the Heresies.* San Francisco: Ignatius, 1990.

Jardine, Murray. *The Making and Unmaking of Technological Society: How Christianity Can Save Modernity from Itself.* Grand Rapids: Brazos, 2004.

Jaspers, Karl. *Kant.* New York: Harcourt Brace Jovanovich, 1957.

Jenson, Robert W. "Karl Barth." In *The Modern Theologians*, edited by David F. Ford, 21–36. Cambridge, MA: Blackwell, 1997.

Johnson, Henry C., Jr. "'Down from the Mountain': Secularization and the Higher Learning in America." *The Review of Politics* 54 (1992) 551–88.

Kant, Immanuel. *The Conflict of the Faculties.* Translated by Mary J. Gregor. Lincoln, NE: University of Nebraska Press, 1979.

———. *Critique of Pure Reason.* In *The Critique of Pure Reason; The Critique of Practical Reason, and Other Ethical Treatises; The Critique of Judgment*, translated by J. M. D. Meiklejohn, et al. 2nd ed. Chicago: Encyclopedia Britannica, 1990.

———. "On a Newly Arisen Superior Tone in Philosophy." In *Raising the Tone of Philosophy: Late Essays by Immanuel Kant, Transformative Critique by Jacques Derrida*, edited by Peter Fenves, 51–82. Baltimore: John Hopkins University Press, 1998.

Karlberg, Stephen, ed. *Max Weber: Readings and Commentary on Modernity.* Malden, MA: Blackwell, 2005.

Kennedy, John F. "Transcript: JFK's Speech on His Religion." September 12, 1960. http://www.npr.org/templates/story/story.php?storyId=16920600.

Keohane, Nannerl O. "Inaugural Address, 23 October 1993." In Keohane, *Higher Ground: Ethics and Leadership in the Modern University*, 218–28. Durham, NC: Duke University Press, 2006.

Kettle, David. *Western Culture in Gospel Context: Towards the Conversion of the West: Theological Bearing for Mission and Spirituality.* Eugene, OR: Cascade, 2011.

Kimbriel, Samuel. *Friendship as Sacred Knowing: Overcoming Isolation.* New York: Oxford University Press, 2014.

Kreeft, Peter. "What Judgment Means to the Pursuit of Wisdom." January 31, 2014. https://www.circeinstitute.org/podcast/podcast-peter-kreeft-what-judgment-means-pursuit-wisdom.

Lakeland, Paul. "Otherness, Difference and the Unity of Purpose: Catholic Education and Postmodernity." Unpublished.

Langford, Jerome J. *Galileo, Science and the Church.* 3rd ed. Ann Arbor, MI: University of Michigan Press, 1999.

Bibliography

Lasch, Christopher. *The True and Only Heaven: Progress and Its Critics*. New York: W. W. Norton, 1991.

Leclercq, Jean. *The Love of Learning and the Desire for God: A Study of Monastic Culture*. New York: Fordham, 1982.

Legaspi, Michael. *The Death of Scripture and the Rise of Biblical Studies*. New York: Oxford University Press, 2011.

Leonard, Bill. "Hegemony or Dissent: Signs of Baptist Identity Amid the Loss of Baptist Culture in the South." Delivered at the Future of Baptist Higher Education Conference, Baylor University, April 18–19, 2005.

Levering, Matthew. *Participatory Biblical Exegesis*. Notre Dame, IN: University of Notre Dame Press, 2008.

Linder, Suzanne C. *William Louis Poteat: Prophet of Progress*. Chapel Hill, NC: University of North Carolina Press, 1966.

Lohfink, Gerhard. *Does God Need the Church? Toward a Theology of the People of God*. Collegeville, MN: Liturgical, 1999.

Lopez, Antonio. "Eternal Happening: God as an Event of Love." In *Love Alone Is Credible: Hans Urs von Balthasar as Interpreter of Catholic Tradition, Volume 1*, edited by David L. Schindler, 75–104. Grand Rapids: Eerdmans, 2008.

Lubac, Henri de. *Medieval Exegesis*. Translated by Mark Sebanc. 4 vols. Grand Rapids: Eerdmans,1998.

———. *The Mystery of the Supernatural*. Translated by Rosemary Sheed. New York: Crossroad, 2013.

———. *Scripture in the Tradition*. Translated by Luke O'Neill. New York: Crossroad, 2000.

Luther, Martin. *On Christian Liberty*. Minneapolis: Fortress, 2003.

MacIntyre, Alasdair. *After Virtue: A Study in Moral Theory*, 2nd ed. Notre Dame, IN: University of Notre Dame Press, 1984.

———."Catholic instead of what?" https://www.youtube.com/watch?v=j7WWMkIOlsw.

———. "A Culture of Choices and Compartmentalization." Presented at the "Culture of Death" conference, Notre Dame Center for Ethics and Culture. University of Notre Dame, October 13, 2000. http://brandon.multics.org/library/Alasdair%20 MacIntyre/macintyre2000choices.xhtml.

Mansfield, Harry C. "Political Correctness." In *Gladly to Learn and Gladly to Teach: Essays on Religion and Political Philosophy in Honor of Ernest L. Fortin, A.A.*, edited by Michael P. Foley and Douglas Kries, 257–70. New York: Lexington, 2002.

Marsden, George M. *The Outrageous Idea of Christian Scholarship*. New York: Oxford University, 1997.

———. *The Soul of the American University: From Protestant Establishment to Established Nonbelief*. New York: Oxford University Press, 1994.

Martin, Craig, and Talal Asad. "Genealogies of Religion, Twenty Years On: An interview with Talal Asad." *Bulletin for the Study of Religion* 43 (2014). https://bulletin. equinoxpub.com/2015/11/genealogies-of-religion-twenty-years-on-an-interview-with-talal-asad/.

Marty, Martin E. *Anticipating Pluralism: The Founders' Vision*. Providence, RI: The Associates of the John Carter Brown Library, 1986.

McClendon, James Wm., Jr. *Ethics: Systematic Theology*, Vol. I. Nashville: Abingdon, 1986.

Mead, Walter B. "A Symposium Encounter: The Philosophies of William Poteat and Michael Polanyi." *Tradition and Discovery, The Polanyi Society Periodical* 35 (2008) 6–13.

Bibliography

Médaille, John C. *Toward a Truly Free Market: A Distributist Perspective on the Role of Government, Taxes, Health Care, Deficits, and More*. Wilmington, DE: Intercollegiate Studies Institute, 2010.

Micklem, Nathaniel. *Reason and Revelation: A Question for Duns Scotus*. New York: Thomas Nelson and Sons, 1953.

Milbank, John. *Being Reconciled: Ontology and Pardon*. London: Routledge, 2003.

———. "The Real Third Way: For a New Metanarrative of Capital and the Associationist Alternative." In *The Crisis of Global Capitalism: Pope Benedict XVI's Social Encyclical and the Future of Political Economy*, edited by Adrian Pabst, 27–70. Cambridge: James & Clark, 2011.

———. *The Suspended Middle: Henri de Lubac and the Debate concerning the Supernatural*. Grand Rapids: Eerdmans, 2005.

———. *Theology and Social Theory: Beyond Secular Reason*. Oxford: Blackwell, 1990.

Mullins, Maire. "'Deeper Down in the Domain of Human Hearts,' Hope in Isak Dinesen's *Babette's Feast*." *Logos* 12 (2009) 16–37.

Myers, Ched. "Embodying the 'Great Story,' An Interview with James McClendon." http://thewitness.org/archive /dec2000/mcclendon.html.

Newman, Elizabeth. "Failure and the Modern Academy." In *Theologies of Failure*, edited by Roberto Daniel Sirvent and Duncan Reyburn. Eugene, OR: Wipf and Stock, forthcoming.

———. "Hospitality and Christian Higher Education." *Christian Scholar's Review* 33 (2003) 75–94.

———. *Untamed Hospitality: Welcoming God and Other Strangers*. Grand Rapids: Brazos, 2007.

Nice, Terrence N. "Schleiermacher on the Scientific Study of Religion." In *Friedrich Schleiermacher and the Founding of the University of Berlin: The Study of Religion as a Scientific Discipline*, edited by Herbert W. Richardson, 45–82. Lewiston, UK: Edwin Mellen, 1991.

O'Brien, David J. "A Catholic Academic Revolution." In *Mission and Identity, A Handbook for Trustees of Catholic Colleges and Universities*, Association of Jesuit Colleges and Universities, 23–35. Washington, DC: Association of Jesuit Colleges and Universities, 2003.

O'Brien, Dennis. "The Disappearing Moral Curriculum." *The Key Reporter* 62 (1997) 4.

Ong, Walter J. *Orality and Literacy, The Technologizing of the Word*. New York: Routledge, 1982.

Pabst, Adrian. "Introduction." In *The Crisis of Global Capitalism: Pope Benedict XVI's Social Encyclical and the Future of Political Economy*, edited by Adrian Pabst, 1–24. Cambridge: James & Clark Co., 2011.

Pecknold, Chad. "Political by Nature: Friendship and the Good Life." The Thomistic Institute, Washington DC, March 2017. Podcast.

Percy, Walker. *Lost in the Cosmos: The Last Self-Help Book*. New York: Farrar, Strauss and Giroux, 1983.

Pickstock, Catherine. *After Writing: On the Liturgical Consummation of Philosophy*. Oxford: Blackwell, 1998.

Pieper, Josef. *Leisure, the Basis of Culture*. New York: Pantheon, 1952.

Polanyi, Michael. "Faith and Reason." *Communio* 28 (2001) 860–74.

———. *Personal Knowledge, Towards a Post-Critical Philosophy*. Chicago: University of Chicago, 1958.

Poteat, William H. "Interpretation of Religion in Modern Western Culture," personal correspondence, 1998.

———. *A Philosophical Daybook: Post-Critical Investigations*. Columbia, MO: University of Missouri Press, 1990.

———. *Polanyian Meditations: In Search of a Post-Critical Logic*. Durham, NC: Duke University Press, 1985.

———. *The Primacy of Persons and the Language of Culture: Essays by William H. Poteat*. Edited by James M. Nickell and James W. Stines. Columbia, MO: University of Missouri Press, 1993.

———. *Recovering the Ground: Critical Exercises in Recollection*. Albany, NY: SUNY Press, 1994.

———. "A Skeleton Key to Arendt's *The Human Condition*," unpublished handout. (Now in the William H. Poteat Archive at Yale Divinity School Library.)

———. "Some Remarks on Walter Mead's essay, 'Poteat's Philosophical Anthropology.'" Unpublished, 1997. (Now in the William H. Poteat Archive at Yale Divinity School Library.)

"Proceedings of the Fourth Annual Meeting of the Baptist State Convention of North Carolina." Cashie Meeting House, Bertie County, November 1–5, 1834. Archived in WFU Presidents' Papers, Samuel Wait, Jr. Z. Smith Reynolds Library, Special Collection and Archives, Wake Forest University, Winston-Salem, NC. https://wakespace.lib.wfu.edu/bitstream/handle/10339/31749/bsc_1834_11.pdf, 1–24.

Radner, Ephraim. *Hope Among the Fragments: The Broken Church and Its Engagement of Scripture*. Grand Rapids: Brazos, 2004.

Reno, R. R. *In the Ruins of the Church: Sustaining Faith in an Age of Diminished Christianity*. Grand Rapids: Brazos. 2002.

Richardson, Herbert, ed. *Friedrich Schleiermacher and the Founding of the University of Berlin: The Study of Religion as a Scientific Discipline*. Lewiston, UK: Edwin Mellen Press, 1991.

Rolnick, Philip A. *Analogical Possibilities: How Words Refer to God*. Atlanta, GA: Scholars, 1993.

Rowland, Tracey. *Culture and the Thomist Tradition: After Vatican II*. London: Routledge, 2003.

Sagan, Carl. *Contact*. New York: Pocket, 1985.

Saint Mary's College, Faculty Assembly Minutes, September 13, 2000.

Scales, Ralph. "The Christian Scholar." Southern Baptist Faculty Conference, Hot Springs, AK, June 26, 1964. Archived in WFU Presidents' Papers, James Ralph Scales. Z. Smith Reynolds Library, Special Collection and Archives, Wake Forest University, Winston-Salem, NC.

Schackner, Bill. "Pitt dropping religious studies graduate classes." *Pittsburgh Post-Gazette*, February 6, 2014. http://www.post-gazette.com/news/education/2014/02/07/Pitt-dropping-religious-studies-graduate-classes/stories/201402070082.

Schindler, David L. *Heart of the World, Center of the Church: Communio Ecclesiology, Liberalism, and Liberation*. Grand Rapids: Eerdmans, 1996.

———. "Introduction," to Henri De Lubac, *The Mystery of the Supernatural*, translated by Rosemary Sheed, xi–xxxi. New York: Crossroad, 2013.

———. "The Meaning of the Human in a Technological Age: *Homo faber, Homo sapiens, Homo amans*." *Communio* 26 (Spring 1999) 80–103.

Bibliography

———. "Modernity and the Nature of a Distinction: Balthasar's Ontology of Generosity." In *How Balthasar Changed My Mind, 15 Scholars Reflect on the Meaning of Balthasar for Their Own Work*, edited by Rodney A. Howsare and Larry S. Chapp, 224–58. New York: Crossroad, 2008.

———. *Ordering Love: Liberal Societies and the Memory of God*. Grand Rapids: Eerdmans, 2011.

———. "On Meaning and the Death of God in the Academy." *Communio* 17 (1990) 192–206.

———. "Sanctity and the Intellectual Life." In *Heart of the World, Center of the Church: Communio Ecclesiology, Liberalism, and Liberation,* by David L. Schindler, 203–20. Grand Rapids: Eerdmans, 1996.

———. "The Significance of Hans Urs von Balthasar in the Contemporary Cultural Situation." In *Glory, Grace, and Culture: The Work of Hans Urs von Balthasar,* edited by Ed Block Jr., 16–36. Mahwah, NJ: Paulist, 2005.

———. "Time in Eternity, Eternity in Time: On the Contemplative-Active Life." *Communio* 18 (1991) 53–68.

———. "2011 11 30 Face to Face with . . . David Schindler—Part 1." https://www.youtube.com/watch?v=3i4HOWHaZ7I, 57.28.

Schindler, David L., ed. *Catholicism and Secularization in America*. Notre Dame, IN: Communio, 1990.

Schleiermacher, Friedrich. *Brief Outline of Theology as a Field of Study*. 3rd ed. Louisville: Westminster John Knox, 2011.

———. *On Religion: Speeches to Its Cultured Despisers*. Translated by John Oman. Louisville: Westminster, 1958.

Schmemann, Alexander. *For the Life of the World*. Crestwood, NY: St. Vladimir's Seminary Press, 1963.

Schor, Juliet B. *The Overworked American: The Unexpected Decline of Leisure*. New York: Basic, 1993.

Schwehn, Mark. "The Academic Vocation: 'Specialists without Spirit, Sensualists without Heart'?" *Cross Currents* 42 (1992) 185–99.

Scott, Giles. "High school teacher: I'm banning laptops in class—and not just because they are distracting." *The Washington Post*, August 5, 2016.

Shea, John. "Here Comes Everybody." *Commonweal* (September 1990) 509–11.

Sheehan, Jonathan. *The Enlightenment Bible: Translation, Scholarship, Culture*. Princeton, NJ: Princeton University Press, 2005.

———. "Enlightenment, Religion and the Enigma of Secularization: A Review Essay." *American Historical Review* 108 (2003) 1061–80.

Shurden, Walter B. *The Baptist Identity: Four Fragile Freedoms*. Macon, GA: Smyth & Helwys, 2013.

Sloan, Douglas. *Faith and Knowledge: Mainline Protestantism and Higher Education*. Louisville: Westminster John Knox, 1994.

Smith, James K. A. *Desiring the Kingdom: Worship, Worldview, and Cultural Formation*. Grand Rapids: Baker Academic, 2009.

Snell, R. J. *Acedia and Its Discontents: Metaphysical Boredom in an Empire of Desire*. Kettering, OH: Angelico, 2015.

Soukup, Paul A. "Orality and Literacy 25 Years Later." *Communication Research Trends, Centre for the Study of Communication and Culture* 26 (2007) 3–33.

Bibliography

"Statement on the Nature of the Contemporary Catholic University," Item #1: "The Catholic University: A True University with Distinctive Characteristics." *The Story of Notre Dame: The Idea of the Catholic University*. Land O'Lakes, Wisconsin, July 23, 1967. Accessed April 25, 2017. http://www.archives.nd.edu/episodes/visitors/lol/idea.htm.

Stroup, John M. "The Idea of Theological Education at the University of Berlin: From Schleiermacher to Harnack." In *Schools of Thought in Christian Tradition*, edited by Patrick Henry, 152–76. Philadelphia: Fortress, 1984.

Surin, Kenneth. "A 'Politics of Speech': Religious Pluralism in an Age of McDonald's Hamburgers." In *Christian Uniqueness Reconsidered: The Myth of a Pluralistic Theology of Religions*, edited by Gavin D'Costa, 192–212. Maryknoll, NY: Orbis, 1990.

Taylor, Charles. *A Secular Age*. Cambridge, MA. Harvard University Press, 2007.

Tice, Terrence N. "Schleiermacher on the Scientific Study of Religion." In *Friedrich Schleiermacher and the Founding of the University of Berlin: The Study of Religion as a Scientific Discipline*, edited by Herbert Richardson, 45–82. Lewiston, UK: Edwin Mellen, 1991.

Wainwright, Geoffrey. *Faith, Hope, and Love, The Ecumenical Trio of Virtues*. Waco, TX: Baylor University Press, 2014.

Wait, Samuel. "Baccalaureate Address, June 20, 1839 To the First Class Graduated as Wake Forest College." Archived in WFU Presidents' Papers, Samuel Wait. Z. Smith Reynolds Library, Special Collection and Archives, Wake Forest University, Winston-Salem, NC.

Weber, Max. *The Protestant Work Ethic and the Spirit of Capitalism*. Translated by Talcott Parsons. Mineola, NY: Dover, 2003.

Weil, Simone. *On Science: Necessity and the Love of God*. New York: Oxford, 1968.

———. *Waiting on God*. London: Routledge and Kegan Paul, 1951.

Wenzel, Siegfried. *The Sin of Sloth: Acedia in Medieval Thought and Literature*. Chapel Hill, NC: University of North Carolina, 1960.

"William H. Poteat." whpoteat.org.

Zizioulas, John D. *Being as Communion: Studies in Personhood and the Church*. Crestwood, NY: St. Vladimir's Seminary Press, 1985.

INDEX OF AUTHORS

Index of Authors

Friedrich, Casper David, 13

Galileo, 44
Galling, Alice, 157
Gandhi, Mahatma, 83n56
Giddens, Anthony, 123–24
Gleason, Philip, 4n9, 17n55
Grant, George, xiii, 2n3, 20n68, 21, 29,
    29n98, 77–78, 78n41, 111–12,
    111n62, 146–47, 147n19, 158n62
Gray, John Henry, 75
Gregory, Brad S., 35n35, 37, 66,
    148n22, 154–58, 155n51
Griffiths, Paul, 40n32, 108–10, 109n54,
    109n55
Guardini, Romano, 82n53

Harnack, Adolf von, 73
Harris, Carl, 29
Harrison, Carol, 81
Hart, David Bentley, 7, 22, 34n13,
    39–40, 41, 61n109
Hauerwas, Stanley, 15, 21, 96n13, 97,
    107, 123, 123n12, 136n61, 144
Havel, Vaclav, 131
Hays, Richard B., 139–140n68
Hearn, Thomas, 19n60
Hearne, Vicki, 1–2
Henry of Ghent, 35
Hesburgh, Theodore, 17–18, 76, 76n33
Humboldt, Wilhelm von, 14

Ignatius, 86
Inazu, John D., 26
Ingham, Mary Beth, 35, 37
Irenaeus, 56, 56n98, 81n50, 86

Jaki, Stanley L., 125
Jardine, Murray, 43n47, 118–19, 121,
    121n7, 124, 124n21
Jasper, Karl, 75n28
Jenson, Robert, 84
Johnson, Henry, 143–44

Kant, Immanuel, 8n23, 57n99, 69,
    70–71, 70–71n9, 73, 74–75,
    75n27, 97, 144, 147n20
Kennedy, John F., 18

Keohane, Nan, 97–98
Kettle, David, 32
Kierkegaard, Søren, 34, 72, 102, 147
Kimbriel, Samuel, 115n70, 151–54,
    158–59
Kreeft, Peter, 113

Lakeland, Paul, 27
Langford, Jerome, 3n4
Lasch, Christopher, 124
Leclercq, Jean, 159, 159–160n68, 161
Legaspi, Michael, 15
Leonard, Bill, 4, 4n7
Levering, Matthew, 125–27, 126n26
López, Antonio, 134
Lord, Albert, 80

MacIntyre, Alasdair, 6n20, 26, 93–96,
    129–130, 135–36, 152n39
Marsden, George, 4, 98–102, 98n21,
    129
Marty, Martin, 24–26, 99
Maurin, Peter, 66
McClendon, James, 9n26, 105
Médaille, John C., 28
Milbank, John, 14n45, 23, 103n39, 143
Mill, John Stuart, 101, 101n32
Milton, John, 100
Murdoch, Iris, 144n5

Neitzsche, Friedrich, 58

O'Brien, David J., 17n55, 20n67
Ong, Walter J., 43n47, 79–80
Origen, 87, 104n41, 146

Pabst, Adrian, 21, 118n1
Paliard, Jacques, 87n69
Pascal, 34
Pecknold, Chad, 150–51, 154
Percy, Walker, xii
Pickstock, Catherine, 37–38, 126
Pieper, Josef, xii, 69–90, 113, 120, 135,
    145, 154
Plato, 132
Polanyi, Michael, 45–46, 45n59
Ponticus, Evagrius, 146
Porter, Noah, 143–44

INDEX OF SUBJECTS

Index of Subjects

"Report of the President's Commission on Education" (Truman), 98
Reynolds, Ed, n45
"rhetoric of nowhere," 93, 97, 114
rhythms
  academic time as market time, 117–120
  academic time as rational and inclusive, 121–23
  academic work vs. leisure, 120–21
  active life, 132–35
  contemplative life, 132–35
  making a difference, 129–132
  rituals of plenitude, 135–39
  scarcity, emptying of time, 123–25
  time, meaning of, 125–29
  time as freedom, 139–142
rituals of plenitude, 135–39

sacraments, 84–86
sacrifice, 72–73
Saint Mary's College, Notre Dame, xi–xii, 20n67, 121–22
"Sanctity and the Intellectual Life" (Schindler), 62–63
scarcity, 123–25
Schleiermacher, Friedrich, 12–16
science
  modern science, 33, 33n6
  positive science, 13–14
  theology as, 13, 13n39, 35, 35n16, 74
scriptural reasoning, 141n76
scripture
  four senses of, 106n47
  linear view of time, 125–27
  use of, 103–8
secular liberalism, 14n45
secularism, 76, 76n34, 121, 131, 155–57
secularization story, 2–9
self, disengaged and porous, 151–52, 153
sin, 65–66, 71–73, 88
singing, grammar of, 79–84
slavery, 105
sloth, 71–72, 72n14, 135, 145
  . See also acedia
social media, 43n47

social responsibility, 122
solitude, theater of, 42–57
The Soul of the American University (Marsden), 4
spiritual/material dualism, 9
stress-free zones, 117
studiousness, 108–13
symbol vs. reality, 55–56

tacit knowing, 45–46, 47, 47n65
taught bodies, 77–79
teaching as if God exists, 1
technology, 59, 77–80, 78n41, 95, 111n62, 142, 142n78
theater of solitude, 42–57
theology
  banished from knowledge-making, 154–55
  mathematics and, 82
  as a science, 13, 13n39, 35, 35n16, 74
time
  academic time as market time, 117–120
  academic time as rational and inclusive, 121–23
  emptying of, 123–25
  as freedom, 139–142
  meaning of, 125–29, 125n23
  and place, dislocation of, 33–34, 34n12
  Trinitarian understanding, 125, 127, 133–35, 134n53
"Time in Eternity, Eternity in Time" (Schindler), 133, 134n53
transcendence of God, 62, 62n113, 62n114
transcendental, term usage, 57n99
transubstantiation, 55, 85
Trinitarian God, 39–40
Trinitarian understanding of time, 125, 127, 133–35, 134n53
truth, 2, 148, 149–150

universal man, 11n32
University of Berlin, 13
University of Dayton, 4, 4n9
University of North Dakota, 20n67
University of Pittsburgh, 71n12

182